Super Shortcut

INSTANT POT®

ALSO BY JEFFREY EISNER

*The Step-by-Step
Instant Pot Cookbook*

*The Lighter Step-by-Step
Instant Pot Cookbook*

*The Simple Comforts
Step-by-Step Instant Pot
Cookbook*

Super
Shortcut

INSTANT POT®

The Ultimate Time-Saving **STEP-BY-STEP** *Cookbook*

SIMPLE AND FLAVORFUL MEALS THAT SERVE 1 TO 6

Jeffrey Eisner

PHOTOGRAPHY BY ALEKSEY ZOZULYA

VORACIOUS

LITTLE, BROWN AND COMPANY
NEW YORK / BOSTON / LONDON

Voracious / Little, Brown and Company
Hachette Book Group
1290 Avenue of the Americas, New York, NY 10104
littlebrown.com

First Edition: April 2023

Voracious is an imprint of Little, Brown and Company, a division of Hachette Book Group, Inc. The Voracious name and logo are trademarks of Hachette Book Group, Inc.

INSTANT POT® and associated logos are owned by Instant Brands Inc. and are used under license.

The publisher is not responsible for websites (or their content) that are not owned by the publisher.

The Hachette Speakers Bureau provides a wide range of authors for speaking events. To find out more, go to hachettespeakersbureau.com or email hachettespeakers@hbgusa.com.

Little, Brown and Company books may be purchased in bulk for business, educational, or promotional use. For information, please contact your local bookseller or the Hachette Book Group Special Markets Department at special.markets@hbgusa.com.

Photographs by Aleksey Zozulya
Food styling by Carol J. Lee

ISBN 9780316485234
LCCN 2022945082

10 9 8 7 6 5 4 3 2 1

CW

Printed in the United States of America

For anyone in a hurry and who
ain't got the time.

These meals require little work
and are all quite sublime.

CONTENTS

(GO!) = DUMP & GO RECIPE

(<5) = 5 INGREDIENTS OR LESS

(<3) = 3 STEPS OR LESS

(air fryer) = AIR FRYER LID

(K) = KETO

(P) = PALEO

(DF) = DAIRY-FREE

(GF) = GLUTEN-FREE

(V) = VEGETARIAN

(VN) = VEGAN

+ = COMPLIANT WITH MODIFICATIONS

INTRODUCTION

IT'S ABOUT TIME

Once upon a time, I worked in the world of advertising and public relations.
I didn't like it.

One night, while I was lying in bed and treating myself to retail therapy to delay the impending night terrors about work the next day, something called an Instant Pot came across my screen. Combining my love for cooking and gadgets, I bought one. Then, I started using it, became passionate about how it made my cooking life so much simpler, and began my blog, *Pressure Luck Cooking*, to create and share Instant Pot recipes with the world. Pouring my soul into this passion project, the odds seemed to be in my favor and so I left my corporate public relations career behind and never looked back.

Now, it's hard to wrap my head around the fact that I have authored three bestselling cookbooks with over 300 recipes and 2,250 photos combined. I've tackled basics, lighter fare, and comfort food in all their simple glories. But even with all those recipes in hundreds of thousands of kitchens, somehow my well hasn't run dry. Once I've brought a book to life, I immediately begin thinking about the recipes in the next one!

But every creator needs an audience to inspire them. I'm here to provide you with a service, and that's why it's so important to *me* to listen to *you*. To ask you what you want and listen to your requests. Because, ultimately, *you* are the decision maker. You have the power to decide whether something is worth your time—or a spot on your dinner plate.

I polled my audience online and asked people at book signings across the country for what they wanted most. Three themes kept coming up:

1. FEWER INGREDIENTS
(less prep, less time, and more budget-friendly)

2. MORE DUMP & GO
(losing the sauté step, creating less work in less time)

3. COOKING TO SERVE 1 TO 2 PEOPLE
(for those in a small household)

All great suggestions. Time is precious—and saving it where we can is always a relief. A lot of folks work hard all day (and sometimes into the night), have families to tend to with the occasional unexpected event or meltdown, or just don't want to be bothered with preparing a meal that's going to require more than a few things tossed into one pot. Often, the microwave or drive-thru takes center stage and we all know that usually doesn't end up being a satisfying or nutritious meal. You deserve better than that! You deserve a homecooked meal done quickly, easily and without hassle. You deserve a shortcut. (You also deserve this book—so if you're just browsing through it in a store: Go on, buy it!)

My good reader, your wish for shortcuts to great meals is answered within this very book—now known as "the green one," where even the *title* is shorter! And because green means "go," this time the recipes are all about simplicity, speed, minimal prep, and fewer ingredients. Plus, I show how to halve each family-style recipe to feed just one or two people.

Super Shortcuts

If you are familiar with my style from the other books, you'll know I often cook with about 15 ingredients per recipe, providing some extra touches to load my dishes with flavor and make them stand out. The ingredients required are widely accessible, affordable, and often include basic spices you likely already have in your cupboard. *But* I wanted to challenge myself to give you dynamite flavor in *true* ten-ingredient-or-less recipes for **every single recipe.** That's right—all 100+ of them! And there are plenty with *five* or less!

No hogwash here, folks. I've seen the "Five Ingredients OR LESS!" books where spices and fridge staples such as milk and butter "don't count" as part of the five ingredients because it is assumed you already have those stocked. Nuh-uh.

No recipe in this book will ever exceed ten required ingredients.

If salt is called for, it's one of the ingredients, just as chicken would be. Equality for all. **The only ingredient I *don't* count as one of the ten (or less) is water**—because it comes right from your faucet. Simple, clear, and honest as that. The only time you may see more than ten ingredients is when they are purely optional: a little extra touch should you wish to go that way. (These optional ingredients print in gray to distinguish them from the required ones.) I also give suggestions for making some of the basic recipes more elaborate with further optional touches in my handy Jeff's Tips section in each recipe.

As for the recipes themselves? I tirelessly tested every recipe to ensure they are all loaded (and I mean *loaded*) with flavor.

The goal of this cookbook is to give you exactly what you asked for: all-new, shareworthy, spectacular recipes done with even fewer ingredients, requiring less time than ever, and added guidance for cooking for fewer people.

In fact, to prove this is my easiest and quickest cookbook ever, I've incorporated three "super shortcuts" into the recipes. Find these icons in many of this book's recipes:

| = DUMP & GO RECIPE | = 5 INGREDIENTS OR LESS | = 3 STEPS OR LESS |

And since so many of us follow different eating lifestyles, this book has something for everyone. Icons also identify dishes that are or can be made **K** (keto), **P** (paleo), **GF** (gluten-free), **DF** (dairy-free), **V** (vegetarian), or **VN** (vegan). A "**+**" next to each icon will be followed by any modification needed to make it that way.

If you strictly follow a specific lifestyle, make sure to use compliant ingredients when making these meals. I did not include nutrition information because how one calculates nutrition info is subjective. Different brands available for a given ingredient can vary and lead to a wide range in the numbers. If you wish to determine nutrition info, I suggest using a reputable nutrition app or online nutrition calculator where you can plug in the exact choices you've made. My blue (*Lighter*) book's introduction covers all of this in detail, although it's always best to consult a doctor or a nutritionist when making dietary decisions.

And so with this fourth baby of mine that you hold in your hands, I now have over 400 recipes and 3,000 photos in the published roster. I'm so incredibly proud of this book because it proves you can make something absolutely delicious and memorable with truly minimal effort, money, mess, and worry. **Less is truly more.**

Time-Saving Tips

Here are five key tips to make your cooking journey as efficient as possible.

1. KEEP YOUR DUCKS IN A ROW. The thought of

organization excites some and scares others. But taking the time to arrange your frequent cooking go-tos can be a huge time saver in the long run. **Line up your most-used spices, oils, and sauces near your stove**—in a cupboard or on the countertop— so they're all easily reachable. You can buy little bleacher-like stands online that can fit in many cupboards so all of your spices are visible.

Or, if you have a smaller kitchen and don't have a lot of space for shelves, a spice rack is great on your countertop or mounted on a wall. Get some canisters for flour, sugar, and cornstarch and also something to corral your go-to utensils such as mixing spoons, wooden spatulas, and

whisks. **Store your measuring cups and spoons in a dedicated drawer.** Knowing where all your kitchen tools are will speed things along and benefit you in the end. And when you're done cooking, **make it a habit to put everything back** in its place. It will make you feel accomplished and will leave you more excited to get back in the kitchen next time.

2. CHECK IN BEFORE CHECKING OUT. When you settle on

the recipe you want to make, check your pantry, cupboards, fridge, and freezer to see what ingredients you already have (and make sure they aren't expired or icky). Then, create a shopping list. I can't tell you how many times I've run to the market before browsing the pantry and then couldn't remember if I had an item or not. So to avoid a second trip, I'd take a gamble and just buy a whole new jar of oregano or roasted peppers or whatever. Of course, when I got home, more often than not I'd find I had plenty of the ingredient. **Do a kitchen audit before shopping** to avoid this.

3. PREP BEFORE YOU STEP. Make sure all your

ingredients are measured, chopped, and ready to go before cooking. To make things extra easy, **do what the French call *mise en place*** and line them up in the same order shown in

THE INSTANT POT CRASH COURSE

If you've never used an Instant Pot before (and since this book's focus is on saving time), here's a super simple visual graphic, which will have you using your pot like a pro in no time!*

1. PLOT THE POT
First and foremost, make sure the stainless steel liner pot is seated in the Instant Pot itself or you'll be in for a messy surprise!

2. PLUG & PLAY
Make sure the cord is plugged in on both ends. On most models, the display will illuminate and read Off (which means the pot actually has power, but isn't doing anything). From there, the pot will begin its job once you choose a function.

3. SAUTÉ AWAY
If a recipe calls for a sauté step, simply hit the Sauté button to get started and adjust the temperature called for (usually More or High). **NOTE:** If your model has a Start button, you'll also need to hit that to begin. If it doesn't, it'll start on its own after a few seconds (the same goes for when pressure cooking and all other functions).

4. SWITCH GEARS
Hit the Cancel button to go back to home base. On most models, the display will read Off and you're ready for the next function.

5. PUT A LID ON IT
Make sure the silicone gasket is in place, secure the lid, and make sure the valve is in the sealing position (some models have a lid that automatically seals itself when closed).

6. PRESSURE LUCK
When it's time to pressure cook, hit the Pressure Cook or Manual button depending on your model. Also, depending on your model, use the +/- buttons, arrow buttons, or knob to adjust the time. Once the display reads On, that means it's building pressure. And once the pin in the lid pops up, it'll shortly begin the countdown for the time you set it for.

7. RELEASE WITH PEACE
When the pressure cooking time is complete, you'll either release the steam immediately, known as a quick release, or allow a natural release for the specified time (meaning you do nothing in that time) and then finish it with a quick release.

8. TRY AN AIR FRY
Should you want your food to have a crispy finish, place the Air Fryer Lid accessory directly on the Instant Pot and choose the function you wish to give it a toasty finish!

And that's all it takes to make your Instant Pot prepare you a meal to remember!

Because your pot has a lot of buttons (with most being pre-sets that I never use), I want to focus *only* on the ones that matter. The chart highlighting key buttons (see page 13) is all you need to pay attention to.

INSTANT POT BASICS

AIR FRYER LID BASICS

*For a more in-depth look at how to use your Instant Pot, see page 264. You can also scan the codes at right to watch my videos.

the ingredients list: That's the order that they are used in the steps. This will prevent any frantic scramble for ingredients, especially once you've begun the sauté process for the recipes which call for it.

4. **CUT IT OUT.** If you're not into cutting your own veggies (like me), have your kids do it for you! I'm only (partially) kidding. But, in many markets you can **find mushrooms, onions, celery, peppers, and carrots pre-chopped or sliced**. This will save you time with most recipes. When it comes to garlic, buy it with the cloves already peeled or minced/crushed (3 cloves = 1 tablespoon). Crushed, minced, or squeeze ginger can also often be found in the produce section or refrigerated/freezer section.

The same goes with chicken: Ask the butcher behind the counter to chop up a whole chicken. Chances are if you ask nicely, they'll do it for you (chop the chicken, not make the soup, that is).

As for shredded cheese, every recipe in this book that calls for it has been made from shredded cheese from a bag. (By the way, an 8-ounce bag yields 2 cups and a 16-ounce/1 pound bag yields 4.) It melts very well when adding and mixing in. You can choose any brand you wish (whatever's on sale is what I usually go for). Now, you can definitely grate your own cheese if you wish to get a bit fancier, but using bagged shredded

cheese will cut out an enormous amount of prep time (and save the inconvenience of shredded knuckles).

And lastly, **if a recipe calls for shrimp,** get a 2-pound bag of frozen raw shrimp (Costco's are the best value). You can get them tail on or off, and they are already peeled and deveined. When it's time to use the shrimp, all you need to do is place the frozen shrimp in a colander and run cold water over them, mixing them around by hand for about 5 minutes. They will thaw completely. This saves an enormous amount of time and work over having to peel and devein shrimp yourself!

5. **CLEAN AND SET BEFORE YOU FORGET.** Chances are Rosie Jetson doesn't live

at your house, so while your food is quietly pressure cooking, **use the downtime** to get some of the stuff we typically don't like to do out of the way. Rinse/clean the utensils and bowls you used prior to pressure cooking. Then, because you're on a roll, get out the serving spoons and platters and set your table. You'll feel *so* much relief post-meal when all you have to do is rinse off your pot and plates, place them in the dishwasher, store any leftovers, and toss things in the trash.

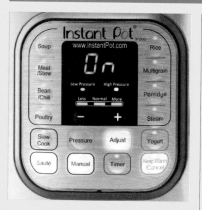

INSTANT POT DUO
(original model)

INSTANT POT DUO
(updated model)

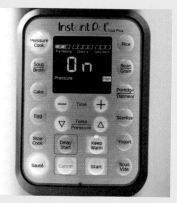

INSTANT POT DUO PLUS
(updated model)

THE DISPLAY

In the older Duo models, the cook time is only displayed in minutes

But in all newer Duos and above, the cook time is displayed with minutes to the right of the colon and hours to the left

The updated Duo Plus uses arrows to adjust the temperature settings and the Start button must be pressed to begin all functions

Some models require a push-dial to set times and functions

When you're done pressure cooking, the display will begin to count up, showing LO:00 or 00:00 for elapsed time

Turn your pot's sound on and off by holding the + and - buttons while the pot is in Off mode

The More You Know

I get many similar questions from people on how to use their Instant Pot, so here are those FAQs, which will likely answer any questions you may have.

I see some of your recipes call for alcohol. That's not for me. What can I use to replace it?

I totally get it. Simply sub more broth for the beer/wine/booze and you're good to go! So if a recipe calls for 1 cup broth and ½ cup wine, simply use 1½ cups broth.

Some recipes only have me pressure cooking some liquid and a few basic ingredients. What's the point?

Good question! You'll notice a few recipes, such as Creamy Coconut Curry Sauce (page 46), Cajun-Style Sauce (page 34), and Spinach & Artichoke Dip (page 242) only require some broth to be pressure cooked with a few spices or veggies. This is done for two reasons:

1. Rather than having to bring a pot of broth on the stove to a boil (and heating up your kitchen with splatters on the stove), pressure cooking it infuses more flavor into the base of the broth while keeping cool.

2. This is a pressure cooking book and therefore we cook it this way because we can!

The bottom of my pot is pretty browned and/or sticky after sautéing. How do I make sure it's smooth so it comes to pressure properly?

This is an important point—especially to avoid the dreaded Burn notice in the middle of the pressure cooking process! It's totally normal for some items (such as bacon and mushrooms) to cause browning on the bottom of your pot in the sauté stage. However, prior to pressure cooking, it's critical the bottom is freed up of as much of that as possible and is nice and smooth. Following my recipes as written will make sure this is the case, but it's worth noting that adding a little liquid—especially Worcestershire sauce or wine, but even broth or lemon juice—while you scrape with a wooden spatula or mixing spoon will greatly help get the browned bits up. It's like magic!

I can't find the exact size ingredient you're calling for. Will that be a problem?

Not at all. Based on where I live and the markets I go to, I'm used to specific (and the most common) sizes for canned items and packaged frozen foods/veggies. So if a recipe in this book calls for, say, a 10-ounce package of frozen corn and you can only find a 16-ounce package, that's fine! Either just use 10 ounces (about two-thirds) from the bag and save the rest—or if you really love corn, add all of it in there! Same for canned goods. If you can only find a 16-ounce can of beans and not a 15.5-ounce can, it will make absolutely no difference.

Also, if I call for a certain item like baby bella mushrooms and you can only find white buttons, those will do absolutely fine! The same with onions—although I call for specific types in my recipes, at the end of the day it really makes very little difference what kind you use. Want to sub a yellow for a red because you bought that huge netted bag on sale? Have at it!

What is a serving size?

A good question with a million different answers. To me, "serving size" is simply a suggestion, because the amount of food you eat is fully dependent on your appetite. Therefore *serving size* doesn't necessarily equal *portion size*. Most recipes will feed *at least* four to six people (and some folks may even claim up to eight). It truly all depends on how large your and your diners' appetites are. Regardless, the recipes in this book are most certainly "family-style," which means that people can serve themselves from a generous portion. So the dish may all be gone in one shot or you'll have some tasty leftovers (which is a benefit of Instant Pot cooking as the flavors are often more vibrant after cooling in the fridge before reheating). Since this book also explains how to adapt each recipe for one or two servings, just follow the instructions within each recipe on how to accomplish that.

Can these recipes be made in any size Instant Pot?

Yes! All the recipes in this book were tested in a 6-quart model but can be done in an 8-quart or 3-quart just as well—but with some adjustments:

For an 8-quart pot, use the same ingredient amounts, but if a recipe calls for only 1 cup of liquid, I usually *add ½ to 1 cup additional broth* than called for due to the volume of the pot. The cook time remains the same; however, it will take longer to come to pressure as there's more space to fill.

For a 3-quart pot, because of its smaller size you'll need to *halve all the ingredients.* You can keep the cook time the same in most circumstances, but because it's smaller, it'll come to pressure more quickly.

Check out the chart below for easy and general reference.

How do I keep my Instant Pot clean?

Bar Keepers Friend will be your and your stainless steel liner pot's bestie; just follow the instructions on the label. You can also place the pressure cooking lid on the top rack of your dishwasher, and the liner pot can go on the bottom rack.

To help get any unwanted aromas out of your silicone sealing ring, wash the ring in the top rack of your dishwasher or soak overnight in vinegar and leave outside to air-dry for a day. It's also a good idea to replace the ring every 6 to 12 months to ensure it is supple and doesn't become loose.

While a sponge could help, I've found the most effective way to get any gunk from under the metal grooves in the outer edges of the top of the pot is to use those super cheap foam brushes you can get from just about any hardware store.

The Practical, Well-Stocked Kitchen

Pantry Staples

This book is about simplicity, and the ingredients I call for match that—especially spices, herbs, seasonings, grains, oils, and vinegars. None are hard to find and all are affordable, and when combined together in a recipe, they really bring the flavors of the dish to life. To make sure you'll always have a large chunk of the ingredients I call for on hand, it's never a bad idea to go to the market (or Costco) and bring them home. They're well worth the investment and since a little often goes a long way, they will last you for many meals to come.

COOKING ADJUSTMENTS BY POT SIZE

POT SIZE	LIQUID AMOUNT	PRESSURE COOK TIME
6-quart (all recipes in this book were made in this size)	As given in the recipes, but if going on your own use 1 cup minimum just to ensure it's enough	As given in the recipes
3-quart	½ cup minimum for roasts and steaming veggies 1 cup minimum for rice 2 cups minimum for pasta	Same as 6-quart (shave off about 10 minutes of cook time for a roast)
8-quart	1½ to 2 cups minimum for roasts and steaming veggies 2 cups minimum for rice 3 cups minimum for pasta	Same as 6-quart

Here is a list of all the pantry staples I strongly suggest keeping on hand, no fancy brands required—though I do specify when I have a favorite.

DRIED HERBS, SPICES, AND SEASONINGS

Cajun/Creole/Louisiana seasoning (I love Tony Chachere's)

Cinnamon, ground

Cumin, both ground and seeds

Garam masala (I like Rani or Swad—easily found online)

Garlic powder

Garlic salt

Italian seasoning

Old Bay seasoning

Onion powder

Oregano, dried

Paprika (some also like smoked)

Parsley, dried

Pepper, black

Pepper, cayenne

Pepper, white, ground

Pepper flakes, crushed red

Sage, dried/ground

Salt, kosher

Salt, seasoned (I use Lawry's)

Sugars (white/granulated, light brown, and dark brown; you can also use the same amount of monk fruit sweetener as a substitute)

Thyme, dried

Turmeric, ground

Zatarain's Concentrated Shrimp & Crab Boil

DAIRY

Butter, salted or unsalted (I use salted in my recipes)

Cheese, cream (by the 8-ounce brick)

Cheese, herb (Boursin; you can also use Alouette, Rondelé, and Laughing Cow)

Cheese, Parmesan, grated

Cream, half-and-half and heavy

Cream, sour

Milk, whole

OILS, VINEGARS, SAUCES, AND OTHER PANTRY STAPLES

Broth (broths made from all varieties of Better Than Bouillon base are my favorite, with low-sodium options if you're watching your sodium intake)

Chili-garlic sauce (my favorite comes from Huy Fong Foods, the same company that makes sriracha)

Coconut milk, unsweetened, light (you should be able to shake the can and it should sound like water)

Cornstarch

Flour, all-purpose; or coconut flour (gluten-free, keto-friendly, and paleo-friendly) or quinoa flour (gluten-free)

Ginger, squeeze (get this at Costco or many markets; it's called "squeeze ginger" and looks like applesauce and is the easiest sub for minced or grated ginger)

Hoisin sauce (check label to ensure brand is gluten-free if necessary)

Honey

Hot sauce (I like Frank's RedHot and Cholula)

Liquid smoke (I prefer hickory flavor but any will do)

Maple syrup, pure

Mustard (Dijon in particular, like Grey Poupon)

Oil, olive (extra-virgin)

Oil, sesame (either toasted or untoasted is fine)

Oyster sauce (check label to ensure brand is gluten-free if necessary)

Pasta (1-pound boxes of your favorites)

Rice (jasmine, brown, and arborio in particular—never the instant kind)

Soy sauce (I use low-sodium; you can also use tamari [which is gluten-free] or coconut aminos [gluten-free and soy-free])

Sriracha

Tomatoes, canned (crushed, diced, paste, and sauce; use no-salt-added for low-sodium intake)

Vinegars (apple cider, balsamic, red wine, rice, and white)

Wines (dry white like sauvignon blanc; dry red like cabernet sauvignon; dry and/or sweet Marsala; and sherry)

Worcestershire sauce

FRUITS & VEGETABLES

Bell peppers (jalapeños and habaneros are also good to have on hand for heat lovers)

Carrots

Garlic (buying pre-peeled cloves or jars of minced garlic is always a time saver. Also, I often call for 3 cloves of crushed or minced garlic (1 tablespoon of jarred minced or crushed garlic is about the equivalent of 3 cloves).

Ginger (see also squeeze ginger, page 16)

Lemons

Limes

Onions (any kind can be used, but I suggest the type I prefer in each recipe)

Spinach (I use baby)

Broth, Herb Cheese, and Cornstarch Slurry

Broth, herb cheese, and cornstarch slurries are, respectively, three key things that greatly enhance a dish in terms of flavor, creaminess (if called for), and thickening. Because of their prominence, let's touch on these three things briefly.

BROTH

You can absolutely make your own broth (and I have recipes in my orange [the original *Step-by-Step Instant Pot*] and blue [*Lighter*] books). But if you don't have any premade, there's no better option than Better Than Bouillon bases. Not only do they have the usual varieties of chicken, beef, and vegetable broth, but they expand to garlic, chili, lobster, ham, and more. They also offer low-sodium and organic options for many of their bases, as well as mock-meat if you're vegan. My recipes give you a few suggested options for the flavor best paired with the dish, but you can choose any that grabs you!

The base is a concentrate in a jar that you mix with water to create broth. Once opened, the concentrate stores in your fridge for quite a long time (taking up very little space). It costs about the same as a quart or two of boxed broth, but makes over 35 cups broth per 8-ounce jar!

To prepare broth using Better Than Bouillon's concentrated base: Mix 1 teaspoon of the base with 1 cup water (it doesn't need to be hot while mixing as it'll be pressure cooked)—the result is 1 cup of seriously flavorful broth!

NOTE When I call for a specific broth variety in a recipe, be it chicken, beef, garlic, or even lobster, I'm merely stating that's the one I used when I created it. But it doesn't have to be that way! Whether you only have one kind of broth in your kitchen or if you have a whole collection and simply want to get creative, make your own rules when it comes to which type you use.

HERB CHEESE

For taking cream cheese to the next level, give an herb cheese such as Boursin or Alouette a try. They're usually found in the market near the deli meats and fancy cheeses (Boursin can also be found in Costco in packs of three at a great price). They often come in various flavors so choose which one you'd like best. Or make your own—see recipe for Garlic Herb Cheese on page 21.

Not only does an herb cheese thicken sauces, pastas, and risottos fantastically, but the rich and creamy flavor it contributes to recipes truly sets it apart from the rest. If you're being more health-conscious, use Greek yogurt instead as a lighter option—roughly ⅔ cup will fill in for a 5.2-ounce package of Boursin or a 6.5-ounce tub of Alouette. But if you just want to use plain, old-fashioned cream cheese anytime Boursin or Garlic Herb Cheese is called for, 4 ounces of an 8-ounce brick will also work.

You'll often find that the liquids remaining in the pot after pressure cooking proteins are on the thin side—in fact in most cases you'll likely have more liquid than when you started due to veggies and proteins releasing water and juices. This is perfectly normal. However, when making a dish with a gravy or sauce, we often will want to thicken that up just before serving. A cornstarch slurry (which is gluten-free) makes that magic happen. All it takes is 1 to 2 tablespoons of cornstarch and an equal amount of cold water mixed together until the consistency is smooth. From there, stir it directly into your sauce along with any dairy finishing touches the recipe may call for, transforming a thin liquid into a rich and spectacular sauce or gravy. Make sure to always mix the slurry together before adding to the pot because just adding the cornstarch to a large pot of liquid will make it clump up immediately and not thicken the sauce.

I personally feel the recipes in this book will give you the perfect consistency when a slurry is called for, but you can also thicken any sauce, gravy, or soup to your liking by simply adding an additional 1 to 2 tablespoons slurry, if desired. Or you can choose to add a slurry to a soup or saucy recipe that doesn't call for one, should you want it quite thick.

Essential Accessories

While the Instant Pot carries the load of the work, no kitchen would be complete without a few other key tools that will become your beloved personal assistants.

1. Bundt pan (a 6-cup nonstick pan fits inside the 6- and 8-quart Instant Pot models)
2. Cheese grater
3. Fine-mesh strainer/colander
4. Food processor or blender
5. Hand or stand mixer
6. Immersion blender (this is heaven-sent for soups as it eliminates messy batch trips to the blender)
7. Juicer (hand-held)
8. Knives (an 8-inch chef's knife for chopping, slicing, and dicing; a paring knife for finely slicing small veggies and getting ribs out of peppers)
9. Ladle
10. Measuring cups and spoons
11. Microplane (amazing for zesting lemons and limes or for topping a dish with some freshly shaved Parmesan)
12. Mixing bowls
13. Mixing spoons and spatulas (wooden and silicone are best for the stainless steel liner pot)
14. Oven mitts/dish towels (to handle a hot pot)
15. Parchment paper rounds
16. Peeler
17. Potato masher

Silicone sling (see page 20)

18. Springform pan (7-inch diameter with 3-inch rim is the best size)
19. Steamer basket (see page 20)
20. Tongs
21. Whisk (silicone is best)
22. Wooden spatula (My main mixing tool of choice, this is what you'll see used in nearly all the step-by-step photos when I stir. It also plays nicely with the stainless steel pot by not scratching it up when stirring/mixing.)

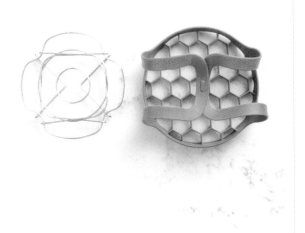

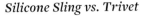

Silicone Sling vs. Trivet

The wire trivet, which comes with many Instant Pots, is a great tool because it elevates eggs, roasts, and pans from resting directly on the bottom of the stainless steel liner pot, which is necessary in most cases. However, it can sometimes be a bit cumbersome to lower a pan and remove it from the Instant Pot when resting on the trivet. That's where the silicone sling comes in. You'll notice that recipes in the dessert chapter (page 248) suggest the sling instead of the trivet. That's because of the ease of lowering it into and raising it out of the pot thanks to the two handles that lock together, plus the lip where a pan can rest without your worrying it may slide off during transport. Silicone slings can be found online and are truly worth every cent.

Steamer Basket

Another accessory to make your life easier is a steamer basket. It makes it so simple to just dump veggies in the pot, such as for my Aligot (page 228), Truffle Hash (page 240), and even other items such as Pierogi Poutine (page 238). It also prevents you from needing a colander since the basket is made of fine mesh.

GARLIC HERB CHEESE

Since the fancy cream cheeses aren't available everywhere and because I want you to get that true flavor experience I've intended in these recipes, I'm sharing how to make your own garlic herb cheese! Not only is this more budget conscious, it tastes just as great as the fancy stuff in the market (if not better since it's homemade).

    This will yield the equivalent of about *five* 5.2-ounce packages of Boursin (one package is approximately ¾ cup). You can also use it as a spread for crackers on your charcuterie board. It will last up to 3 weeks in your fridge and can be frozen for future use. All it takes are the following:

- **2 (8-ounce) bricks cream cheese, softened for 2 hours at room temperature (don't microwave)**
- **2 sticks (8 ounces) salted butter, softened for 2 hours at room temperature (don't microwave)**
- **¼ cup grated Parmesan cheese**
- **3 cloves garlic, minced or pressed**
- **1 teaspoon dried parsley**
- **1 teaspoon dried dill**
- **½ teaspoon garlic powder**
- **½ teaspoon dried thyme**
- **½ teaspoon dried basil**
- **½ teaspoon black pepper**
- **½ teaspoon Italian seasoning**

Simply add all the ingredients to a large mixing bowl. Take a silicone, rubber, or wooden mixing spoon and mix it all together, folding it over until well combined with even seasoning distribution. (NOTE: You can also use a hand mixer if that's easier, but I find that the familiar consistency is best achieved when mixed by hand.)

GENERAL COOKING CHARTS

These charts will come in handy when you want to make your own creations. Just bear in mind that these are loose guidelines, as the dish or sauce you're making may require slightly altered ratios and times depending on what you're making and adding to each dish (be it meat or veggies).

PASTA

PASTA	PASTA:LIQUID RATIO BY POUND:CUP	PRESSURE COOK TIME AT HIGH PRESSURE	RELEASE
Short pasta (macaroni, penne, ziti, farfalle, rotini, cavatappi, cellentani, campanelle, or medium shells)	1:4	6 minutes	Quick
Linguine or egg noodles	1:4	6 minutes	Quick
Spaghetti	1:4	8 minutes	Quick
Rigatoni	1:4	8 minutes	Quick
Bucatini	1:4	12 minutes	Quick

- *If making whole-wheat pasta, cut the package's suggested minimum cook time in half, then subtract 1 minute for softer pasta or 2 minutes for al dente pasta.*
- *If making gluten-free pasta, halve the suggested Pressure Cook time in the chart above.*
- *You can't pressure cook chickpea or lentil pasta. It will turn to mush. Believe me, I've tried.*
- *If making pasta without a sauce, drain the excess liquid before serving.*
- *If using a long noodle such as spaghetti or linguine, you must break it in half before adding to the pot. True, some Italian grandmothers may chase you with their rolling pins for doing so, but if you don't, it won't fit or cook properly.*
- *Always add 2 tablespoons butter or oil to the pot to prevent sticking.*
- *Be mindful of doubling pasta because that's double the starch, which could cause some bubbly sputtering from the valve when releasing the pressure. Remember, each of my recipes will feed up to six (some would argue eight), but if you really want to double a pasta dish, do it in an 8-quart pot since there's more room. When doubling a pasta—especially if it contains veggies and proteins—I'd only add an additional half of the given amount of broth and seasonings. This will prevent the dish from becoming too soupy with liquids from the veggies and proteins, or too spicy or salty from the seasonings (but this can be a trial and error process depending on the recipe). The cook time would remain the same as written.*

POULTRY

MEAT (2–4 POUNDS)	PRESSURE COOK TIME AT HIGH PRESSURE WITH 1 CUP OF LIQUID AND MEAT RESTING ON TRIVET	RELEASE
Chicken breasts (boneless or bone-in), 1 inch thick	12 minutes	Quick
Chicken breasts (boneless), ¼ inch thick	8 minutes	Quick
Chicken breasts (boneless), cut into bite-size pieces	5 minutes	Quick
Chicken thighs (bone-in or boneless)	8 minutes	Quick
Chicken thighs (boneless), cut into bite-size pieces	5 minutes	Quick
Chicken drumsticks	6 minutes	Quick
Chicken, whole	25 minutes	15-minute natural followed by quick
Duck breast or leg, confit	10 minutes	5-minute natural followed by quick
Duck, whole	30 minutes	15-minute natural followed by quick
Turkey, whole	40–50 minutes	12-minute natural followed by quick
Turkey breast (boneless or bone-in)	35 minutes	12-minute natural followed by quick

- *All cook times are the suggested general times and will vary based on the quality, cut, and size of meat, as well as the dish you are using it in.*
- *For frozen cuts of meat, add 10–15 minutes of cook time. For a frozen whole chicken, duck, or turkey, thaw before cooking.*

RICE & GRAINS

GRAIN (ALL RINSED FOR 90 SECONDS)	GRAIN:LIQUID RATIO BY CUP:CUP	PRESSURE COOK TIME AT HIGH PRESSURE	RELEASE
White rice (jasmine, basmati, or long-grain)	1:1	3 minutes	10-minute natural followed by quick
Brown rice*	1:1	15–25 minutes	5- to 10-minute natural followed by quick (If going for 15 minutes, do a 10-minute natural release; for 25 minutes, do a 5-minute natural release. As the pressure time increases, the natural release time decreases—so adjust accordingly if cooking within this 10-minute range.)
Arborio rice (risotto)	1:2	6 minutes	Quick
Wild rice	1:2	25 minutes	15-minute natural followed by quick
Quinoa	1:1	1 minute	10-minute natural followed by quick
Barley	1:1½	15 minutes	10-minute natural followed by quick
Couscous (not quick-cooking)	1:2½	6 minutes	Quick
Polenta (not quick-cooking)	1:4	9 minutes	Quick
Oats (steel-cut)	1:2	3 minutes	15-minute natural followed by quick

- *For brown rice, you can go for 15 minutes with a 5-minute natural release for al dente rice and 25 minutes with a 10-minute natural release for softer rice.
- Cook your grains in broth instead of water to really enhance the flavor!
- Some people use a special rice measuring cup when measuring their rice, but I've found it works just as well to use a regular measuring cup, the same as you would with liquid, for the ratios above.

MEAT

MEAT (3–6 POUNDS)	PRESSURE COOK TIME AT HIGH PRESSURE WITH 1 CUP OF LIQUID AND MEAT RESTING ON TRIVET	RELEASE
Beef roast (chuck, bottom, rump, round, brisket), whole	60–75 minutes	15-minute natural followed by quick
Beef roast (chuck, bottom, rump, round, brisket), cut into bite-size pieces	15–20 minutes	15-minute natural followed by quick
Beef stew meat, cut into bite-size pieces	10–18 minutes (the longer, the more tender)	5-minute natural followed by quick
Beef short ribs (boneless or bone-in)	45 minutes	15-minute natural followed by quick
Beef spare ribs (back)	30 minutes	15-minute natural followed by quick
Pork baby back ribs (back loin)	30 minutes	10-minute natural followed by quick
Pork spare ribs (St. Louis style)	30 minutes	10-minute natural followed by quick
Pork shoulder/butt	60–90 minutes	10-minute natural followed by quick
Pork tenderloin, cut into ½-inch-thick medallions	8 minutes	10-minute natural followed by quick
Pork chops (boneless or bone-in), ¾ inch thick	8 minutes	10-minute natural followed by quick
Lamb shanks	40 minutes	15-minute natural followed by quick

- All cook times are the suggested general times and will vary based on the quality, cut, and size of meat, as well as the dish you are using it in.
- For frozen cuts of meat that are bite-size or larger chunks, add 5–10 minutes of cook time. For a frozen whole roast or pork shoulder, I strongly suggest thawing before cooking, but if you just don't have the time for that, or simply forgot and have a hungry crew to feed, add another 15–20 minutes of cook time for a roast between 3 and 6 pounds.

SEAFOOD

SEAFOOD (1–3 POUNDS)	PRESSURE COOK TIME AT HIGH PRESSURE WITH 1 CUP OF LIQUID AND SEAFOOD RESTING ON TRIVET	RELEASE
General fish (salmon, halibut, cod, mahi-mahi, haddock, tilapia, etc.), ¼ to 1 inch thick	3–4 minutes	Quick
Large/jumbo shrimp, tail on	0–1 minute	Quick
Lobster tail	4 minutes	Quick
Snow crab legs	2 minutes	Quick
King crab legs	3 minutes	Quick
Mussels, fresh	2 minutes	Quick
Clams, fresh	2 minutes	Quick

• All cook times are the suggested general times and will vary based on the quality and size of the seafood, as well as the dish you are using it in.

• If using frozen seafood, increase the Pressure Cook Time by 1 minute for shrimp and 2 minutes for everything else.

BEANS & LEGUMES

1 POUND DRIED (RINSED)	PRESSURE COOK TIME AT HIGH PRESSURE, SOAKED IN SALTED WATER FOR 6–8 HOURS, THEN COOKED WITH 4 CUPS WATER OR BROTH	PRESSURE COOK TIME AT HIGH PRESSURE, UNSOAKED, COOKED WITH 4 CUPS WATER OR BROTH	RELEASE
Black	15–20 minutes	20–25 minutes	15-minute natural followed by quick
Black-eyed peas	10–15 minutes	30–35 minutes	15-minute natural followed by quick
Cannellini, great northern, or navy	10–15 minutes	35–45 minutes	15-minute natural followed by quick
Chickpea/garbanzo	15–20 minutes	40–45 minutes	15-minute natural followed by quick
Kidney	15–20 minutes	20–25 minutes	15-minute natural followed by quick
Lima	15–20 minutes	25–30 minutes	15-minute natural followed by quick
Pinto	10–15 minutes	30–35 minutes	15-minute natural followed by quick
Red	15–20 minutes	25–30 minutes	15-minute natural followed by quick
Lentils (brown)	N/A	10 minutes	Quick
Split peas (green or yellow)	N/A	6 minutes	15-minute natural followed by quick

• All cook times are the suggested general times and may vary based on the dish you are using the beans in.

VEGETABLES

VEGETABLE	PRESSURE COOK TIME AT HIGH PRESSURE WITH 1 CUP OF LIQUID AND VEGGIES RESTING ON TRIVET OR IN STEAMER BASKET	RELEASE
Artichokes, whole	12 minutes	Quick
Asparagus	1 minute	Quick
Beets (larger require more time)	15–25 minutes	Quick
Bell peppers, whole	3 minutes	Quick
Broccoli florets	1 minute	Quick
Brussels sprouts	2 minutes	Quick
Cabbage, whole head	8 minutes	Quick
Carrots	2 minutes	Quick
Cauliflower, whole head	4 minutes	Quick
Celery	3 minutes	Quick
Corn, on the cob	3 minutes	Quick
Eggplant, sliced	2 minutes	Quick
Green beans	3 minutes	Quick
Greens (collards, kale, spinach, etc.)	4 minutes	Quick
Okra	2 minutes	Quick
Onions, sliced	4 minutes	Quick
Peas	1 minute	Quick
Potatoes, peeled and cubed	6 minutes	Quick
Potatoes, whole	15 minutes	10-minute natural followed by quick
Squash (butternut or acorn), halved	6–10 minutes	Quick
Sweet potatoes	10–15 minutes	10-minute natural followed by quick
Tomatoes, whole	3 minutes	Quick
Zucchini, sliced	2 minutes	Quick

• *All cook times are the suggested general times and may vary based on the dish you are using the vegetables in.*

• *If veggies are frozen, add 1–2 minutes more.*

1

SAUCES
FOR NOW & LATER

Whether you're working with meats, veggies, or starches, a great sauce can be the thing that elevates a dish from good to outstanding.

Not only do sauces work well immediately after they're prepared, they also keep for weeks in the refrigerator (where the flavors really come together) or freezer—making them perfect for now and later.

Every flavor-packed sauce in this chapter will go from the pot to the table in just about an hour—no all-day stovetop simmering here. And each will yield 2 to 4 quarts! So grab an apron and some napkins because we're about to get saucy.

= DUMP & GO RECIPE

 = 5 INGREDIENTS OR LESS

 = 3 STEPS OR LESS

 = AIR FRYER LID

 K = KETO

P = PALEO

 DF = DAIRY-FREE

 GF = GLUTEN-FREE

V = VEGETARIAN

 VN = VEGAN

✛ = COMPLIANT WITH MODIFICATIONS

CLASSIC ★ RED SAUCE

K
P
DF
GF
VN

A classic Italian-style marinara (or red sauce) is all it takes to transform any pasta or chicken preparation into a magnificent meal to remember. I have a more robust, garlic-laden marinara in my orange (original *Step-by-Step*) book, but I wanted to give you a simpler red sauce here. This healthy recipe is lightning-quick compared to an all-day stovetop simmer.

Prep Time	Sauté Time	Pressure Building Time	Pressure Cook Time	Total Time	Serves
5 MIN	8 MIN	10–15 MIN	5 MIN	30 MIN	4–6

½ cup extra-virgin olive oil

1 large Spanish or yellow onion, diced

12 cloves garlic, minced or pressed

2 (28-ounce) cans whole peeled tomatoes, with their juices (San Marzano are the best, if you want to get a little fancy)

2 cups vegetable or garlic broth (e.g., Garlic Better Than Bouillon)

2 tablespoons Italian seasoning

1–2 tablespoons seasoned salt (start with 1 and add more to taste)

1 tablespoon garlic powder

1½ teaspoons sugar (optional)

1 (6-ounce) can tomato paste

1 Add the olive oil to the Instant Pot. Hit Sauté and Adjust so it's on the More or High setting. After 3 minutes of heating, add the onion and sauté for 3 minutes, until translucent. Add the garlic and sauté for 2 minutes more.

2 Pour in the canned tomatoes, broth, and Italian seasoning and stir well.

3 Secure the lid and move the valve to the sealing position. Hit Cancel followed by Manual or Pressure Cook on High Pressure for 5 minutes. Quick release when done.

JEFF'S TIPS If you wish to give this sauce a kick, add some ground black pepper, cayenne pepper, or crushed red pepper flakes to taste in Step 4.

Of course, as with any sauce, you can feel free to taste and add any seasonings you wish when adding the final ingredients in Step 4.

4 Take a potato masher and mash the tomatoes up to the desired chunkiness. Stir in the seasoned salt, garlic powder, sugar (if using), and tomato paste (**see Jeff's Tips**).

5 You can serve immediately with pasta, chicken, or veggies, but the longer it cools, the more it will thicken. If storing for future use, allow to fully cool before doing so.

To Serve 1–2 Simply halve the recipe. Cook times remain the same.

BOLOGNESE SAUCE

 K
 P
 DF
 GF

Bolognese is a fragrant Italian sauce loaded with meat and infused with a key ingredient: wine. The meat simmers in the wine for a bit until the wine reduces, then we add tomatoes and give it a smooth, slightly creamy finish (or leave the dairy out if you like). My orange (original *Step-by-Step*) book has an acclaimed Bolognese recipe in which the pasta cooks in the sauce, but if it's just the sauce you seek (making it done even more quickly), this is the recipe for you. Here, I use more tomatoes than traditionally called for as well as heavy cream instead of milk for a richer taste.

Prep Time	Sauté Time	Pressure Building Time	Pressure Cook Time	Total Time	Serves
5 MIN	20 MIN	10–15 MIN	5 MIN	40 MIN	4–6

1/2 cup extra-virgin olive oil

1 large Spanish or yellow onion, diced

2 large carrots, peeled and diced

6 cloves garlic, minced or pressed

1 1/2 pounds ground meat of your choice (I like a mix of veal, pork, and beef)

1 cup dry red wine (like a cabernet sauvignon; and see Jeff's Tips)

2 (28-ounce) cans crushed tomatoes (San Marzano are the best, if you want to get a little fancy)

1 cup beef or garlic broth (e.g., Garlic Better Than Bouillon)

1 tablespoon Italian seasoning

1 tablespoon seasoned or celery salt

1/2 cup heavy cream or half-and-half (optional)

1 (5.2-ounce) package Boursin cheese (any flavor), or 3/4 cup Garlic Herb Cheese (page 21), cut into chunks (optional)

1 Add the olive oil to the Instant Pot. Hit Sauté and Adjust so it's on the More or High setting. After 3 minutes of heating, add the onion and carrot and sauté for 3 minutes, until slightly softened. Add the garlic and meat and sauté for 3 minutes more, until the meat is lightly browned and crumbled. Leave those juices in the pot—they enhance the flavor profile.

2 Add the wine and let the meat simmer for 10 minutes (this step is important as it infuses the meat with rich flavor). Scrape the bottom of the pot occasionally to loosen any browned bits.

3 Add the crushed tomatoes, broth, and Italian seasoning. Stir until well combined.

4 Secure the lid and move the valve to the sealing position. Hit Cancel followed by Manual or Pressure Cook on High Pressure for 5 minutes. Quick release when done.

5 Stir in the seasoned or celery salt, cream (if using), and Boursin (if using) until well combined.

6 You can serve immediately over pasta or veggies, but the longer it cools, the more it will thicken. If storing for future use, allow to fully cool before doing so.

JEFF'S TIPS While I love a Bolognese with a slightly creamy finish, some prefer it without. Feel free to simply omit the cream and Boursin.

If you don't wish to use wine, sub an additional cup of broth and have the meat simmer in that.

To make the flavor slightly more complex, use ¾ cup dry red wine plus ¼ cup dry white in lieu of the full cup of red.

To Serve 1-2 Simply halve the recipe. Cook times remain the same.

VODKA SAUCE

One of the most popular pasta dishes on any Italian-American menu is a classic penne alla vodka. And is that a surprise? It's basically a red sauce with a kiss of rich dairy, giving it a pinkish hue and the most satisfying of flavors. My Instant Pot version delivers those delicious results with no hassle or mess. And don't worry about the vodka—the sauce won't taste like it. Its main contribution is to make the sauce more cohesive, which allows the tomatoes to flow nicely with the creamy finish in a beautiful, smooth texture.

Prep Time	Sauté Time	Pressure Building Time	Pressure Cook Time	Total Time	Serves
5 MIN	7 MIN	10–15 MIN	5 MIN	30 MIN	4–6

2 tablespoons (¼ stick) salted butter

2 large shallots, diced

6 cloves garlic, minced or pressed

½ cup vodka

2 (28-ounce) cans whole peeled tomatoes, with their juices (San Marzano are the best, if you want to get a little fancy)

Leaves from 2 bunches fresh basil

1 cup heavy cream or half-and-half

1 cup grated Parmesan cheese

1 (5.2-ounce) package Boursin cheese (any flavor), or ¾ cup Garlic Herb Cheese (page 21), or 4 ounces brick cream cheese, cut into chunks (optional)

1 tablespoon seasoned salt or Cajun/Creole/Louisiana seasoning (I use Tony Chachere's)

1 Add the butter to the Instant Pot. Hit Sauté and Adjust so it's on the More or High setting. Once melted and bubbling, add the shallots and garlic and sauté for 3 minutes, until fragrant.

2 Add the vodka and let simmer for 1 minute. Deglaze (scrape the bottom of the pot) to get up any browned bits at this time.

3 Pour in the tomatoes and stir until well combined. Top with the basil, but *do not stir*.

4 Secure the lid and move the valve to the sealing position. Hit Cancel followed by Manual or Pressure Cook on High Pressure for 5 minutes. Quick release when done.

5 Blend with an immersion blender until the consistency is a mix of smooth and slightly chunky.

6 Stir in the cream, Parmesan, and Boursin (if using) until fully melted into the sauce. Add the seasoned salt and stir.

7 You can serve immediately with pasta, roasts, chicken, or veggies, but the longer it cools, the more the flavors will come together. If storing for future use, allow to fully cool before doing so.

To Serve 1–2 Simply halve the recipe. Cook times remain the same.

JEFF'S TIPS Some enjoy their vodka sauce with diced pancetta, guanciale, or thick-cut bacon tossed in. If that's you, double the butter and sauté about 8 ounces of chosen pork for 3 to 5 minutes just before adding the shallots in Step 1. Then, deglaze (scrape the bottom of the pot) when adding the vodka in Step 2. The pork won't necessarily be crispy, but rather on the chewier side.

For a thicker sauce, just before Step 6, mix 2–3 tablespoons each of both cornstarch and cold water in a bowl to form a slurry. Hit Sauté so the pot bubbles and stir in the slurry, until thickened. Then, continue with the recipe.

CAJUN-STYLE
· SAUCE ·

K + *(if you're okay with a cornstarch slurry)*

GF

V + *(if using garlic or vegetable broth)*

I recently went to this cute, cozy restaurant in the country and they had an amazing dish of a spicy, flavor-filled cream sauce draped over a trio of meats—chicken, filet mignon, and shrimp—resting on a bed of rice and veggies. When I asked the owner what was in it, she responded, "cream and Cajun." That didn't help much. But the sauce was beyond addictive and tastes amazing with just about anything. So I had to come up with my own rendition of it to share with you, starting with plenty of garlic and my favorite Cajun spice blend.

Prep Time	Sauté Time	Pressure Building Time	Pressure Cook Time	Total Time	Serves
5 MIN	8 MIN	10–15 MIN	3 MIN	30 MIN	4–6

2 tablespoons (¼ stick) salted butter

12 cloves garlic, sliced into thin slivers

4 cups chicken or garlic broth (e.g., Garlic Better Than Bouillon)

1 tablespoon Cajun/Creole/Louisiana seasoning (I use Tony Chachere's), divided

1 tablespoon dried parsley flakes

5 tablespoons cornstarch plus 5 tablespoons cold water

1 cup heavy cream or half-and-half

1 cup grated Parmesan cheese

½–1 teaspoon each of cayenne pepper, smoked paprika, and/or crushed red pepper flakes, to taste (optional)

1 Add the butter to the Instant Pot. Hit Sauté and Adjust so it's on the More or High setting. Once melted and bubbling, add the garlic and sauté for 5 minutes, until lightly browned.

2 Add the broth, 1½ teaspoons of the Cajun seasoning, and the dried parsley. Stir until well combined and scrape to remove any browned bits from the bottom of the pot.

3 Secure the lid and move the valve to the sealing position. Hit Cancel followed by Manual or Pressure Cook on High Pressure for 3 minutes. Quick release when done.

4 Meanwhile, mix together the cornstarch and cold water in a bowl to form a slurry.

5 Hit Cancel and then Sauté and Adjust to the More or High setting. Once bubbling, immediately stir in the slurry. Then add the remaining 1½ teaspoons Cajun seasoning along with the cream and Parmesan, and stir until fully combined into the sauce. Hit Cancel to turn the pot off.

6 If you want this sauce spicy, stir in cayenne or crushed red pepper to taste. Start with ½ teaspoon of either the cayenne or red pepper flakes and go from there. You can serve immediately over roasts, chicken, seafood, rice, veggies, or pasta, but the longer it cools, the more it will thicken. If storing for future use, allow to fully cool before doing so.

 JEFF'S TIPS One difference between Cajun and Creole cooking is that Creole cooks often use tomatoes in recipes whereas Cajun cooks generally don't. In order to make this a Creole-style sauce, add 1–2 (14.5-ounce) cans drained diced tomatoes in Step 5 when adding the dairy.

Once a cornstarch slurry is mixed into a sauce and the sauce is refrigerated, it can become quite thick. Heating it up will bring it right back to its proper consistency.

 To Serve 1–2 Simply halve the recipe. Cook times remain the same.

STIR-FRY SAUCE

 K + *(if you're okay with wine and a cornstarch slurry)*

 P + *(if you're okay with wine and a cornstarch slurry)*

GF

V

Many Asian cuisines are known for incredible stir-fries: This sweet and savory garlic sauce is a simple way to bring some of those beloved flavors to your Instant Pot. With its combination of hoisin (sweet) and oyster (savory) sauces, it is perfect over any protein, long-form noodle, or combination of stir-fried veggies, and will keep you coming back for more.

Prep Time	Sauté Time	Pressure Building Time	Pressure Cook Time	Total Time	Serves
5 MIN	9 MIN	10–15 MIN	5 MIN	30 MIN	4–6

1/4 cup vegetable oil

1 large white or yellow onion, sliced into 1/4-inch-thick strands

3 red and/or green bell peppers (see Jeff's Tips), sliced into 1/4-inch-thick strands

12 cloves garlic: 6 crushed or minced, 6 sliced into thin slivers

1/2 cup sherry or Shaoxing wine (or see Jeff's Tips)

3 1/2 cups vegetable or garlic broth (e.g., Garlic Better Than Bouillon)

3 tablespoons cornstarch plus 3 tablespoons cold water

1/2 cup hoisin sauce

1/2 cup oyster sauce

1 Add the oil to the Instant Pot. Hit Sauté and Adjust so it's on the More or High setting. After 3 minutes of heating, add the onion, peppers, and all the garlic and sauté for 5 minutes, until translucent.

2 Add the wine and let simmer for 1 minute longer, deglazing (scraping the bottom of the pot) to get up any browned bits. Add the broth and stir.

3 Secure the lid and move the valve to the sealing position. Hit Cancel followed by Manual or Pressure Cook on High Pressure for 5 minutes. Quick release when done.

4 Meanwhile mix together the cornstarch and cold water in a bowl to form a slurry.

5 When the lid comes off, give it a stir. Hit Cancel and then Sauté and Adjust to the More or High setting. Once bubbling, immediately stir in the slurry until thickened. Add the hoisin and oyster sauces. Stir until fully combined. Hit Cancel to turn the pot off. Pour over noodles, rice, any protein, and/or veggies of your choice!

 JEFF'S TIPS Use virtually any pepper you wish here and feel free to add more than what the recipe calls for. For a spicier sauce, be bold and add a diced jalapeño, red chile, or even (dare I say it) habanero chile in Step 1 while sautéing.

If you don't want to use wine, add another ½ cup of broth.

Once a cornstarch slurry is mixed in and the sauce is refrigerated, it can become quite thick. Heating it up will bring it right back to its proper consistency.

 To Serve 1–2 Simply halve the recipe. Cook times remain the same.

TUSCAN SAUCE

DUMP & GO!

K + *(if you're okay with wine and a cornstarch slurry)*

GF

V + *(if using garlic or vegetable broth)*

This is the ultimate cream sauce: Loaded with spinach, garlic, and Parmesan, it's like a trip to the Italian countryside right in your Instant Pot. It's similar to an Alfredo, but even more vibrantly flavored. It will work gloriously when tossed with thin and flowy angel hair pasta or thick and tubular ziti.

Prep Time	Pressure Building Time	Pressure Cook Time	Sauté Time	Total Time	Serves
5 MIN	10–15 MIN	5 MIN	2 MIN	25 MIN	4–6

2 tablespoons (¼ stick) salted butter

1 cup dry white wine (like a sauvignon blanc), optional (see Jeff's Tips)

2 cups chicken, garlic, or mushroom broth (e.g., Garlic or Mushroom Better Than Bouillon)

1 tablespoon Italian seasoning

2 tablespoons garlic powder, divided

8–12 ounces baby spinach

3 tablespoons cornstarch plus 3 tablespoons cold water

1½ cups heavy cream or half-and-half

1 cup grated Parmesan cheese

1 (5.2-ounce) package Boursin cheese (any flavor), or ¾ cup Garlic Herb Cheese (page 21), cut into chunks (optional)

1 Add the butter, wine (if using), broth, Italian seasoning, and 1 tablespoon of the garlic powder to the Instant Pot and stir. Top with the spinach but *do not stir*. (NOTE: It may seem like a lot of spinach, but trust me—it cooks down.)

2 Secure the lid and move the valve to the sealing position. Hit Cancel followed by Manual or Pressure Cook on High Pressure for 5 minutes. Quick release when done.

3 Meanwhile, mix together the cornstarch and cold water in a bowl to form a slurry.

4 When the lid comes off, you'll see the spinach will have cooked down dramatically. Give it a stir. Hit Cancel and then Sauté and Adjust to the More or High setting. Once bubbling, immediately stir in the slurry. Then add the cream, the remaining 1 tablespoon garlic powder, the Parmesan, and Boursin (if using). Stir until fully melded into the sauce. Hit Cancel to turn the pot off.

5 You can serve immediately over roasts, chicken, seafood, rice, veggies, and pasta, but the longer it cools, the more it will thicken. If storing for future use, allow to fully cool before doing so.

JEFF'S TIPS If you want to load this sauce up with mushrooms (which I sometimes do), add another 2 tablespoons (¼ stick) butter (so 4 tablespoons total) and 1 pound sliced baby bella or white mushrooms in Step 1. Sauté for 5 minutes.

If you don't wish to use wine, sub an additional cup of broth.

Once a cornstarch slurry is mixed in and the sauce is refrigerated, it can become quite thick. Heating it up will bring it right back to its proper consistency.

To Serve 1–2 Simply halve the recipe. Cook times remain the same.

MARSALA
· SAUCE ·

K + *(if you're okay with wine and a cornstarch slurry)*

P + *(if using olive oil)*

DF + *(if using olive oil)*

GF

V + *(if using garlic or vegetable broth)*

Ah, Marsala—that lovely, iconic Italian sauce loaded with the flavor of sweet Marsala wine and mushrooms galore. My recipes for chicken Marsala and its pasta counterparts are big hits, so I wanted to include a quick-and-dirty solo-sauce recipe in this shortcuts cookbook. The sauce is commonly served over chicken, but will also delight when cascading over any pasta, grain, protein, or veggie.

Prep Time	Sauté Time	Pressure Building Time	Pressure Cook Time	Total Time	Serves
10 MIN	10 MIN	10–15 MIN	3 MIN	35 MIN	4–6

4 tablespoons (½ stick) salted butter or ¼ cup extra-virgin olive oil

1 pound baby bella or white mushrooms, sliced

2 large shallots, diced

6 cloves garlic, minced or pressed

2 cups Marsala wine (use dry for a more savory sauce and sweet for a very sweet sauce; cooking Marsala will also work)

2 cups chicken, garlic, or mushroom broth (e.g., Garlic or Mushroom Better Than Bouillon)

1 tablespoon Italian seasoning

¼ cup cornstarch plus ¼ cup cold water

1 Add the butter or olive oil to the Instant Pot. Hit Sauté and Adjust so it's on the More or High setting. Once melted and bubbling, add the mushrooms and shallots and sauté for 5 minutes, until the mushrooms are lightly browned. Add the garlic and sauté for 1 minute longer.

2 Add the wine and deglaze (scrape the bottom of the pot), freeing up any browned garlic and mushrooms. Allow to simmer for 1 minute.

3 Add the broth and Italian seasoning and stir. Secure the lid and move the valve to the sealing position. Hit Cancel followed by Manual or Pressure Cook on High Pressure for 3 minutes. Quick release when done.

4 Meanwhile, mix together the cornstarch and cold water in a bowl to form a slurry.

5 When the lid comes off, give it a stir. Hit Cancel and then Sauté and Adjust to the More or High setting. Once bubbling, immediately stir in the slurry until thickened. Hit Cancel to turn the pot off.

JEFF'S TIPS

If you want this Marsala sauce a touch creamy, in Step 5 after you've added the slurry, add up to ½ cup of either heavy cream or half-and-half, or a 5.2-ounce package of Boursin.

Once the slurry is mixed in and the sauce is refrigerated, it can become quite thick. Heating it up will bring it right back to its proper consistency.

To Serve 1–2

Simply halve the recipe. Cook times remain the same.

LEMON PARMESAN SAUCE

When life gives you lemons, make this sauce. It's an irresistible concoction that has all the beauty of an Alfredo with the added brightness of lemons, marrying refreshing citrus flavors with cheese and cream. Of course, you can tone down the dairy should you wish (see Jeff's Tips). One ladle of this sunny sauce is all it takes to make any dish exciting—from chicken to shrimp, and rice to pasta.

Prep Time	Sauté Time	Pressure Building Time	Pressure Cook Time	Total Time	Serves
5 MIN	6 MIN	10–15 MIN	3 MIN	25 MIN	4–6

4 tablespoons (½ stick) salted butter

2 large shallots, diced

3½ cups chicken or garlic broth (e.g., Garlic Better Than Bouillon)

Juice and grated zest of 3 lemons

1 tablespoon dried parsley

2 tablespoons cornstarch plus 2 tablespoons cold water

3 large eggs

1 cup heavy cream or half-and-half

1 cup grated Parmesan cheese

1 Add the butter to the Instant Pot. Hit Sauté and Adjust so it's on the More or High setting. Once melted and bubbling, add the shallots and sauté for 3 minutes, until translucent.

2 Add the broth, lemon juice, and dried parsley and stir.

3 Secure the lid and move the valve to the sealing position. Hit Cancel followed by Manual or Pressure Cook on High Pressure for 3 minutes. Quick release when done.

4 Meanwhile, in one bowl, mix together the cornstarch and cold water to form a slurry. In another bowl, whisk together the eggs and cream.

5 When the lid comes off, give it a stir. Hit Cancel and then Sauté and Adjust to the More or High setting. Once bubbling, immediately stir in the slurry until thickened. Gently stir in the creamy egg mixture followed by the Parmesan and lemon zest. Hit Cancel to turn the pot off.

JEFF'S TIPS

You can cut down on this sauce's richness by simply omitting the cream and Parmesan in Step 4 and you'll still have a magnificent egg lemon sauce (while keeping it dairy-free if you also swap the butter with 2 tablespoons olive oil in Step 1). If you want it thicker, just add 1–2 tablespoons additional cornstarch slurry until you've reached the desired consistency.

Once a cornstarch slurry is mixed in and the sauce is refrigerated, it can become quite thick. Heating it up will bring it right back to its proper consistency.

To Serve 1–2

Simply halve the recipe. Cook times remain the same.

·SIMPLY·
SUNDAY SAUCE

A Sunday sauce (or "gravy") is a staple in many Italian-American households. Often a family affair, it's a red sauce that is simmered in a pot on the stove all Sunday (and sampled by those who pass by) as the house fills with the aromas that conjure memories of the past. What makes Sunday sauce special is that it contains meat—*lots* of meat. Here we take some shortcuts to make it in about an hour, and use sausage and short ribs to create unforgettably rich flavor.

Prep Time	Sauté Time	Pressure Building Time	Pressure Cook Time	Natural Release Time	Total Time	Serves
15 MIN	10 MIN	10–15 MIN	25 MIN	15 MIN	1 HR 15 MIN	4–6

- 1/4 cup extra-virgin olive oil
- 1 large Spanish or yellow onion, diced
- 12 cloves garlic: 6 crushed or minced, 6 sliced into thin slivers
- 2 pounds Italian sausage (sweet or hot, or a mix of the two, or see Jeff's Tip); 1 pound with the casings removed, 1 pound with each link cut into 1/2-inch pieces

- 6 cups marinara sauce (I like the Rao's and Victoria brands, but you can also use my Classic Red Sauce, page 28)
- 1 cup beef or garlic broth (e.g., Garlic Better Than Bouillon)
- 11/2 pounds short ribs
- Leaves from 1 bunch fresh basil

- 1 (6-ounce) can tomato paste
- 1 tablespoon dried oregano
- 1/2 cup grated Parmesan cheese (optional, and you can also do this to taste)

1 Add the oil to the Instant Pot. Hit Sauté and Adjust so it's on the More or High setting. After 3 minutes of heating, add the onion and garlic. Sauté for 3 minutes, until translucent.

2 Add the sausage and stir until lightly browned, 3–5 minutes.

3 Pour in the marinara and broth and stir until well combined. Nestle in the short ribs and top with the basil but *do not stir.*

4 Secure the lid and move the valve to the sealing position. Hit Cancel followed by Manual or Pressure Cook on High Pressure for 25 minutes. When done, allow a 15-minute natural release followed by a quick release.

5 Using tongs, remove the short ribs to a cutting board and carefully slide the meat off the bone, then slice the meat into bite-size pieces.

6 Using a ladle, skim off about 2 cups of the drippings from the top of the pot and discard.

7 Add the tomato paste, oregano, and Parmesan (to taste, if using) and stir until fully integrated into the sauce. Return the sliced short rib meat back to the pot, giving it all a final stir before serving over pasta. (NOTE: This sauce will come together more once it cools—so I suggest letting it rest a solid 15 minutes before serving. And once refrigerated, the flavors *really* come together nicely.)

JEFF'S TIP The Italian sausage and short ribs provide such deep flavor to the sauce, but you can load it up with any meat you like (be it ground beef, veal, or pork). Just don't exceed a total of 3½ pounds of meat or the pot will have issues coming to pressure.

CREAMY COCONUT CURRY SAUCE

K + (if you're okay with a cornstarch slurry)

GF

V

With all the rich spices and deep flavors Indian cuisine employs, it's no surprise that its influence is responsible for some of the most flavorful and memorable sauces around. With this rich curry-based sauce, we highlight the flavor profiles of the many Indian classics that rely on simple ingredients. It's all about the coconut milk base, yogurt, and a key Indian spice blend, garam masala. It pairs wonderfully with meat, chicken, seafood, rice, and samosas!

Prep Time	Sauté Time	Pressure Building Time	Pressure Cook Time	Total Time	Serves
5 MIN	6 MIN	10–15 MIN	3 MIN	25 MIN	4–6

- 4 tablespoons (½ stick) salted butter
- 1 large Vidalia (sweet) onion, diced
- 2 (14.5-ounce) cans unsweetened coconut milk (shake can vigorously to mix before opening; it should be thin like water, not thick and lumpy)

- 2 (14.5-ounce) cans diced tomatoes, with their juices
- 2 tablespoons garam masala (see Jeff's Tips), divided
- 3 tablespoons cornstarch plus 3 tablespoons cold water

- 2 tablespoons curry powder
- 1–3 teaspoons seasoned salt
- ½ cup heavy cream or half-and-half
- ½ cup Greek yogurt

1 Add the butter to the Instant Pot. Hit Sauté and Adjust so it's on the More or High setting. Once melted and bubbling, add the onion and sauté for 3 minutes, until translucent.

2 Add the coconut milk, diced tomatoes, and 1 tablespoon of the garam masala and stir.

3 Secure the lid and move the valve to the sealing position. Hit Cancel followed by Manual or Pressure Cook on High Pressure for 3 minutes. Quick release when done.

4 Meanwhile mix together the cornstarch and cold water in a bowl to form a slurry.

5 When the lid comes off, give the sauce a stir. Hit Cancel and then Sauté and Adjust to the More or High setting. Once bubbling, immediately stir in the slurry until thickened. Add the remaining 1 tablespoon garam masala, the curry powder, seasoned salt (start with 1 teaspoon), cream, and yogurt. Stir until fully combined. Taste and decide if you want to add more seasoned salt. Hit Cancel to turn the pot off.

JEFF'S TIPS

Garam masala is an Indian spice blend that is available at many international and Indian-centric markets. It's also easily available online. The brands I strongly recommend are Rani and Swad.

Once a cornstarch slurry is mixed in and the sauce is refrigerated, it can become quite thick. Heating it up will bring it right back to its proper consistency.

To Serve 1–2

Simply halve the recipe. Cook times remain the same.

2

SOUPS & STEWS

Soup can be one of the most foolproof and rewarding dishes to make in the Instant Pot: Not only is it nearly impossible to mess up, but it's easy to customize and experiment with. You can add whatever seasonings, spices, and goodies you wish to any existing soup recipe and adapt it to create your own masterpiece.

This chapter will set you up to make some seriously satisfying and spectacular soups with minimal ingredients in lightning-quick fashion!

 = DUMP & GO RECIPE

 = 5 INGREDIENTS OR LESS

 = 3 STEPS OR LESS

 = AIR FRYER LID

 = KETO

 = PALEO

 = DAIRY-FREE

 = GLUTEN-FREE

 = VEGETARIAN

 = VEGAN

 = COMPLIANT WITH MODIFICATIONS

HAM & CHEESE CHOWDER

One afternoon in the winter of 2022, I was craving a toasted, melty ham and cheese sandwich... but I also wanted a thick and hearty soup. A light bulb went off and I felt inspired to transform the hammiest and cheesiest ham and cheese sandwich into the most decadent chowder. To add to the challenge, I wanted to do it with less than ten ingredients (just seven in this case, to be exact). The end result tasted so great and was so simple, it was borderline surreal. Scoop it with some garlic toast or a buttery, toasty croissant.

DUMP & GO!

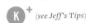
K ⁺ (see Jeff's Tips)

GF

Prep Time	Pressure Building Time	Pressure Cook Time	Sauté Time	Total Time	Serves
5 MIN	10–15 MIN	3 MIN	3 MIN	25 MIN	4–6

- **4 cups chicken or ham broth (e.g., Ham Better Than Bouillon)**
- ¼ cup sherry wine (optional, but if not using, sub an additional ¼ cup broth)
- **2 pounds Idaho (russet) potatoes (about 2–3 of them), peeled and diced** (NOTE: You can also use baby potatoes and quarter them without peeling.)

- **3 tablespoons cornstarch plus 3 tablespoons cold water**
- **2 cups heavy cream or half-and-half**
- **1 (5.2-ounce) package Boursin cheese (any flavor), or ¾ cup Garlic Herb Cheese (page 21), cut into chunks**

- **4 cups (1 pound) shredded cheese (see Jeff's Tips), plus more for topping** (I used half Swiss and half Cheddar, but you can use any kind you like)
- **1½ pounds ham of your choice, cut into ¼-inch cubes** (ask the deli counter to slice the ham into three thick slices of ½ pound each)

1 Add the broth, sherry (if using), and potatoes to the Instant Pot. Stir well.

2 Secure the lid, move the valve to the sealing position, hit Cancel, and then hit Manual or Pressure Cook on High Pressure for 3 minutes. Quick release when done.

3 Meanwhile, mix together the cornstarch and cold water in a bowl to form a slurry.

4 Hit Cancel and then hit Sauté and Adjust so it's on the More or High setting. Once bubbling, stir in the cornstarch slurry and let bubble for about 30 seconds. Turn the heat off the pot—the soup will have thickened into a chowder consistency almost immediately.

5 Add the cream and Boursin. In batches, whisk in the shredded cheese. Stir until fully combined and then stir in the ham.

6 Ladle the soup into bowls and serve topped with more cheese.

JEFF'S TIPS This makes a wonderfully *thick* and *rich* chowder! For a thinner chowder, lessen the slurry to 1–2 tablespoons each of cornstarch and water. You can start with less and always add more.

You don't need to use all the cheese: Start with 2 cups and work your way up. But I like it super cheesy.

To make it lighter on the carbs (and keto), sub a large head of cauliflower for the potatoes. Remove the stalk, chop up the florets, and add them to the pot when you would the potatoes, but reduce the pressure cook time to 1 minute (instead of 3).

Top the soup with a few small drops of liquid smoke to give it an extra smoky flavor!

If you make the recipe as written, refrigerated leftovers are going to really thicken. When reheating, simply add more broth or cream to your liking and stir until it's the desired consistency.

To Serve 1–2 Simply halve the recipe. Cook times remain the same.

CHICKEN SOUP
· WITH *WILD* RICE ·

In a song from her and Maurice Sendak's musical *Really Rosie*, legendary singer-songwriter Carole King sings, "Happy once, happy twice, happy chicken soup with rice." And, of course, she knows exactly what she's talking about. In the case of this creamy, rice-y, and oh-so-simple variation on chicken soup, I use wild rice for that perfect bite: mildly nutty, beautifully textured, and vibrantly colored. Side note: When my first book tour stopped in Minneapolis, the friendly crowd let me know that wild rice is big in Minnesota—so this one is for them!

Prep Time	Sauté Time	Pressure Building Time	Pressure Cook Time	Total Time	Serves
10 MIN	8 MIN	10–15 MIN	35 MIN	1 HR 10 MIN	4–6

- **4 tablespoons (½ stick) salted butter**
- **2 medium carrots, peeled and diced**
- **3 ribs celery, diced**
- **6 cups chicken broth**
- **1 cup wild rice (no need to rinse, and see Jeff's Tips)**

- **1–2 tablespoons Creole/Cajun/ Louisiana seasoning (I use Tony Chachere's) or seasoned salt, divided**
- **2 teaspoons dried sage**

- **2–3½ pounds boneless, skinless chicken breasts and/or thighs** (NOTE: I use an equal portion of each. The more chicken used, the more of a stew-like consistency. Go for 1½–2 pounds if you want it more soupy.)
- **2 cups heavy cream or half-and-half**
- **½ cup all-purpose flour**

1 Add the butter to the Instant Pot and hit Sauté and Adjust so it's on the More or High setting. Once melted and bubbling, add the carrots and celery and sauté for 5 minutes.

2 Add the broth, rice, 1 tablespoon of the Creole seasoning (or seasoned salt), and sage. Stir, then nestle in the chicken, making sure it's submerged in the broth.

3 Secure the lid, move the valve to the sealing position, hit Cancel, and then hit Pressure Cook or Manual at High Pressure for 35 minutes. Quick release when done.

4 Meanwhile, in a separate bowl, whisk together the cream and flour until thickened.

5 Using tongs, remove the chicken to a bowl, then shred with two forks (it will fall apart) or use a hand mixer to *really* make your job easier.

6 Hit Cancel followed by Sauté and Adjust so it's on the More or High setting. Once bubbling, stir the creamy flour mixture into the pot. Keep stirring until combined and let bubble for 2 minutes before hitting Cancel to turn the pot off. Return the chicken to the pot and stir. Taste the soup. If you feel it needs more Creole seasoning or seasoned salt, add up to another tablespoon now (but do it in teaspoon increments so as to not oversalt).

7 Ladle into bowls and serve with crusty French or Italian bread.

 To Serve 1-2 Simply halve the recipe. Cook times remain the same.

 JEFF'S TIPS For a very thick and hearty soup (like a stew or creamy chicken cacciatore), use 3½ pounds chicken and 1½ cups wild rice. For a thinner soup, use no more than 2 pounds chicken and ¾ cup wild rice. Same cook time regardless of amounts used.

You don't need to use wild rice exclusively (it is pricier than most but it's also extra delicious)—you can use a wild rice blend instead, but it won't be as prominent as wild rice on its own.

SAUSAGE GNOCCHI SOUP

When sizzling sausage and gentle gnocchi play together in a luscious broth, all is right in the world. This beautiful soup, like a richer, thicker version of my popular Sausage & Spinach Soup from the orange (original *Step-by-Step* book, is so loaded with stunning color and hearty flavor, it's going to immediately become one of your favorites. Feel free to substitute any kind of uncooked sausage for the Italian (although hot Italian sausage is where the special color and flavor come from).

Prep Time	Sauté Time	Pressure Building Time	Pressure Cook Time	Total Time	Serves
5 MIN	8 MIN	10–15 MIN	5 MIN	30 MIN	4–6

- 4 tablespoons (1/2 stick) salted butter
- 2 pounds Italian sausage (sweet or hot or a mix of the two; and see Jeff's Tips); 1 pound with the casings removed, 1 pound with each link cut into 1/2-inch pieces
- 6 cups chicken broth
- 2 teaspoons dried thyme

- 5–8 ounces baby spinach or chopped kale
- 2 cups heavy cream or half-and-half
- 1/2 cup all-purpose flour
- 1–2 pounds gnocchi of your choice (I used potato gnocchi. This is usually found in the market at either room temperature in an airtight container near the deli section, or frozen in a bag in the freezer section—either is fine!)

- 1 (5.2-ounce) package Boursin cheese (any flavor), or 3/4 cup Garlic Herb Cheese (page 21), cut into chunks
- 1 1/2 teaspoons Creole/Cajun/Louisiana seasoning (I use Tony Chachere's) or seasoned salt (optional, taste the soup first before deciding to add)

1 Add the butter to the Instant Pot and hit Sauté and Adjust so it's on the More or High setting. Once melted and bubbling, add all the sausage and sauté for 5 minutes, until the loose sausage is crumbled and lightly browned.

2 Add the broth and thyme and stir well. Top with the spinach or kale but *do not stir*. Secure the lid, move the valve to the sealing position, hit Cancel, and then hit Pressure Cook or Manual at High Pressure for 5 minutes. Quick release when done.

3 Meanwhile, in a separate bowl, whisk together the cream and flour until smooth.

4 Hit Cancel and then hit Sauté and Adjust so it's on the More or High setting. Once bubbling, stir the creamy flour mixture into the pot followed by the gnocchi and let boil for 2–3 minutes, until the gnocchi are cooked. Hit Cancel to turn the pot off and then hit Keep Warm.

5 Stir the Boursin into the pot, then taste the soup and add the Creole seasoning (or seasoned salt) if desired. Keep stirring until combined. Ladle into bowls and serve.

JEFF'S TIPS If your market carries ground Italian sausage already out of the casings, feel free to use that!

As seen, I give you a range of how much gnocchi to use. A pound will give you a good amount, but 2 pounds will really load this soup up into something between a stew and a pasta dish. Also bear in mind that if you have leftovers, gnocchi will continue to absorb the liquid around them, making the soup very thick and more pasta-like once cooled. To make it soupy again, simply add a bit more broth and/or cream to your liking when reheating on the stove or on Sauté in your Instant Pot.

To Serve 1–2 Simply halve the recipe. Cook times remain the same.

CREAMY TORTELLINI SOUP

If you're wishing for ultimate comfort in the form of a soup loaded with stuffed pasta purses in a creamy, cheesy, tomatoey broth but want it done with the push of a button, just call me Genie Jeffrey because your wish is granted. When I released this recipe one winter, it got so much love the snow melted. And with just two steps, you may find yourself making it on the regular.

DUMP & GO! 3 STEPS OR LESS!

V + (if using meat-free tortellini and vegetable broth)

Prep Time	Pressure Building Time	Pressure Cook Time	Total Time	Serves
5 MIN	10–15 MIN	1 MIN	17 MIN	4–6

4 cups chicken or vegetable broth

2 (8-ounce) cans (or more, see Jeff's Tips) tomato sauce (not the same as pasta sauce)

2 teaspoons Italian seasoning

20 ounces fresh tortellini of your choice

Leaves from 1 bunch fresh basil

10 ounces grape or cherry tomatoes

1½ cups heavy cream or half-and-half

2 cups shredded Cheddar cheese

1 (5.2-ounce) package Boursin cheese (any flavor), or ¾ cup Garlic Herb Cheese (page 21), cut into chunks (optional)

2–4 tablespoons hot sauce (optional)

1 Add the broth, tomato sauce, and Italian seasoning to the Instant Pot and stir well. Add the tortellini but *do not stir*—just smooth them out. Top with the basil leaves, followed by the tomatoes and again, *do not stir*. Secure the lid, move the valve to the sealing position, and then hit Pressure Cook or Manual at High Pressure for 1 minute. Quick release when done.

2 Stir in the cream, Cheddar, Boursin (if using), and hot sauce (if using, and start with less; you can always add more). Stir until combined. If you want the soup to be warmer after adding the cold dairy, simply hit Cancel and then Sauté and bring to the desired temperature before serving. Then, hit Cancel again to turn the pot off.

 JEFF'S TIPS Want to make this soup very zesty? In addition to the optional hot sauce, sub 2 cups of your favorite Bloody Mary mix for the tomato sauce (I like Zing Zang and Mr & Mrs T brands).

If you find you want more tomato in the soup, simply add 1–2 cups additional tomato sauce, Bloody Mary mix, or even Classic Red Sauce (page 28, or your favorite brand of marinara) in Step 2 for it to be a bit chunkier.

 To Serve 1–2 Simply halve the recipe. Cook times remain the same.

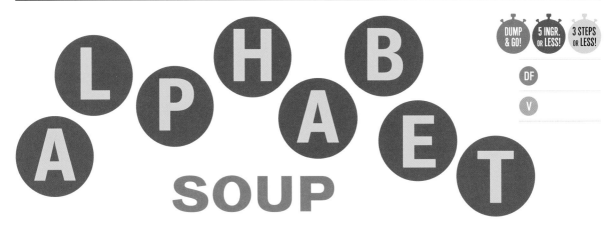

ALPHABET SOUP

When the kids refuse to eat their veggies, cook them up in a basic, yet very tasty (and educational) soup with the letters of the alphabet floating in their bowl! Just know that if you find the words Q-U-I-C-K, E-A-S-Y, and/or D-E-L-I-C-I-O-U-S in there, it's no coincidence. And if you're a grown-up and think the letters are too juvenile, I gotcha. Try ditalini, tubettini (little tubes), or pastina (little stars) instead.

Prep Time	Pressure Building Time	Pressure Cook Time	Total Time	Serves
2 MIN	10–15 MIN	2 MIN	15 MIN	4–6

6 cups vegetable broth

1 (14.5-ounce) can diced tomatoes, with their juices (try to use a brand with basil, garlic, and oregano in it)

20–30 ounces frozen vegetable mix (usually has carrots, peas, corn, green beans, and sometimes lima beans)

½ cup alphabet pasta (see Jeff's Tip)

1–3 teaspoons seasoned salt, to taste (optional)

1 Add the broth, diced tomatoes, frozen veggies, and pasta to the pot. Stir well. Secure the lid, move the valve to the sealing position, and hit Pressure Cook or Manual at High Pressure for 2 minutes. Quick release when done.

JEFF'S TIP I suggest using only ½ cup pasta because while it may not look like a lot in its uncooked state, the pasta expands and absorbs the broth significantly as it cooks. If you have kids who *really* want lots of letters in their soup, you can use ¾ cup or even up to 1 cup pasta, but I'd suggest serving the whole pot upon cooking. Otherwise, the pasta will continue to absorb the broth as it rests, making any leftover soup mostly pasta—but again, some kids may prefer this (anything that gets them to eat their veggies, right?). Of course, you can always add more broth if you find too much of it has been absorbed by the pasta while resting.

To Serve 1–2 Simply halve the recipe. Cook times remain the same.

2 If using, stir in the seasoned salt (start with 1 teaspoon and add more to taste). Ladle the soup into bowls and practice for tomorrow's spelling test.

CREAM OF ONION SOUP

 ⁺ *(see Jeff's Tips)*

French onion soup is a perennial favorite, and for good reason: With that crust of bubbling cheese resting on top of a bed of spongy, yet crusty bread in a deep, onion-laden broth, who could resist? Here we're taking the best elements of that soup and turning it into a cream of onion soup—the broth becomes smooth and rich and the cheese is infused *into* the soup rather than resting on top of it. If you have leftovers, you can even skip reheating them as this soup can be served as a rendition of a vichyssoise—a cold, French-style potato and onion soup!

Prep Time	Sauté Time	Pressure Building Time	Pressure Cook Time	Total Time	Serves
15 MIN	18–25 MIN	10–15 MIN	5 MIN	50 MIN	4–6

8 tablespoons (1 stick) salted butter

8 onions (or more, see Jeff's Tips), cut lengthwise into strips (I used 2 Vidalia (sweet), 2 Spanish, 2 yellow, and 2 red, but you can use any kind you wish)

5 cups vegetable, garlic, or onion broth (e.g., Garlic or Sautéed Onion Better Than Bouillon)

2 pounds Idaho (russet) potatoes (about 2–3 of them), peeled and diced

2 teaspoons dried thyme

1 cup heavy cream or half-and-half

2 tablespoons onion powder

1 tablespoon garlic salt or seasoned salt

1 (5.2-ounce) package Boursin cheese (any flavor), or ¾ cup Garlic Herb Cheese (page 21), cut into chunks

2–4 cups shredded mozzarella or Swiss cheese (see Note, Step 5)

1 Place the butter in the Instant Pot and hit Sauté and Adjust so it's on the More or High setting. Once the butter's melted and bubbling, add the onions, coat well with the butter, and sauté (stirring occasionally) for 15–25 minutes, until very softened into a pasta-like consistency. (NOTE: This step is important so don't skip it. You can stop at 15 minutes, but the longer you sauté, the more buttery and flavorful the onions will be.)

2 Add the broth, potatoes, and thyme and stir well. Secure the lid and move the valve to the sealing position. Hit Cancel followed by Manual or Pressure Cook at High Pressure for 5 minutes. Quick release when done.

3 With a slotted spoon, remove about 1½–2 cups of the onions (not the potatoes) and place in a bowl. Set aside for the time being.

4 With an immersion blender, blend everything in the pot together for about 1 minute, until pureed. (You can use a regular blender, but an immersion blender is so much easier since you don't have to transfer the soup to a blender and then back into the pot.)

5 Add the cream, onion powder, garlic salt, Boursin, and shredded cheese. Whisk until the cheese is totally melted into the soup. (NOTE: Start with 2 cups cheese, whisk, and if you feel you want more, add up to another 2 cups.)

6 Lastly, return the reserved onions to the pot and stir until fully incorporated. Ladle the soup into bowls and top with a few additional sprinkles of shredded cheese, if desired. If you like, take it to the next level by serving the soup in a sourdough bread bowl and topping it with caramelized onions (**see Jeff's Tips**), additional thyme, and/or some cheese toast/croutons.

 JEFF'S TIPS *Optional but worthwhile step:* Since this is a variation on an onion soup, it's a nice touch to have some caramelized onions as a garnish when served. This is simple to do: Cut 2 additional Vidalia (sweet) and/or yellow onions into thin slices. While the soup's pressure cooking, use just enough vegetable oil to coat the bottom of a cast-iron skillet or frying pan. Heat the pan on the stove over medium-high heat until the oil is hot. Add the onions and sauté for 15–20 minutes, until caramelized and slightly charred on the edges. They should be nice and syrupy when done. Use these to top the soup when serving in Step 6. It'll take this dish from already spectacular to out of this galaxy.

Want it less carb-y (and keto)? Use a head of chopped-up cauliflower instead of the potatoes.

To Serve 1–2 Simply halve the recipe. Cook times remain the same.

SINGAPORE
CHICKEN NOODLE
SOUP

A great chicken noodle soup is one of those things that just make everything better. Here, I wanted to do a variation reminiscent of a Singapore noodle dish: light, yet hearty and intensely flavored with hints of sesame, ginger, and curry powder. For noodles, we use the rice variation in order to keep it more faithful to Asian cuisine. Any soup that requires both a spoon and chopsticks is pure joy in my book.

Prep Time	Sauté Time	Pressure Building Time	Pressure Cook Time	Total Time	Serves
10 MIN	8 MIN	10–15 MIN	10 MIN	40 MIN	4–6

¼ cup sesame oil

12 ounces baby carrots, cut into ¼-inch pieces

10 ounces shiitake or baby bella mushrooms, sliced (optional, see Jeff's Tips)

2 bunches scallions, sliced, divided (plus some reserved for garnish)

6 cloves garlic, minced or pressed

1 tablespoon minced ginger (I use squeeze ginger); or 2 teaspoons ground ginger

6 cups chicken, garlic, or onion broth (e.g., Garlic or Sautéed Onion Better Than Bouillon)

2 tablespoons curry powder, divided (optional)

1 whole (4–5 pound) chicken, skin on, chopped into quarters (you can ask the butcher to do this for you)

8–16 ounces rice noodles of your choice (I suggest medium or large size, see Jeff's Tips)

1–2 tablespoons seasoned salt

¼ cup low-sodium soy sauce, tamari, or coconut aminos (optional)

1 Add the sesame oil to the Instant Pot and hit Sauté and Adjust so it's on the More or High setting. After 2–3 minutes of heating, add the carrots, mushrooms (if using), and half of the sliced scallions and sauté for 5 minutes. Add the garlic and ginger and sauté for 1 minute longer.

2 Add the broth and 1 tablespoon of the curry powder (if using), stir everything well, and nestle in the chicken. Secure the lid, move the valve to the sealing position, hit Cancel, and then hit Pressure Cook or Manual at High Pressure for 10 minutes. Quick release when done.

3 When the lid comes off the pot, remove the chicken with tongs and set aside to cool. Once cooled, pull the chicken meat from the bones and discard the bones, skin, and cartilage (or save to make bone broth). Shred the meat and set aside.

CONTINUES

4 Rice noodles are delicate and disintegrate when pressure cooked, so to make them perfect we are going to cook them off pressure—with two options!

To cook the noodles separate from the soup (prevents broth loss): While the soup is pressure cooking in Step 2, bring a pot of water to a boil and then turn the heat off so it stops boiling. Add the noodles and let sit for about 8 minutes, stirring occasionally, and they should cook perfectly. Taste a noodle. If it's at just a slight al dente texture, drain the noodles immediately so they don't overcook.

To cook the noodles in the soup (they will continue to absorb more broth as they sit): After the broth pressure cooks for 10 minutes, add the noodles to the pot and let rest, stirring occasionally, for about 8 minutes—the heat of the soup should cook them perfectly. After 8 minutes, taste a noodle. If not the texture you like, let them soak until you're happy with them. (NOTE: If you follow this method and you have leftovers, just be mindful that when stored in the fridge, this soup will morph into a soft noodle dish once the delicate rice noodles have absorbed most of the broth!)

5 Return the chicken to the pot. Stir in the remaining sliced scallions, the remaining curry powder (if using), and seasoned salt (start with 1 tablespoon). Taste it. If you want more salt, add up to another tablespoon seasoned salt and/or the soy sauce (which will also darken the soup). If you cooked the noodles separately, place some in a bowl and ladle in the soup. If you cooked the noodles in the soup, simply ladle all at once into a bowl. Top with additional scallions, if desired.

 JEFF'S TIPS Not into mushrooms? You can simply omit them, or swap in any veggies you wish—be it snow peas, water chestnuts, or baby corn. Simply add them in Step 1 and sauté with the other veggies.

Eight ounces of noodles is more than you'd think and is the amount I recommend for 4 servings of noodle soup. But if you're into oodles of noodles, use up to 16 ounces.

If you'd prefer egg noodles over rice noodles, follow the first cooking option for rice noodles, but continue to let the water boil after you've placed them in the pot rather than just relying on the heat of the soup or water to cook them. Egg noodles are not as delicate as rice noodles and require boiling to cook. If cooking the egg noodles directly in the Instant Pot, that can be achieved by hitting the Sauté button and Adjusting to the More or High setting. Cook until tender.

 To Serve 1–2 Simply halve the recipe. Cook times remain the same.

SHORTCUT SHORT RIB STEW

K + (See Jeff's Tip)
P + (See Jeff's Tip)
DF
GF

While I couldn't include my fan-favorite Short Rib Chili in this book since it has quite a few ingredients (feel free to find it on my blog, it's well worth it!), I *did* use it as inspiration for a tasty challenge: Create something just as delicious with only a few ingredients. Hence, a *shortcut* stew so easy and flavor-filled it's worthy of being in print. Shortcut Short Rib Stew, it's a pleasure to meet you.

Prep Time	Sauté Time	Pressure Building Time	Pressure Cook Time	Natural Release Time	Total Time	Serves
10 MIN	15 MIN	10–15 MIN	35 MIN	15 MIN	1 HR 30 MIN	4–6

- 3–4 pounds short ribs
- 1 tablespoon kosher salt
- 5 tablespoons extra-virgin olive oil, divided
- 2 large carrots, peeled and sliced into ¼-inch-thick disks

- 1 large Spanish or yellow onion, diced
- 2½ cups beef broth
- 2 (14.5-ounce) cans diced tomatoes, with their juices
- 1½ pounds white baby potatoes (white, red, or mixed), skins on, quartered

- 1 (6-ounce) can tomato paste
- 1–2 tablespoons of one of the following seasonings:
  - *Chili Better Than Bouillon*
  - *Cajun/Creole/Louisiana seasoning (I use Tony Chachere's)*
  - *Seasoned salt*

1 Rub the short ribs with the kosher salt.

2 Add 3 tablespoons of the olive oil to the Instant Pot and hit Sauté and Adjust so it's on the More or High setting. After 3 minutes of heating, add the short ribs in batches (if necessary) and flash-sear for about 30 seconds on each side, until lightly browned. Use tongs to remove to a plate and set aside.

3 Add the remaining 2 tablespoons olive oil to the pot. After 2 minutes of heating, add the carrots and onion and sauté for 5 minutes, scraping the bottom of the pot to get up any browned bits.

CONTINUES

4 Add the broth and diced tomatoes and stir well, once again scraping the bottom of the pot. Then nestle in the seared short ribs and top with the potatoes but *do not stir*. Secure the lid, move the valve to the sealing position, hit Cancel, and then hit Pressure Cook or Manual at High Pressure for 35 minutes. When done, allow a 15-minute natural release followed by a quick release.

5 Use tongs to gently transfer the short ribs to a cutting board. They will be so tender the meat will slide right off the bone. Take a knife and slice the meat into bite-size pieces and then return to the pot.

6 Stir in the tomato paste and one of the seasonings of your choice (start with 1 tablespoon and add more to taste) until combined. Let rest for 10 minutes until the stew thickens. Ladle into bowls and serve with a crusty baguette or garlic knots.

JEFF'S TIP If you want to make this keto or paleo, forget the potatoes and sub diced bell peppers or mushrooms in their place: Sauté with the carrots and onion in Step 3.

ELOTE CHOWDER

GF⁺ *(see Jeff's Tips)*

Elote is a beloved Mexican street food staple in which mayo is slathered on grilled corn, then topped with lime, chili powder, and cotija cheese. Given the similar bases of dairy and corn, I thought an elote-inspired corn chowder would make for a great twist on the classic, and if my audience's response was any indication, it did. See Jeff's Tips for additional seasoning suggestions to make it even more irresistible.

Prep Time	Sauté Time	Pressure Building Time	Pressure Cook Time	Total Time	Serves
10 MIN	5 MIN	10–15 MIN	5 MIN	30 MIN	4–6

- 4 tablespoons (½ stick) salted butter
- 1 yellow onion, diced
- 2 large poblano or green bell peppers, diced
- 3 tablespoons all-purpose flour

- 3 cups chicken or garlic broth (e.g., Garlic Better Than Bouillon)
- 1 tablespoon sherry wine (optional)
- 1 pound baby potatoes (or see Jeff's Tips), skin on, quartered
- 16–24 ounces frozen corn kernels
- 1 cup heavy cream or half-and-half

- 1 cup crumbled cotija cheese (if you can't find cojita, use grated Parmesan cheese or finely crumbled feta), plus more for topping
- 1 (approximately 1-ounce) packet taco seasoning
- 1–2 teaspoons chili powder, plus more for topping (optional)

1 Add the butter to the Instant Pot, hit Sauté, and Adjust so it's on the More or High setting. Once melted, add the onion and pepper and sauté for 3–5 minutes, until slightly softened.

2 Add the flour and quickly stir to coat the veggies. Add the broth and stir, scraping the bottom of the pot to get any browned bits up.

3 Add the sherry (if using), potatoes, and corn. Stir well. Secure the lid, move the valve to the sealing position, hit Cancel, and then hit Manual or Pressure Cook on High Pressure for 5 minutes. Quick release when done.

4 Hit Cancel followed by Sauté and Adjust so it's on the More or High setting. Once bubbling, add the cream, cotija, taco seasoning, and chili powder (if using). Stir until combined and then hit Cancel to turn the pot off. Ladle the soup into bowls and top with more cotija and chili powder, if desired.

JEFF'S TIPS

You can also use Idaho (russet) potatoes. Just make sure you peel them and then cut into cubes or bite-size pieces.

To make this gluten-free, skip the flour in Step 2 and add a slurry of 3 tablespoons cornstarch plus 3 tablespoons cold water in Step 4 once the pot's bubbling and just before you add the dairy.

If you want to season this your own way, feel free to: your chowdah, your rules! Try out the following:

- Sliced chorizo or bite-size pieces of boneless, skinless chicken thighs or breasts (add while sautéing the veggies in Step 1)

- The juice of a lime (add in Step 2 with the broth)

- Everything But the Elote seasoning from Trader Joe's (add to taste in Step 4)

- Shrimp (add after the dairy in Step 4; once curled and opaque, they're done)

To Serve 1–2

Simply halve the recipe. Cook times remain the same.

BEAN & ESCAROLE SOUP

3 STEPS OR LESS!

DF

GF

V + *(if using garlic broth and plant-based sausage—or no sausage at all)*

This beans-and-greens soup is an Italian classic. Don't be fooled by the short list of ingredients: It is anything but a boring soup. Plus, it's quite nutritious, packed with beans and leafy escarole, a member of the endive family. I love adding Italian sausage, but I've made that optional in case you'd like to keep it vegetarian. It's just as delicious either way, especially with a freshly baked bread of your choice.

Prep Time	Sauté Time	Pressure Building Time	Pressure Cook Time	Total Time	Serves
5 MIN	7 MIN	10–15 MIN	3 MIN	25 MIN	4–6

2 tablespoons extra-virgin olive oil, plus more for drizzling

1 pound Italian sausage (sweet or hot or a mix of the two) or a plant-based sausage, casings removed (optional)

1–2 bunches escarole, tougher white bottoms discarded, roughly chopped

6 cloves garlic, minced or pressed

6 cups chicken or garlic broth (e.g., Garlic Better Than Bouillon)

2 teaspoons black pepper (freshly ground is best here), plus more for topping

2 (15.5-ounce) cans cannellini, navy, or great northern beans (or <u>see Jeff's Tips</u>), drained and rinsed

1/4–1/2 cup grated Parmesan cheese (optional)

Seasoned salt, to taste (<u>see Jeff's Tips</u>), optional

1 Add the oil to the Instant Pot and hit Sauté and Adjust so it's on the More or High setting. If using sausage, after 2–3 minutes of heating, add it and sauté for 3 minutes, until crumbled and lightly browned. Add the escarole and garlic and sauté for 1–2 minutes, until the escarole is wilted. (NOTE: If using two bunches of escarole, add them in two batches. Otherwise, it can get crowded in the pot. Once the first batch wilts, add the second and sauté another 1–2 minutes until wilted.)

2 Add the broth and pepper and stir well. Top with the beans but *do not stir.* Just smooth them out with a mixing spoon. Secure the lid, move the valve to the sealing position, hit Cancel, and then hit Pressure Cook or Manual at High Pressure for 3 minutes. Quick release when done.

3 If using, stir in the Parmesan (start with 1/4 cup and add up to 1/2 cup if desired). Taste the soup. If at this point you feel it needs seasoned salt, start by adding 1 teaspoon, stir and taste, then increase from there, up to 1 tablespoon. Ladle the soup into bowls and serve topped with more pepper and a drizzle of olive oil, if desired.

JEFF'S TIPS

AVOID OVERSALTING: The amount of seasoned salt needed here depends on whether or not you include sausage and Parmesan in the soup. Both are quite salty, so they'll likely satisfy the soup's savory capacity. If you added one or both, make sure you really taste the broth in Step 3 before adding seasoned salt. If you didn't use sausage or Parmesan, you'll likely want to add 1–3 teaspoons. Regardless, all taste buds are different so do it to personal preference.

If you feel like using a darker bean, by all means, mix it up and use your favorite. Just make sure they're drained and rinsed before adding in Step 2.

To Serve 1–2

Simply halve the recipe. Cook times remain the same.

CHICKEN TACO CHILI

 K ＋ (See Jeff's Tips)

 P ＋ (See Jeff's Tips)

 DF

 GF

I make it a mission to always have a chili represented in each of my books. This time around, it's one inspired by chicken tacos! Once I created and tasted this hearty dish, I immediately knew it earned a place in this cookbook. Loaded with ground chicken, beans, salsa verde, and taco seasoning, this delightful dish will make Taco Tuesday that much more exciting.

Prep Time	Sauté Time	Pressure Building Time	Pressure Cook Time	Total Time	Serves
10 MIN	10 MIN	10–15 MIN	5 MIN	40 MIN	4–6

- **3 tablespoons extra-virgin olive oil**
- **1 large Spanish or yellow onion, diced**
- **3 poblano or green bell peppers, diced**
- **2 pounds ground chicken (or see Jeff's Tips)**

- **4 cups chicken broth**
- **2 cups salsa verde (green salsa) of your choice, divided**
- **2 (approximately 1-ounce) packets taco seasoning, divided**
- **2 (15.5-ounce) cans cannellini, navy, or great northern beans, drained and rinsed**

- **3–4 tablespoons cornstarch plus 3–4 tablespoons cold water**
- **About 16 ounces canned diced green chiles, with their juices (these cans come in various sizes so just get enough to total approximately 16 ounces)**

1 Add the olive oil to the Instant Pot and hit Sauté and Adjust so it's on the More or High setting. After 3 minutes of heating, add the onion and peppers and sauté for 3 minutes, until softened.

2 Add the ground chicken and sauté for another 3–5 minutes, until crumbled and slightly cooked.

3 Add the broth, 1 cup of the salsa verde, and 1 packet of the taco seasoning. Stir well, scraping the bottom of the pot. Top with the beans but *do not stir*. Just smooth them out with a mixing spoon. Secure the lid, move the valve to the sealing position, hit Cancel, and then hit Pressure Cook or Manual at High Pressure for 5 minutes. Quick release when done.

4 Meanwhile, mix together the cornstarch and cold water in a bowl to form a slurry.

5 Hit Cancel and then hit Sauté and Adjust so it's on the More or High setting. Once bubbling, stir in the cornstarch slurry and the chili will immediately thicken. Stir in the diced green chiles, the remaining 1 cup salsa verde, and the remaining packet of taco seasoning. Hit Cancel to turn the pot off.

6 Ladle into bowls and top with some shredded Mexican cheese blend, sliced avocado, and/or fresh cilantro, if desired.

JEFF'S TIPS Yes, it's *Chicken* Taco Chili, but use any ground meat you wish (such as turkey, beef, veal, or pork). You can also use 2 pounds boneless/skinless chicken thighs and/or breasts in place of ground chicken. Just skip Step 2, add the chicken pieces in Step 3 after stirring the pot but just before adding the beans, and remove the cooked chicken to a mixing bowl with tongs at the end after pressure cooking. Shred the chicken with two forks (or a hand mixer) and return the meat to the pot in Step 5 when adding the remaining salsa and taco seasoning.

For an extra chili flavor kick, add 1–2 tablespoons Chili Better Than Bouillon *or* 2 teaspoons chili powder in Step 5 when adding the final ingredients.

If you want this a touch creamy, add ½ cup heavy cream or half-and-half in Step 5 when adding the salsa and taco seasoning.

To make it keto, paleo (and Texan), simply omit the beans.

To Serve 1–2 Simply halve the recipe. Cook times remain the same.

EGG DROP WONTON SOUP

  DUMP & GO! · 3 STEPS OR LESS!

 DF

 V + *(if using garlic or vegetable broth and vegetable wonton and if you are okay with eggs)*

Egg drop soup and wonton soup are two beloved classics of Asian-American cuisine, which happens to also be the kind of food I crave the most. This recipe was inspired by my dad, who loves adding wontons to his egg drop soup. We're going to simplify things further by using store-bought frozen wontons, making this soup as quick and easy as it is sublime.

Prep Time	Pressure Building Time	Pressure Cook Time	Sauté Time	Total Time	Serves
5 MIN	10–15 MIN	3 MIN	5 MIN	25 MIN	4–6

6 cups chicken, vegetable, or garlic broth (e.g., Garlic Better Than Bouillon)

1½ teaspoons ground ginger

1½ teaspoons seasoned salt

1 teaspoon garlic powder

1½ teaspoons sesame oil

10 ounces frozen corn (optional)

1 bunch scallions, sliced, with some reserved for topping the soup

½ teaspoon turmeric

1½–2 pounds frozen wontons of your choice (see Jeff's Tips)

2–3 tablespoons cornstarch plus 2–3 tablespoons water, mixed together to form a slurry (see Jeff's Tips)

3 large eggs plus 3 egg whites, beaten in a bowl

1 Add the broth, ground ginger, seasoned salt, garlic powder, sesame oil, and corn (if using) to the Instant Pot. Secure the lid, move the valve to the sealing position, and hit Manual or Pressure Cook at High Pressure for 3 minutes. Quick release when done.

2 Hit Cancel and then Sauté and Adjust so it's on the More or High setting. Add the scallions and turmeric. Once the soup begins to bubble, add the frozen wontons and let them cook for 5 minutes. Then add the cornstarch slurry and stir for another minute until the soup has thickened. (For a thinner soup, see Jeff's Tips.)

3 Hit Cancel again to turn off the heat. Once the bubbles die down, simultaneously pour in the beaten eggs with one hand while gently raking the eggs through the soup with a large serving fork in the other hand. Do this for about 1 minute, until the eggs are cooked through and beautiful egg ribbons form. Ladle into bowls and top with some additional scallions (and chow mein noodles if you desire).

JEFF'S TIPS I have the wonderful luxury of living near Flushing, Queens (in NYC), which arguably has some of the greatest Chinese food in the States. That means I can go to my favorite wonton shop (which happens to be White Bear, get the #6), and buy their wontons frozen, which is exactly what I use for this soup. But since not everyone lives near Flushing, you can easily go to an Asian market (H Mart is my jam) or many other supermarkets and use any frozen wontons or dumplings you wish (Costco has some good ones). You can use mini or regular size. Of course, you can also make and freeze my wontons from my yellow (*Simple Comforts*) book.

For a thinner soup, start with 2 tablespoons each of cornstarch and water for the slurry. If after stirring in Step 2 you decide you want it thicker, then add another tablespoon of each.

To Serve 1–2 Simply halve the recipe. Cook times remain the same.

MUSHROOM BARLEY
· SOUP ·

Beef and barley soup is just about the most rustic and hearty soup there is, but for those who don't eat meat, mushrooms can make an amazing meat substitute for a robust, vegetarian-friendly barley soup. There's also something very satisfying about using minimal ingredients, time, and effort to make such a grand soup that tastes like it required hours of simmering. You can also give it a slightly creamy finish—and, as with all my dishes, it is customizable so you can really make it your own.

 V + *(if you're okay with Worcestershire sauce)*

Prep Time	Sauté Time	Pressure Building Time	Pressure Cook Time	Total Time	Serves
15 MIN	11 MIN	10–15 MIN	25 MIN	1 HR 5 MIN	4–6

- 4 tablespoons (½ stick) salted butter
- 2 pounds mushrooms (I used 1 pound sliced baby bella and 1 pound sliced portobellos), chopped into bite-size pieces
- 1 yellow onion, diced

- 12 ounces baby carrots, cut into ¼-inch pieces
- 6 cups vegetable, garlic, or mushroom broth (e.g., Garlic or Mushroom Better Than Bouillon)
- ¾–1 cup barley, rinsed (see Jeff's Tips)

- 2 teaspoons dried thyme
- 1½ teaspoons seasoned salt, plus more in Step 4 if desired
- 2 tablespoons Worcestershire sauce
- ½–1 cup heavy cream or half-and-half (optional)

1 Add the butter to the Instant Pot, hit Sauté, and Adjust so it's on the More or High setting. Once the butter's melted and bubbling, add the mushrooms, onion, and carrots and sauté for about 8 minutes, until the mushrooms begin to brown.

2 Add the broth, barley, thyme, and seasoned salt. Give it a good stir, scraping any browned bits up from the bottom of the pot.

3 Secure the lid, move the valve to the sealing position, hit Cancel, and then hit Manual or Pressure Cook for 25 minutes. Quick release when done.

4 Stir in the Worcestershire sauce and taste. Add more seasoned salt if desired (start with 1 teaspoon). Also, if you decide you want the creamy finish, now's the time to add the cream or half-and-half.

5 Ladle into bowls and feel free to top with some freshly ground pepper or drizzle on some truffle oil, then serve with rustic bread.

JEFF'S TIPS The longer this soup sits after cooking, the more the barley will absorb the broth, reducing the amount of liquid. Feel free to add more broth or cream when reheating.

The cream, as stated, is optional. But if you're into that and want to make it even more indulgent and out-of-this-world, add a package of Boursin or ¾ cup Garlic Herb Cheese (page 21) in Step 4 and stir until combined. This will make it a truly next-level Cream of Mushroom Barley Soup!

You can also add up to 1 cup of any chopped veggies of your choice in Step 1 when sautéing the mushrooms, carrots, and onion. Be it diced celery, any pepper variety, or whatever other veggies you enjoy!

To Serve 1–2 Simply halve the recipe. Cook times remain the same.

FANCY
(BUT NOT REALLY)

INSTANT RAMEN

DUMP & GO! **5 INGR. OR LESS!**

DF

V + (if using a vegetarian broth and ramen variety)

At one point or another, most of us had to live on ramen noodles, the only variation is whether or not you are the kind of person who actually enjoyed that time of your life. If you are (and even if you aren't), this recipe is for you—because we're taking those ramen packets and glamming them up with just *four* more ingredients, plus optional toppings to add a slightly fancy touch with deep flavor. For the broth, I like to use a combination of beef and chicken.

Prep Time	Pressure Building Time	Pressure Cook Time	Sauté Time	Total Time	Serves
5 MIN	10–15 MIN	6–8 MIN	10–15 MIN	30–40 MIN	4–6

6 cups any broth of your choice, divided

4–6 large eggs

1/2 cup hoisin sauce

1 tablespoon sesame oil

3 (3-ounce) packages any instant ramen noodles of your choice, with their seasoning packets

OPTIONAL TOPPINGS

Bean sprouts (canned or fresh)

Fresh cilantro

Sliced scallions

Sliced jalapeños

Sriracha

Fish sauce

1 Add the trivet and 1 cup of the broth to the Instant Pot. Place the eggs on the trivet. Secure the lid, move the valve to the sealing position, and hit Manual or Pressure Cook at **Low Pressure** for 6 minutes for runny yolks, or 8 minutes for slightly runny, yet firmer yolks. Quick release when done. (NOTE: In order to get that perfect runny yolk, you set your Pot to Low Pressure instead of High; it's my only recipe that calls for this. Adjust by hitting the Pressure Button; or, if your display screen is a touchscreen or has a knob, adjust by using those.)

2 Using tongs, carefully transfer the eggs to an ice bath and cool for 90 seconds. While the eggs cool, remove the trivet from the pot and hit Cancel followed by Sauté and Adjust so it's on the More or High setting. Add the remaining 5 cups broth, the hoisin sauce, and sesame oil to the pot.

3 While the broth is heating, *gently* smash each egg and *gently* roll it around the countertop until it's cracked, then *gently* peel the shell off. Slice each egg in half longways and set aside.

4 After 5 minutes of heating, add the ramen noodles with their packet contents to the pot. Let the heat of the broth cook the ramen for 5–10 minutes, stirring often to break up the noodles as they absorb some of the broth and soften. Hit Cancel to turn the pot off.

5 Use tongs to place the noodles into bowls, then ladle over some broth. Top with an egg, then any optional toppings to make it fancy, if desired.

JEFF'S TIPS

If you don't fancy eggs in your ramen (and to make this even faster), instead of following Step 1 as is, simply start by adding the full 6 cups of broth to the pot along with the hoisin sauce and sesame oil and cook at High Pressure for 1 minute with a quick release. Then, jump to Step 4. Due to it having just been pressure cooked, the broth will already be hot enough to cook the noodles in 5–10 minutes with frequent stirring without requiring the Sauté function.

If you want more noodles and less broth, add an additional 3-ounce packet of ramen and its seasoning packet.

To Serve 1–2 Simply halve the recipe. Cook times remain the same.

③ PASTA

The thought of making a complete pasta meal in your Instant Pot might raise an eyebrow of a first-time user. But trying just one of these recipes is all it takes to convince you that this method of cooking pasta embodies exactly what this book is about: shortcuts. One pot, no draining, zero fuss, and *all* of the flavor.

The fascinating thing about this gold mine of a chapter is that you'll discover some of the best pasta dishes you'll ever have—not just pasta cooked under pressure, but any pasta—while greatly limiting the ingredients. And *that's* amore.

 = DUMP & GO RECIPE

 = 5 INGREDIENTS OR LESS

 = 3 STEPS OR LESS

♨ = AIR FRYER LID

K = KETO

P = PALEO

DF = DAIRY-FREE

GF = GLUTEN-FREE

V = VEGETARIAN

VN = VEGAN

[+] = COMPLIANT WITH MODIFICATIONS

LINGUINE LA PARMA

DF⁺ (see Jeff's Tips)

V⁺ (see Jeff's Tips)

VN⁺ (see Jeff's Tips)

This pasta, inspired by one of my favorite Italian restaurants, has it all: a spicy red sauce made with pancetta, guanciale, or bacon that is tossed with linguine and some Parmesan. If you're a spicy pasta lover, it'll bring you sassy joy. And if you don't want it spicy, I've got you covered in Jeff's Tips.

Prep Time	Sauté Time	Pressure Building Time	Pressure Cook Time	Total Time	Serves
5 MIN	15 MIN	10–15 MIN	6 MIN	36 MIN	4–6

- 6 tablespoons extra-virgin olive oil, divided (plus more for drizzling if desired)
- 8 ounces diced pancetta, guanciale, or bacon
- 1 red or yellow onion, diced
- 9 cloves garlic, minced or pressed

- 2½ cups chicken or garlic broth (e.g., Garlic Better Than Bouillon)
- ½ cup hot sauce (I use Frank's RedHot)
- 3½ cups marinara sauce (I like the Rao's and Victoria brands, but you can also use my Classic Red Sauce, page 28), preferably at room temperature, divided

- ½–1 teaspoon crushed red pepper flakes (or more if you want it spicier, less for milder), optional
- 1 pound linguine (see Jeff's Tips)
- ⅓ cup heavy cream or half-and-half
- ½ cup grated Pecorino Romano or Parmesan cheese, plus more for topping

1 Add 3 tablespoons of the olive oil to the Instant Pot. Hit Sauté and Adjust so it's on the More or High setting. After 3 minutes of heating, add the pancetta and sauté for about 8 minutes, until it begins to get crispy. Remove with a slotted spoon, place in a paper towel–lined bowl, and set aside; but leave the oil and pancetta juices in the pot.

2 Add the remaining 3 tablespoons olive oil to the pot and then the onion and garlic and sauté for 3 minutes. As the onions sweat, scrape the bottom of the pot so the sticky layer of browned pancetta bits is incorporated into the onions: The bottom of the pot should be nice and clear.

3 Add the broth and hot sauce. Stir well, giving the bottom of the pot a final scrape. Then, add 1½ cups of the marinara sauce and the red pepper flakes (if using). Stir once more.

4 Break the linguine in half and layer in a crisscross fashion so it's mostly submerged in the sauce, but *do not stir*. Secure the lid and move the valve to the sealing position. Hit Cancel followed by Manual or Pressure Cook on High Pressure for 6 minutes (**see Jeff's Tips**). Quick release when done and give the pot a good stir. (NOTE: The linguine may be a little clumped together and perhaps a bit al dente but that's how it should be. It will separate and continue to cook as it's stirred.)

5 Return the pancetta to the pot and stir in the remaining 2 cups marinara sauce along with the cream and grated cheese. Let rest for 5 minutes. Serve topped with additional cheese and a drizzle of olive oil, if desired.

JEFF'S TIPS The pancetta can be left out to make this vegetarian (if that happens, only use 3 tablespoons olive oil since you're skipping Step 1) and the Parmesan and cream can be left out to make it dairy-free. Leaving out all these things will make it vegan.

If you want a thicker noodle, try spaghetti or bucatini/perciatelli (same noodle, different names). It's like a hollow, super fat spaghetti, and has a great texture. Simply adjust the cook time to 8 minutes for spaghetti or 12 minutes for bucatini.

For me, 6 minutes is the right pressure cook time, but if you want your linguine a bit softer upon quick releasing, pressure cook for 7 minutes.

To keep this linguine mild, simply adjust the broth to 3 cups instead of 2½, leave out the hot sauce, and forgo the optional red pepper flakes.

To Serve 1–2 Reduce the broth to 2 cups but halve all the other ingredients. Cook times remain the same.

WHOLESALE CLUB
PASTA

Whenever I go to Costco (aka my happy place), I always have to peruse their wondrous Take-and-Bake section. They have a pasta dish loaded with sausage in a white wine and Parmesan sauce, not unlike my acclaimed Sausage & Shells from the orange (original *Step-by-Step*) book. Instead of the richer dairy finish of my Sausage & Shells, the sharper wine sauce creates a lighter, yet very satisfying experience. I've re-created it for you here and simply call it Wholesale Club Pasta since that's where the idea was born.

Prep Time	Sauté Time	Pressure Building Time	Pressure Cook Time	Total Time	Serves
5 MIN	8 MIN	10–15 MIN	6 MIN	30 MIN	4–6

- 4 tablespoons (½ stick) salted butter
- 2 pounds Italian sausage (sweet, hot, or a mix), sliced into ½-inch pieces (see Jeff's Tips)
- 9 cloves garlic, minced or pressed

- 1½ cups dry white wine (like a chardonnay, or see Jeff's Tips), divided
- 1½ cups chicken or garlic broth (e.g., Garlic Better Than Bouillon)
- 2 teaspoons dried Italian seasoning

- 1 pound orecchiette (Frisbee/ear-shaped pasta, see Jeff's Tips)
- 10–20 ounces grape or cherry tomatoes
- 5–8 ounces baby spinach
- ½–1 cup grated Parmesan cheese

1 Add the butter to the Instant Pot. Hit Sauté and Adjust so it's on the More or High setting. Once melted and bubbling, add the sausage and garlic and sauté for 5 minutes, until the sausage is lightly browned.

2 Add ½ cup of the wine and deglaze (scrape the bottom of the pot) so any browned bits come up. The bottom of the pot should be nice and clear.

3 Add the remaining 1 cup wine, plus the broth and Italian seasoning. Stir well.

4 Add the pasta but *do not stir.* Just smooth it out with a mixing spoon so it's mostly submerged in the broth. Top with the tomatoes and spinach and still *do not stir.* Secure the lid and move the valve to the sealing position. Hit Cancel followed by Manual or Pressure Cook on High Pressure for 6 minutes. Quick release when done. (NOTE: Once it's done pressure cooking, some of the pasta may appear clumped together, but stirring it up will quickly separate it.)

5 Stir in the Parmesan cheese (start with ½ cup and then decide if you want more) and serve.

JEFF'S TIPS To easily cut raw sausage, pop it into the freezer for 5–10 minutes before slicing. This will help it keep its form.

The wine makes the flavor of this sauce, but you can also swap it out for another 1½ cups broth.

Orecchiette is pretty easy to find in most markets, but either medium shells or a small penne will work great as a substitute. Same cook time.

To Serve 1–2 Keep the broth at 1½ cups but halve all the other ingredients Cook times remain the same.

PEPPERONI PIZZA PASTA

The only thing better than transforming a pepperoni pizza into a pasta is doing it with just five ingredients. This pasta gives you the best parts of a slice (the cheese and pepperoni), is way better than popping a frozen pie into the oven, and will be sure to satisfy the most hungry of appetites. For extra oomph, I love giving it a bubbly-brown-cheese and pepperoni-loaded broiled top for an instantly Instagrammable classic dinner.

Prep Time	Pressure Building Time	Pressure Cook Time	Optional Broiling Time	Total Time	Serves
5 MIN	10–15 MIN	5 MIN	5–10 MIN	25 MIN	4–6

3 cups chicken or garlic broth (e.g., Garlic Better Than Bouillon)

3½ cups marinara sauce (I like the Rao's and Victoria brands, but you can also use my Classic Red Sauce, page 28), preferably at room temperature, divided

1 pound regular or large elbow macaroni

2–4 cups shredded mozzarella cheese (see Jeff's Tips), plus more for the pizza-style finish if you like

1 (6-ounce) package pepperoni, diced or kept as whole slices

1 Add the broth and 1½ cups of the marinara sauce to the Instant Pot and stir well. Add the pasta but *do not stir*. Just smooth it out so it's mostly submerged.

2 Secure the lid and move the valve to the sealing position. Hit Cancel followed by Manual or Pressure Cook on High Pressure for 5 minutes. Quick release when done and give the pot a good stir.

3 Stir in the cheese (start with 2 cups and add up to 2 more, if desired). Once it's melted into the pasta and becomes a bit stretchy, add the remaining 2 cups marinara sauce and the pepperoni (reserving some for topping for a pizza-style finish if you like). Let rest for 5 minutes and either serve, or...

JEFF'S TIPS How cheesy you want this pasta is up to you (and there are no rules here since this *is* a pizza-inspired pasta, after all). In Step 3, start with 2 cups shredded cheese and if you want more, add up to 2 cups more! Add the extra cheese in Step 4 if you want it as part of the topping.

In lieu of the marinara or red sauce, you can choose any sauce variety you wish! Be it a jarred pizza sauce or one from the sauce chapter (page 26), especially the Vodka Sauce!

4 **For a pizza-style finish:** Evenly top the finished pasta with 1–2 cups mozzarella and reserved pepperoni slices. Add the Air Fryer Lid to your Instant Pot and Broil (400°F) for 5–10 minutes, until the cheese is bubbly and browned. Alternatively, you can place the pasta in a casserole dish and broil in the oven until the cheese is golden brown.

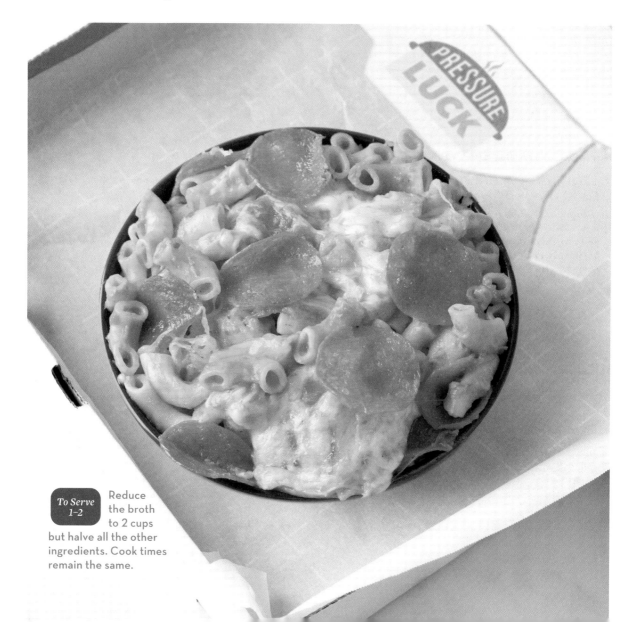

To Serve 1–2 Reduce the broth to 2 cups but halve all the other ingredients. Cook times remain the same.

THE FOUR C'S SPAGHETTI

CREAMY CHEESY CHICKEN & CHIVE

This ultimate creamy, cheesy spaghetti loaded with chicken and chives has come to be known amongst my followers as Four C's Spaghetti. It tastes like Cheddar and sour cream potato chips and is about as simple to make as reaching into a bag and grabbing a handful. And the super satisfying pasta dish is a sure-fire hit with kids and grown-ups alike.

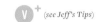 **V**+ *(see Jeff's Tips)*

Prep Time	Sauté Time	Pressure Building Time	Pressure Cook Time	Total Time	Serves
5 MIN	6 MIN	10–15 MIN	8 MIN	30 MIN	4–6

8 tablespoons (1 stick) salted butter, divided

1½–2 pounds boneless, skinless chicken breasts or thighs, cut into bite-size pieces

6 cloves garlic, minced or pressed

4 cups chicken or garlic broth (e.g., Garlic Better Than Bouillon)

1 pound spaghetti

2 cups shredded Cheddar or Colby Jack cheese

¼ cup grated Parmesan cheese, plus more for topping

¼ cup sour cream

2 bunches fresh chives, thinly sliced, some reserved for topping

1 Add 4 tablespoons of the butter to the Instant Pot. Hit Sauté and Adjust so it's on the More or High setting. Once melted and bubbling, add the chicken and garlic and sauté for 2–3 minutes, until the chicken is pinkish-white in color.

2 Add the broth, then break the spaghetti in two and layer it in the pot in a crisscross fashion so it's mostly submerged in the broth, but *do not stir*. Top with the remaining 4 tablespoons butter, cut into a few pats for even distribution over the pasta.

3 Secure the lid and move the valve to the sealing position. Hit Cancel followed by Manual or Pressure Cook on High Pressure for 8 minutes. Quick release when done and give the pot a good stir. (NOTE: The spaghetti may be a little clumped together and perhaps a bit al dente but that's how it should be. It will separate and continue to cook as it's stirred.)

4 Add the cheeses and stir until well combined, followed by the sour cream. Let rest for 5 minutes and allow to thicken.

5 Lastly, add the chives and give it a final stir. Top with additional chives and additional grated Parmesan, if desired.

JEFF'S TIPS

Make it vegetarian by skipping the chicken and using garlic or vegetable broth. You can also sub in mushrooms in place of (or in addition to) the chicken. Just add in Step 1 while sautéing the garlic.

If you want to sub sliced chicken sausage (or Italian sausage) for the chicken, go for it! Everything else remains as is in the recipe.

If you want to pay homage to the song "On Top of Spaghetti," add meatballs: Skip the chicken and instead of sautéing in Step 1, add 1–1½ pounds frozen meatballs of your choice and then continue with Step 2, but top the spaghetti with 8 tablespoons butter instead of 4 since we didn't add it in Step 1.

Don't jive with chives? Leave 'em out!

To Serve 1–2 Reduce the broth to 2½ cups but halve all the other ingredients. Cook times remain the same.

CACIO E PEPE

PEARLS

Cacio e pepe ("cheese and pepper") has become all the rage here in the States, probably in part because it's loaded with satisfying flavor while requiring minimal ingredients. It's usually made with a longer noodle such as spaghetti (which I do in my *Simple Comforts* book), but here, I wanted to share a more playful and kid-friendly variation on the Roman staple by using a pearl-shaped pasta called acini di pepe, which means "seeds of pepper" in Italian. The pasta itself doesn't have pepper in it—it's just shaped like peppercorns, which is fitting, as pepper is a key ingredient in this easy, cheesy dish.

Prep Time	Pressure Building Time	Pressure Cook Time	Total Time	Serves
2 MIN	10–15 MIN	6 MIN	20 MIN	4–6

3½ cups chicken or garlic broth (e.g., Garlic Better Than Bouillon)

1 pound acini di pepe (pasta pearls)

8 tablespoons (1 stick) salted butter, divided into 1-tablespoon pats

1 cup either grated Parmesan or Pecorino Romano or a mix of the two, plus more for serving

1 tablespoon freshly cracked black pepper (see Jeff's Tips), plus more to taste

1 Add the broth and pasta to the Instant Pot and stir well. Top with 4 pats of the butter.

2 Secure the lid and move the valve to the sealing position. Hit Cancel followed by Manual or Pressure Cook on High Pressure for 6 minutes. Quick release when done and give the pot a good stir.

3 Stir in the remaining 4 pats butter, the Parmesan, and pepper. Taste it and see if you want more pepper; if you do, add it now and stir. Serve immediately topped with additional cheese and pepper, if desired.

JEFF'S TIPS For best results, try to use freshly cracked black pepper since it's a key ingredient to making a cacio e pepe sing. But you can use pre-ground if that's all you have.

If you want to liven this dish up with even more serious flavor, add a pound or two of Italian sausage (sweet or hot, casings removed). In this case, due to oils released by the sausage, reduce the butter from a full stick (8 tablespoons) to a half (4 tablespoons). Before Step 1, add 2 tablespoons (¼ stick) salted butter, hit Sauté and Adjust to the More or High setting. Once melted, add 1–2 pounds ground sausage and sauté until crumbled and lightly browned. Then add the broth and scrape the bottom of the pot to get up any browned bits. Finally, add the pasta but *do not stir* (just smooth it out with a mixing spoon). From there, follow the recipe as written from Step 2, stirring in the remaining 2 tablespoons butter instead of 4 in Step 3.

Because of how cheesy it is and how quick the pasta is to absorb the sauce, Cacio e Pepe is a dish best eaten immediately. If you have leftovers, I'd suggest adding some milk or cream when reheating in order to reconstitute the sauce.

To Serve 1–2 Reduce the broth to 2½ cups but halve all the other ingredients. Cook times remain the same.

FRENCH ONION MAC & CHEESE

Look, the truth is that if you slap the words "French Onion" on any recipe, you'll have my attention. This "grown-up" rendition of mac and cheese has been given the French onion treatment with syrupy-sweet onions and the use of Swiss or Gruyère (or even mozzarella) in place of Cheddar. From there, we toss it all with campanelle or pasta shells—essentially making it the greatest, ooey-est, gooey-est, and richest mac and cheese ever—but one that is still super easy to make.

Prep Time	Sauté Time	Pressure Building Time	Pressure Cook Time	Total Time	Serves
5 MIN	15–20 MIN	10–15 MIN	6 MIN	40 MIN	4–6

- **6 tablespoons (¾ stick) salted butter**
- **2 Vidalia (sweet) onions, sliced into ¼-inch-thick strips**
- **1 tablespoon light or dark brown sugar**
- **½ cup dry red wine, like a pinot noir** (NOTE: If you don't wish to use wine, add another cup of broth.)

- **3½ cups vegetable, onion, or garlic broth** (e.g., Sautéed Onion or Garlic Better Than Bouillon)
- **1 pound campanelle or medium shells**
- **½ cup heavy cream or half-and-half**
- **2 teaspoons garlic powder**

- **1 (5.2-ounce) package Boursin cheese (any flavor) or ¾ cup Garlic Herb Cheese (page 21)**
- **3 cups shredded Swiss, Gruyère, and/or mozzarella cheese**
- Packaged fried onions, for topping (optional, I use French's)

1 Add the butter to the Instant Pot. Hit Sauté and Adjust so it's on the More or High setting. Once melted and bubbling, add the onions and brown sugar and sauté for 15–20 minutes, until they are nicely softened into a pasta-like consistency. (NOTE: *Do not skimp on this step because the worst thing ever is to have crunchy, undercooked onions in a pasta.*)

2 Next, add the wine and deglaze (scrape the bottom of the pot) to get up any browned bits. Let simmer for a minute. Follow by adding the broth. Stir well.

3 Lastly, add the pasta but *do not stir.* Just allow it to be as submerged as possible under the liquid by smoothing out with a mixing spoon.

4 Secure the lid and move the valve to the sealing position. Hit Cancel followed by Manual or Pressure Cook on High Pressure for 6 minutes. Quick release when done and give the pot a good stir. You'll see some liquid left in the pot and this is exactly what we want as it will be the base for our sauce.

5 Add the cream, garlic powder, Boursin, and shredded cheese. Gently stir it in with the pasta for about 2 minutes, until fully incorporated into a stretchy and wondrous sauce. If you want it smoother, feel free to add a little more cream until the desired consistency is reached.

6 Transfer to bowls and top with fried onions, if desired.

 JEFF'S TIP When reheating any leftovers, mix in a few splashes of milk or cream with the pasta.

 To Serve 1–2 Reduce the broth to 2½ cups but halve all the other ingredients. Cook times remain the same.

ZIPPY ZITI

There's nothing like tubular pasta in a buttery garlic-Parmesan sauce, especially with some cream and red sauce added to the mix...well, perhaps except for when you make it unbelievably easy and flavorful with minimal ingredients. This one earned its name due to how fast it is to make. Check out Jeff's Tips on how to liven it up even more.

 (see Jeff's Tips)

 (if using garlic broth)

Prep Time	Pressure Building Time	Pressure Cook Time	Total Time	Serves
2 MIN	**10–15 MIN**	**6 MIN**	**20 MIN**	**4–6**

4 cups chicken or garlic broth (e.g., Garlic Better Than Bouillon)

2 teaspoons Italian seasoning (optional)

1 pound ziti or ziti rigati

4 tablespoons (½ stick) salted butter, divided into 4 pats

1 cup Parmesan cheese, plus more for topping if desired

2 teaspoons garlic powder

½ cup heavy cream or half-and-half (for a lighter, thinner sauce) or 5.2-ounce package Boursin or ¾ cup Garlic Herb Cheese, page 21 (for a richer, thicker sauce)

2 cups marinara sauce (I like the Rao's and Victoria brands, but you can also use my Classic Red Sauce, page 28), preferably at room temperature

1 Add the broth and Italian seasoning (if using) to the Instant Pot. Stir well. Add the ziti but *do not stir*. Just smooth it out so it's mostly submerged. Top with 2 pats of the butter.

2 Secure the lid and move the valve to the sealing position. Hit Cancel followed by Manual or Pressure Cook on High Pressure for 6 minutes. Quick release when done and give the pot a good stir.

JEFF'S TIPS This recipe is remarkably customizable. Feel free to add any spices you wish in Step 1 or Step 3: 1–2 teaspoons of each of your favorites should do the trick.

If you want it dairy-free, skip the butter, cheese, and cream/Boursin.

For a meaty touch, at the end of Step 1 add (approximately) a 24-ounce package of frozen meatballs on top of the pasta and butter but *do not stir.*

3 Stir in the remaining 2 pats of butter, followed by the Parmesan, garlic powder, cream, and marinara sauce. Let rest for 5 minutes before serving with more Parmesan for topping and some toasty garlic bread, if desired.

To Serve 1–2 Reduce the broth to 2¾ cups but halve all the other ingredients. Cook times remain the same.

VOLCANO CARBONARA

If you enjoyed my creamy, meaty, eggy Spaghetti Carbonara in the orange book, you're going to love this spin with a thicker, hollowed-out noodle known as bucatini (or perciatelli). Oh, and the name doesn't lie...because this carbonara is *spicy*! (Although it doesn't *have* to be—see Jeff's Tips.)

Prep Time	Sauté Time	Pressure Building Time	Pressure Cook Time	Total Time	Serves
5 MIN	15 MIN	10–15 MIN	12 MIN	45 MIN	4–6

1/3 cup extra-virgin olive oil

8–10 ounces pancetta or thick-cut bacon, diced

6 cloves garlic, minced or pressed

2 teaspoons cayenne pepper *or* crushed red pepper flakes *or* a mix of the two, plus more for serving (see Jeff's Tips)

1/4 cup dry white wine (like a sauvignon blanc)

5 1/2 cups chicken or garlic broth (e.g., Garlic Better Than Bouillon)

1 pound bucatini or perciatelli

4 tablespoons (1/2 stick) salted butter, cut into 4 pats

3 large eggs

1 cup grated Parmesan or Pecorino Romano *or* a mix of the two

1/2–1 cup heavy cream or half-and-half (optional)

1 Pour the oil in the Instant Pot and hit Sauté and Adjust so it's on the More or High setting. After 3 minutes of heating, add the pancetta and sauté for 8–10 minutes, until it begins to brown and get slightly crispy. Use a slotted spoon to remove the pancetta to a paper towel–lined bowl and set aside.

2 Add the garlic and cayenne and/or red pepper flakes to the pot and sauté for 3 minutes more. Reserve 1–2 tablespoons of the oil for serving (see Step 7). The bottom of the pot will be quite brown and sticky by now. That's about to change.

3 Add the wine and deglaze (scrape the bottom of the pot), freeing any browned bits from the sautéing of the pancetta. (NOTE: If you prefer not to use wine, use an additional 1/4 cup broth instead.)

CONTINUES

4 Add the broth to the pot and stir well. Break the pasta in half and add it to the pot in a crisscross fashion, but *do not stir*. Just smooth it out with a spoon to make sure it's mostly covered (it's okay if some of it sticks out). Top with the pats of butter. Secure the lid, move the valve to the sealing position, hit Cancel, and then hit Pressure Cook or Manual on High Pressure for 12 minutes. Quick release when done.

5 While the pasta's cooking, whisk the eggs in a mixing bowl and then gradually whisk in the grated cheese until the mixture becomes quite thick. Set aside.

6 When the lid comes off the pot, give everything a good stir. (NOTE: The pasta may be a little clumped together and perhaps a bit al dente but that's how it should be. It will separate and continue to cook as it's stirred. It also may appear soupy, but not to worry: It's about to get quite thick!) Hit Cancel followed by Sauté on the More or High setting. Pour in the egg and cheese mixture with one hand while stirring aggressively and continuously with the other for 1–2 minutes, until the egg appears cooked. If using the cream, stir it in now (start with ½ cup and add up to ½ cup more if desired).

7 Return the reserved pancetta and oil to the pot, give the pasta a final toss, and hit Cancel to turn off the heat. Serve immediately, topped with an additional sprinkling of the cayenne or crushed red pepper flakes, if you dare.

JEFF'S TIPS How much spicy "lava" you want to erupt from this volcano carbonara is in your court. Start with the 2 teaspoons of cayenne and/or red pepper flakes in Step 2. After stirring in the reserved oil and cooked pancetta in Step 7, give the pasta a taste just before serving. From there, you can decide to stir in additional pepper in 1-teaspoon increments until it achieves your spicy desires.

If you don't want it spicy, leave out the cayenne and/or red pepper flakes altogether.

The bucatini will continue to absorb the sauce and egg mixture as it rests and cools. The cream will keep it nice and saucy.

You can also use spaghetti or linguine. If you do, reduce the amount of broth to 5 cups and pressure cook on High Pressure in Step 4 for 8 minutes for spaghetti or 6 minutes for linguine.

To Serve 1–2 Halve the recipe but leave the broth amount the same. Cook times remain the same.

CHUCKWAGON WHEELS

V⁺ *(see Jeff's Tips)*

Sometimes in addition to wanting fabulous-tasting food, we also want to have fun with it. Inspired by the retro computer game *The Oregon Trail*, this complete pasta dish features wagon wheels in a tomato-based meat sauce with a smooth, cheesy finish. It tastes like a Western-style lasagna. It's called Chuckwagon Wheels and it's a bandwagon you're about to get on (dysentery-free, of course).

Prep Time	Sauté Time	Pressure Building Time	Pressure Cook Time	Total Time	Serves
5 MIN	9 MIN	10–15 MIN	6 MIN	30 MIN	4–6

¼ cup extra-virgin olive oil

1 medium yellow onion, diced

1½ pounds ground meat (see Jeff's Tips)

1 tablespoon Worcestershire sauce

3½ cups beef or garlic broth (e.g., Garlic Better Than Bouillon)

3½ cups marinara sauce (I like the Rao's and Victoria brands, but you can also use my Classic Red Sauce, page 28), preferably at room temperature, divided

1 (approximately 1-ounce) packet taco seasoning

1 pound wagon wheel or mini wagon wheel pasta (see Jeff's Tips)

3 cups shredded Cheddar cheese

1 (5.2-ounce) package Boursin cheese (any flavor) or ¾ cup Garlic Herb Cheese (page 21), cut into chunks

1 Add the olive oil to the Instant Pot. Hit Sauté and Adjust so it's on the More or High setting. After 3 minutes of the oil heating, add the onion and sauté for 2–3 minutes, until translucent.

2 Add the ground meat and break it up with a wooden spatula or spoon. Sauté for 3 minutes, until it becomes crumbled and lightly browned.

3 Add the Worcestershire sauce and deglaze (scrape the bottom of the pot) to get any browned bits up.

CONTINUES

4 Add the broth, 1½ cups of the marinara sauce, and the taco seasoning. Stir well. Add the pasta but *do not stir*. Simply smooth out with a mixing spoon so it's submerged.

5 Secure the lid, move the valve to the sealing position, and hit Cancel followed by Manual or Pressure Cook at High Pressure for 6 minutes. Quick release when done.

6 Add the remaining 2 cups marinara sauce and the cheeses. Stir until combined. Serve with crusty Italian bread.

JEFF'S TIPS For the ground meat, I use ground chuck (hence the name of the recipe), but you can absolutely feel free to use any protein you wish, be it ground sirloin, turkey, veal, chicken, pork sausage, or a plant-based "meat" (like Impossible or Beyond—which will make it vegetarian).

If you can't find wagon (or mini wagon) wheel pasta, any short-form pasta (such as macaroni, bow ties, gemelli, cavatappi, mezze penne, or ziti rigati) will do. Same cook time.

To Serve 1–2 Reduce the broth to 2½ cups but halve all the other ingredients. Cook times remain the same.

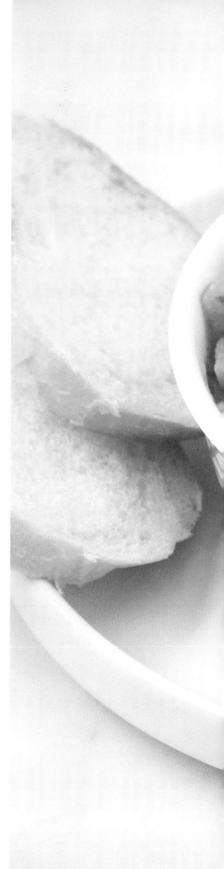

GINGER-SCALLION · NOODLES

Sometimes, all it takes are super basic ingredients to create something so unforgettable that it must be tasted to be believed. For this flavorful Cantonese-style dish, we infuse oil with ginger, scallion, and soy sauce (or tamari) and toss it with some pressure-cooked spaghetti. It couldn't be easier to make and it's something I could eat every day. The ginger-scallion oil is also incredible spooned over rice. It's a vegan dish as written, but check out Jeff's Tips for how to glamify it with additional veggies and proteins of your choice.

Prep Time	Sauté Time	Pressure Building Time	Pressure Cook Time	Total Time	Serves
5 MIN	6 MIN	10–15 MIN	8 MIN	30 MIN	4–6

THE NOODLES

2 tablespoons sesame oil

1 bunch scallions, sliced into ½-inch strands

3 cups vegetable or garlic broth (e.g., Garlic Better Than Bouillon)

1 pound spaghetti

THE GINGER-SCALLION OIL

4-inch knob ginger, peeled and roughly chopped

1 bunch scallions, sliced and roughly chopped

⅔ cup vegetable oil

2 teaspoons low-sodium soy sauce, tamari, or coconut aminos

½ teaspoon kosher salt

1 Add the sesame oil to the Instant Pot. Hit Sauté and Adjust so it's on the More or High setting. After 3 minutes of the oil heating, add the scallions and sauté for 2–3 minutes, until softened.

2 Add the broth, break the spaghetti in half, and layer crisscross fashion so it's mostly submerged in the broth but *do not stir*. Secure the lid, move the valve to the sealing position, and hit Cancel followed by Manual or Pressure Cook at High Pressure for 8 minutes. Quick release when done.

3 While the spaghetti's cooking, add the ginger and scallion to a food processor or blender. Pulse/blend until finely minced. Transfer to a salad dressing shaker or large bowl and add the vegetable oil, soy sauce, and salt. Shake or mix until well combined.

4 When the lid comes off, give the pot a good stir. (NOTE: The spaghetti may be a little clumped together and perhaps a bit al dente but that's how it should be. It will separate and continue to cook as it's stirred.) Pour the ginger-scallion oil all over the noodles, stir, and let rest for 5 minutes before serving. Top with additional scallions or remnants from the oil, if desired.

 JEFF'S TIPS The point of this book is to keep the ingredient lists to ten or less, but I know some folks love their noodles loaded with veggies and proteins.

Here are more veggie options for sautéing in Step 1 (if needed, add 1–2 tablespoons more sesame oil):

1 medium yellow onion, diced

8–16 ounces shiitake mushrooms, sliced

1 large or 2 medium carrots, cut into ¼-inch-thick matchsticks

1 large bell pepper of your choice, seeded and diced

6 ounces snow peas

1 (8-ounce) can water chestnuts, drained

1 (8-ounce) can bamboo shoots, drained

Or, you can be lazy and just use up to a 24-ounce bag of frozen veggies, be it classic veggies or an Asian stir-fry mix

Here are a few optional touches to add in Step 4 when adding the ginger-scallion oil to the noodles:

1–2 tablespoons hoisin sauce

2–4 teaspoons soy sauce (or tamari or coconut aminos)

1–2 teaspoons crushed red pepper flakes

And here's how you can add some proteins of your choice:

1½ pounds chicken thighs or thinly sliced breasts, cut into bite-size pieces: Add in Step 1 with the veggies and sauté until pinkish-white in color, about 2 minutes—but reduce the broth to 2½ cups since they will release juices.

2 pounds flank steak, cut into bite-size pieces: Add in Step 1 with the veggies and sauté until lightly browned on the edges—but reduce the broth to 2½ cups since the steak will release juices.

1–2 pounds frozen raw shrimp, peeled and deveined: Add in Step 4 when adding the ginger-scallion oil. Once curled and opaque, the shrimp are cooked.

 To Serve 1–2 Reduce the broth to 2¼ cups but halve all the other ingredients. Cook times remain the same.

SAUSAGE CURLS

No matter how hard the three little pigs tried to protect their houses from the Big Bad Wolf, we all know how that turned out. But since this is my book and I make the rules, I'm writing a different ending: In my version, one piggy decides to build their house out of cavatappi—a pasta shaped like a squiggly pigtail—and uses the leftovers to make this very dish, which they offer to Mr. Wolf. He is so delighted by the porky pasta in pink sauce that he forgets all about his original plan. Instead of huffing and puffing, he inhales bowl after bowl of pasta until he is so stuffed he can't move. And so Mr. Wolf and the three little pigs become the best of friends. The End.

Prep Time	Sauté Time	Pressure Building Time	Pressure Cook Time	Total Time	Serves
5 MIN	8 MIN	10–15 MIN	6 MIN	30 MIN	4–6

- **4 tablespoons (½ stick) salted butter, divided**
- **2 large shallots, diced**
- **2 pounds Italian sausage (I use a mix of sweet and hot), sliced into ½-inch chunks (<u>see Jeff's Tips</u>)**
- **3½ cups marinara sauce (I like the Rao's and Victoria brands, but you can also use my Classic Red Sauce, page 28), preferably at room temperature, divided**

- **3½ cups chicken or garlic broth (e.g., Garlic Better Than Bouillon)**
- **Leaves from 1 bunch fresh basil, some chopped and reserved for garnish**
- **1 pound cavatappi or cellentani**
- **¼ cup heavy cream or half-and-half**
- **½ cup grated Parmesan cheese, plus more for topping**

- **1 (5.2-ounce) package Boursin cheese (any flavor), ¾ cup Garlic Herb Cheese (page 21), or 4 ounces brick cream cheese, cut into chunks**

SPICY OPTIONS (USE UP TO ALL THREE, IF YOU DARE!)
- ¼ teaspoon crushed red pepper flakes
- ¼ teaspoon cayenne pepper
- 1–2 tablespoons hot sauce

1 Add 2 tablespoons of the butter to the Instant Pot, hit Sauté and Adjust so it's on the More or High setting. Once melted and bubbling, add the shallots and sauté for 2 minutes, until just softened. Add the sausage and sauté for 3 minutes longer, until the sausage is just lightly browned (it should not be fully cooked at all).

2 Add 1½ cups of the marinara sauce, all of the broth, and the basil leaves. Stir until well combined.

3 Top with the pasta but *do not stir*. Just smooth it out with a mixing spoon or spatula so it's mostly submerged in the sauce. Top with the remaining 2 tablespoons butter cut into pats.

4 Secure the lid, move the valve to the sealing position, and hit Cancel followed by Manual or Pressure Cook on High Pressure for 6 minutes. Quick release when done.

5 Add the remaining 2 cups marinara sauce, the heavy cream, Parmesan, and Boursin (or cream cheese). If using any or all of the optional spicy ingredients, add those now as well. Stir until the dairy is fully combined into the sauce. Let the pasta rest for about 5 minutes to come together before serving topped with additional Parmesan and basil, if desired.

JEFF'S TIPS

Like a sponge, pasta always continues to absorb the liquids or sauces that coat it—even after cooking. If you have leftovers, just heat it up in your Instant Pot on Sauté and stir in a little milk or cream to revive the sauciness!

To easily slice a sausage link, pop it in the freezer for 5–10 minutes and it will slice without the meat coming out of the casing—a total game changer!

To Serve 1-2

Reduce the broth to 2½ cups but halve all the other ingredients. Cook times remain the same.

PASTA · BIANCA ·

If it's a cheesy pasta you crave with no red sauce required, allow me to share Pasta Bianca with you. Made up of a trio of white cheeses (ricotta, mozzarella, and Parmesan), this dish is reminiscent of an Alfredo, but cheesier, more textured, and more lavish—especially with a drizzle of truffle oil to finish it off. You'll probably want some soft bread sticks or garlic knots on hand. And if you *do* prefer a red sauce presence, I throw in a tip on how to easily turn the pasta into a vegetarian-style ziti!

 (if using garlic broth)

Prep Time	Pressure Building Time	Pressure Cook Time	Total Time	Serves
2 MIN	10-15 MIN	6 MIN	20 MIN	4-6

1 pound penne, mezze penne, or campanelle (or <u>see Jeff's Tips</u>)

4 cups chicken or garlic broth (e.g., Garlic Better Than Bouillon)

4 tablespoons (½ stick) salted butter, cut into 4 pats

2 cups ricotta cheese (a 15-ounce tub will do)

4 cups shredded mozzarella cheese

1 cup grated Parmesan cheese

3 large eggs

1 tablespoon dried basil, plus more for topping

1-2 tablespoons extra-virgin olive oil or truffle oil (see Jeff's Tips), plus more for drizzling (optional)

1 Add the pasta and broth to the Instant Pot, making sure the pasta is submerged as best as possible in the broth. Top with the butter. Secure the lid and move the valve to the sealing position. Hit Cancel followed by Manual or Pressure Cook on High Pressure for 6 minutes. Quick release when done and give the pot a good stir.

2 Meanwhile, add the ricotta, mozzarella, Parmesan, eggs, and dried basil to a large bowl and mix until combined.

3 Add the cheese mixture to the pot and stir until combined. Taste the pasta. If you decide you want to add the oil, do it now (start with 1 tablespoon) and stir once more. Serve immediately with additional drizzled oil, if desired.

JEFF'S TIPS

Any short-form pasta that scoops up a sauce nicely will do. This includes ziti, penne, mezze penne, mostaccioli, and medium shells. Same cook time.

Obviously using truffle oil is a much different flavor profile (and much more intense) than olive oil, but both complement this dish nicely. If using, choose whichever you prefer.

To easily turn this pasta into a vegetarian-friendly (un)baked ziti (or whatever short-form pasta you use): Add some Classic Red Sauce (page 28) or store-bought marinara (preferably at room temperature) in Step 3 after stirring in the cheese. How much you want to add is up to you—so just add, stir, and taste until you're content. You can also have the best of both worlds by adding some red sauce to individual bowls of the pasta or to leftovers!

To Serve 1–2

Reduce the broth to 2¾ cups but halve all the other ingredients. Cook times remain the same.

BARBECUE CHICKEN PASTA

There are few things as American as barbecue chicken. But a few chickens got together, ditched crossing the road, and bought one-way tickets from Barbecue-land to Italy and fell in love with pasta. This colorful dish satisfies a serious comfort craving and is a huge crowd-pleaser. Goes great with cornbread!

Prep Time	Sauté Time	Pressure Building Time	Pressure Cook Time	Total Time	Serves
10 MIN	8 MIN	10–15 MIN	5 MIN	35 MIN	4–6

2 tablespoons (¼ stick) salted butter

1 red onion, diced

1½ pounds boneless, skinless chicken thighs and/or breasts, cut into bite-size chunks

3 cups chicken or ham broth (e.g., Ham Better Than Bouillon)

1 (14.5-ounce) can diced tomatoes

1 pound rotini

12- to 16-ounce jar sliced banana peppers, drained, some peppers reserved for topping (optional)

10 ounces frozen corn

2–4 cups shredded Cheddar cheese

1 cup barbecue sauce (I use Sweet Baby Ray's)

Bacon bits, for topping (optional)

1 Add the butter to the Instant Pot. Hit Sauté and Adjust so it's on the More or High setting. Once melted and bubbling, add the onion and sauté for 2 minutes, until softened.

2 Add the chicken and sauté until pinkish-white in color, 2–3 minutes longer.

3 Add the broth and diced tomatoes to the pot and stir well.

4 Add the pasta but *do not stir*. Top with the banana peppers (if using) and corn (again, *no stirring*). Hit Cancel followed by Manual or Pressure Cook at High Pressure for 5 minutes. Quick release when done and stir the pasta.

5 Add the cheese (**see Jeff's Tip**) and barbecue sauce and stir until combined. Let rest for 5 minutes for everything to come together.

6 Serve in bowls and top with additional banana peppers, cheese, and bacon bits, if desired.

JEFF'S TIP When adding the cheese in Step 5, start with 2 cups. If you feel you want it cheesier, you can definitely add up to another 2 cups!

To Serve 1–2 Reduce the broth to 2 cups but halve all the other ingredients. Cook times remain the same.

BUFFALO RANCH BOW TIES

This pasta dish is a super simple mac and cheese with a buffalo sauce infusion. Bow ties (farfalle) work nicely here because the cheesy sauce clings to the grooves, but medium shells, ziti rigati, or mezze penne are also good since the sauce gets scooped up in the hollows (same cook time for all). Feel free to give this buffalo some wings by adding some chicken, ground meat, or shrimp—check out Jeff's Tips for how.

DUMP & GO! 3 STEPS OR LESS!

V+ *(if using garlic broth)*

Prep Time	Pressure Building Time	Pressure Cook Time	Total Time	Serves
2 MIN	10–15 MIN	6 MIN	20 MIN	4–6

1 pound farfalle (bow ties) (NOTE: For some strange reason, this specific pasta usually only comes in a 12-ounce package instead of 16 ounces. You may need to get two boxes for the full pound/16 ounces.)

3½ cups chicken or garlic broth (e.g., Garlic Better Than Bouillon)

½ cup buffalo wing sauce, plus more for topping

4 tablespoons (½ stick) salted butter, cut into 4 pats

2–4 cups shredded cheese of your choice (I like a sharp Cheddar or Colby Jack)

½ cup ranch dressing (I like Hidden Valley)

½ cup grated Parmesan cheese

A few splashes of milk or cream (optional, for additional smoothness)

Blue cheese crumbles, for topping (optional)

1 Add the pasta and broth to the Instant Pot and stir, making sure the pasta is mostly submerged in the broth. Top with the buffalo sauce and pats of butter.

2 Secure the lid and move the valve to the sealing position. Hit Manual or Pressure Cook on High Pressure for 6 minutes. Quick release when done.

To Serve 1–2 Reduce the broth to 2½ cups but halve all the other ingredients. Cook times remain the same.

 3 Give the pot a good stir. You'll see some liquid left in the pot and this is exactly what we want as it will be the base for our sauce. Add the shredded cheese (start with 2 cups), ranch, and Parmesan and stir until melded into the pasta. If you want it cheesier, add up to 2 more cups. If you want a creamier sauce, add a few splashes of milk or cream. Serve topped with blue cheese crumbles and additional buffalo sauce, if desired.

JEFF'S TIPS

To cluck this pasta up, in place of Step 1, add 2 additional tablespoons (¼ stick) salted butter to the pot, hit Sauté and Adjust to the More or High setting. Once melted, add 1–2 pounds ground chicken (or any ground meat of your choice) and sauté until crumbled and lightly browned. Then, add the broth and scrape the bottom of the pot to get up any browned bits. Then, add the pasta (but *do not stir*) and top with the buffalo sauce and 4 pats of butter. From there, follow the recipe as written from Step 2.

For a quicker chicken solution, you can keep Step 1 as is and just add 1–2 pounds of shredded precooked rotisserie chicken in Step 3.

For a shrimpy touch, add 1 pound peeled raw shrimp in Step 3 while stirring in the cheese (you can hit Sauté and Adjust to the Normal or Medium setting to give the pot a bit more heat here). Once curled and opaque, the shrimp are done.

Reheat any leftovers by adding a few splashes of milk or cream and mixing it into the pasta.

SMOKY

This is perhaps one of the most simple, unique, and outrageous pasta dishes I've ever created, thanks to a broth made with not one but *two* wines (but see Jeff's Tips to make it wine-free or to change the wine up), plus an extra-special, creamy smoked paprika finish. The scallions provide a slightly bitter twang which I feel is a fragrant touch, but I've made them optional if that's not your style.

V+ *(if using onion or garlic broth)*

Prep Time	Sauté Time	Pressure Building Time	Pressure Cook Time	Total Time	Serves
5 MIN	8 MIN	10–15 MIN	6 MIN	30 MIN	4–6

1/3 cup extra-virgin olive oil

12 cloves garlic, peeled and halved

2 bunches scallions, sliced into 1-inch pieces (optional), with some reserved for garnish

1 cup Marsala wine (sweet or dry, but any will do—see Jeff's Tips)

1/2 cup sherry wine

2 cups chicken, onion, or garlic broth (e.g., Sautéed Onion or Garlic Better Than Bouillon)

1 pound medium pasta shells

1/4 cup heavy cream or half-and-half

2 teaspoons liquid smoke

1 (5.2-ounce) package Boursin cheese (any flavor) or 3/4 cup Garlic Herb Cheese (page 21), cut into chunks

1 tablespoon smoked paprika, plus more for topping

1 Pour the oil in the Instant Pot and hit Sauté and Adjust so it's on the More or High setting. After 3 minutes of heating, add the garlic and sauté for 3 minutes, until lightly browned. If using, add the scallions and sauté them in the oil for another 2 minutes.

2 Add both wines and, if necessary, deglaze the bottom of the pot, freeing it from any browned bits from the sautéing of the garlic.

3 Once the wine's bubbling, add the broth to the pot and stir well. Add the pasta but *do not stir*. Just smooth it out with a spoon to make sure it's mostly covered (it's okay if some of it sticks out). Secure the lid, move the valve to the sealing position, hit Cancel, and then hit Pressure Cook or Manual on High Pressure for 6 minutes. Quick release when done.

JEFF'S TIPS

The combination of the Marsala and sherry wines is what makes this pasta so incredibly special. However, if you're not into cooking with wine, just nix them and sub in an additional 1½ cups broth (so 3½ cups broth total). In Step 2, add 1 cup of the broth to deglaze the pot before adding the remaining 2½ cups in Step 3.

Try it with merlot in place of the Marsala. It will change the flavor profile into something a bit drier and give a much darker hue to the pasta. It works, though!

4 Add the cream, liquid smoke, Boursin or herb cheese, and smoked paprika. Stir until fully combined. Let rest for 3–5 minutes to thicken. Top with reserved sliced scallions and smoked paprika, if desired.

To Serve 1–2

Keep the broth at 2 cups but halve all the other ingredients. Cook times remain the same.

DAN DAN–STYLE NOODLES

DUMP & GO! **3 STEPS OR LESS!**

 DF + *(see Jeff's Tips)*

 GF + *(if using rice noodles, per Jeff's Tips)*

 VN + *(if using garlic or onion broth)*

If you're looking for a simple spicy noodle dish, this is the one. My noodles, inspired by the Szechuan staple, apply the flavor profile I love so much to a different type of noodle. The recipe lets you choose from three options of long-form pastas, from fat to thin. Whichever you go with, it's all about that final sauce featuring a vibrant, red chili oil (with a touch of optional sweetness), ending in an addictive bowl of stunning noodles to devour with a pair of chopsticks. The perfect meal for curling up on the couch in sweats on a chilly day and watching your favorite flick. To make this with a traditional Chinese noodle, check out Jeff's Tips.

Prep Time	Pressure Building Time	Pressure Cook Time	Total Time	Serves
5 MIN	**10–15** MIN	**6–12** MIN (SEE STEP 2)	**25–32** MIN	**4–6**

4 cups chicken, onion, or garlic broth (e.g., Sautéed Onion or Garlic Better Than Bouillon)

1 pound bucatini/perciatelli, spaghetti, or linguine (or see Jeff's Tips)

4 tablespoons (½ stick) salted butter, sliced into 4 pats (see Jeff's Tips)

5–8 ounces baby spinach

¼–½ cup smooth peanut butter (optional)

¼ cup pad thai sauce or sweet soy sauce (optional)

⅔ cup chili oil (I use a mix of chili oil itself and a chili oil with crushed chilis already in it—see Jeff's Tip, page 115, top right)

2 tablespoons sesame oil

1–3 tablespoons chili garlic sauce

½–1 teaspoon crushed red pepper flakes (optional, add more or less to taste)

1 Pour the broth in the Instant Pot. Break the pasta in half and lay in the pot in a crisscross fashion but *do not stir.* (NOTE: You must break the pasta for it to fit in the pot and cook properly. Once you're eating them, the strands will still feel plenty long.)

2 Top the pasta with the butter pats and spinach. Secure the lid, move the valve to the sealing position, and hit Manual or Pressure Cook on High Pressure for the following times: 12 minutes for bucatini/perciatelli, 8 minutes for spaghetti, or 6 minutes for linguine. Quick release when done. (NOTE: When the lid comes off, some of the pasta may appear fused together. This will easily come apart once you stir a bit with a wooden spatula and use it to separate any strands until the pasta easily comes independent.)

JEFF'S TIP There are tons of chili oil options out there and what you choose is totally up to you. I will say I love the Lao Gan Ma brand (Spicy Chili Crisp, in particular!) that you can find in many Asian markets and online. In lieu of the chili oil, you can use a pre-made dan dan noodle sauce found in many Asian markets and online.

3 Add the peanut butter (if using), pad thai/sweet soy sauce (if using), chili oil, sesame oil, and 1 tablespoon chili garlic sauce. Stir until all the noodles are coated and adopt that gorgeous, glistening red color. Taste it. If you decide you want it spicier, add 1–2 tablespoons more chili garlic sauce and/or some crushed red pepper flakes (start with 1 teaspoon and you can always add more). Goes great with an icy Coke!

To Serve 1–2 Reduce the broth to 2½ cups but halve all the other ingredients. Cook times remain the same.

JEFF'S TIPS To keep this dairy-free, in lieu of the butter, add 2 more tablespoons of sesame oil on top of the pasta in Step 2 before topping with the spinach.

If you want to add some protein, add pre-cooked rotisserie chicken or raw shrimp in Step 3. If using shrimp, stir until opaque and curled.

TRADITIONAL TIP! If you wish to make this with 1 pound rice stick/banh pho noodles (large size) or white, Asian-style wheat noodles (medium thick) in place of the Italian pasta, forget the Instant Pot. Omit the butter and broth and skip Steps 1 and 2 completely. Add about 8 cups water to a pot on your stove and bring to a boil. After 8–10 minutes of heating, when the water is nearly boiling, turn your burner off. Add the noodles and cook according to the package instructions. You can also add the spinach if you wish. Once the noodles are flowy and soft to the bite, drain the noodles (and spinach, if using) through a colander. Add the drained contents to a large bowl, then add all the remaining ingredients as listed. Toss until the noodles are fully coated in the sauce and serve.

4

RICE & GRAINS

When made in the Instant Pot, rice is so nice, you'll want to make it twice...or thrice. From numerous fried rices to creamy risottos, this selection of recipes couldn't be easier, quicker, or more satisfying. They will soon be on frequent rotation as mains, sides, or maybe even a little snack.

= DUMP & GO RECIPE

 = 5 INGREDIENTS OR LESS

 = 3 STEPS OR LESS

 = AIR FRYER LID

 K = KETO

P = PALEO

 DF = DAIRY-FREE

 GF = GLUTEN-FREE

V = VEGETARIAN

 VN = VEGAN

+ = COMPLIANT WITH MODIFICATIONS

WHITE OR BROWN RICE

DUMP & GO!

5 INGR. OR LESS!

DF

GF

VN + *(if using water or vegetable broth)*

This recipe, which is also in my first two books, has to be re-shared in this volume. It will give you the perfect rice every time with just *two* ingredients. Side note: unless instructed otherwise, when any recipe calls for white or brown rice, make sure to always rinse it for 90 seconds.

WHITE RICE

Prep Time	Pressure Building Time	Pressure Cook Time	Natural Release Time	Total Time	Serves
2 MIN	5-10 MIN	3 MIN	10 MIN	25 MIN	4-6

BROWN RICE

Prep Time	Pressure Building Time	Pressure Cook Time	Natural Release Time	Total Time	Serves
2 MIN	5-10 MIN	25 MIN	10 MIN	45 MIN	4-6

2 cups white (jasmine, basmati, or long-grain) or brown rice (do not use instant rice)

2 cups water (or, for more flavor, a broth of your choice—chicken or vegetable preferred)

1 Place the rice in a fine-mesh strainer and rinse it under cold water for 90 seconds, shaking it around until the water filtering through goes from cloudy to clear. (NOTE: Do *not* skip this step as it keeps your rice from becoming mushy.)

2 Place the rinsed rice and water (or broth) in the Instant Pot and stir.

JEFF'S TIP

For more al dente brown rice, pressure cook for 15 minutes with a 5-minute natural release.

To Serve 1–2

Simply halve the recipe. Cook times remain the same.

3 Secure the lid, move the valve to the sealing position, and hit Manual or Pressure Cook on High Pressure for 3 minutes for white rice, 25 minutes for brown (**see Jeff's Tip**). When done, allow a 10-minute natural release followed by a quick release.

4 Remove the lid, fluff with a fork, and serve.

SAUSAGE RISOTTO

Risotto is one of the greatest shortcut recipes the Instant Pot has to offer—mainly because it's truly a "set it and forget it" experience—avoiding the babysitting that the stovetop version traditionally requires. This hearty risotto basically takes two of my most popular recipes: Sausage & Shells and Sausage & Spinach Soup (both from my first book) and turns them into a simplified risotto, so if you're into either of those, you're gonna really love this.

(see Jeff's Tip; and if you use onion or garlic broth)

Prep Time	Sauté Time	Pressure Building Time	Pressure Cook Time	Total Time	Serves
5 MIN	8 MIN	10–15 MIN	6 MIN	30 MIN	4–6

3 tablespoons salted butter

2 pounds Italian sausage (sweet, hot, or a mix), casings removed

2 large shallots, diced

3 cloves garlic, minced or pressed

½ cup dry white wine (like a sauvignon blanc)

2 cups arborio rice

4 cups chicken, onion, or garlic broth (e.g., Onion or Garlic Better Than Bouillon)

5–8 ounces baby spinach

1 (5.2-ounce) package Boursin cheese (any flavor) or ¾ cup Garlic Herb Cheese (page 21), cut into chunks

½ cup grated Parmesan cheese

1 Add the butter to the Instant Pot and hit Sauté and Adjust so it's on the More or High setting. Once the butter's melted, add the loose sausage and shallots and sauté for about 3 minutes, until the sausage crumbles and becomes lightly browned. Add the garlic and sauté 1 minute longer.

2 Add the wine, bring to a simmer, and simmer for another minute before adding the rice. Sauté for 1 minute.

3 Add the broth and stir. Top with the baby spinach but *do not stir*. Secure the lid, move the valve to the sealing position, hit Cancel, and then hit Manual or Pressure Cook at High Pressure for 6 minutes. Quick release when done.

JEFF'S TIP
In lieu of the Italian sausage, you can use any type of sausage your heart desires. In fact, go ahead and use any form of ground meat; or use a plant-based meat to make it vegan.

To Serve 1–2
Simply halve the recipe. Cook times remain the same.

4 Stir in the Boursin and Parmesan and let the risotto rest for up to 5 minutes to thicken before serving.

· UNSTUFFED ·
BURRITO RICE

3 STEPS OR LESS!

 DF

 GF

 VN + *(if using plant-based meat, see Jeff's Tips)*

Burrito bowls are all the rage these days and seeing as they focus on the burrito filling (which is the best part anyway) while saving a few carbs, it's no guess why. That said, this recipe sort of happened by accident. I was experimenting with a taco-like porridge recipe, but when it was done, I discovered it was just like the creamy inside of an outrageously dressed burrito. And so, I give you the most delicious accident ever: Unstuffed Burrito Rice.

Prep Time	Sauté Time	Pressure Building Time	Pressure Cook Time	Natural Release Time	Total Time	Serves
5 MIN	7 MIN	5–10 MIN	25 MIN	20 MIN	1 HR 5 MIN	4–6

3 tablespoons extra-virgin olive oil

1½–2 pounds ground beef or meatloaf mixture (see Jeff's Tips)

2 (approximately 1-ounce) packets taco seasoning

6½ cups water

1½ cups jasmine rice (do not rinse)

10–20 ounces frozen corn (optional)

2 (15.5-ounce) cans beans of your choice (optional, and see Jeff's Tips), drained and rinsed

1–2 tablespoons Creole/Cajun/Louisiana seasoning (I use Tony Chachere's) or seasoned salt (start with 1 tablespoon and add more to taste)

Optional toppings (such as shredded cheese, sour cream, tortilla strips) or flour or corn tortillas

1 Pour the oil in the Instant Pot and hit Sauté and Adjust so it's on the More or High setting. After 3 minutes of heating, add the meat and sauté for 3–5 minutes, until crumbled and lightly browned, leaving the juices in the pot. Add the taco seasoning and mix until the meat is coated, about 1 minute more.

2 Add the water, rice, and corn (if using) to the pot and stir well. Top with the beans (if using) but *do not stir*. Secure the lid, move the valve to the sealing position, hit Cancel, and then hit Pressure Cook or Manual on High Pressure for 25 minutes. When done, allow a 20-minute natural release followed by a quick release.

3 Stir in the Creole seasoning or seasoned salt. The rice will thicken almost immediately. Serve topped with shredded cheese, tortilla strips, and a dollop of sour cream, if desired. Or, of course, serve rolled up in tortillas of your choice.

JEFF'S TIPS

You can use any type of ground meat you wish, be it pork, turkey, chicken, or plant-based such as Impossible or Beyond (which will make it vegan). 1½ pounds will make these unstuffed burritos meaty and 2 pounds will make it super meaty.

For the beans, I use 1 can of red kidney and 1 can of black.

To make this extra cheesy, rather than just topping the individual bowls, stir 2–4 cups shredded Mexican or taco blend cheese in with the seasoning in Step 3.

To Serve 1–2

Simply halve the recipe. Cook times remain the same.

CHICKEN TERIYAKI FRIED RICE

This fried rice is perfect for an easy, all-in-one meal for busy weeknights because it's a cinch to prepare and will make the whole family happy. The frozen vegetable blend adds nutrition and variety while shaving the time spent standing over your cutting board. To make things even more simple, I suggest my favorite teriyaki brand for the sauce, but I also give you an option to make your awesome own in Jeff's Tips.

(if using a gluten-free teriyaki sauce)

Prep Time	Sauté Time	Pressure Building Time	Pressure Cook Time	Natural Release Time	Total Time	Serves
10 MIN	3–5 MIN	5–10 MIN	2 MIN	10 MIN	30 MIN	4–6

2 tablespoons sesame oil

2½ pounds boneless, skinless chicken thighs, cut into ¼-inch-thick strips

1 large white or yellow onion, diced

2 cups chicken or garlic broth (e.g., Garlic Better Than Bouillon)

2 cups jasmine rice, rinsed

10–20 ounces frozen vegetable blend (one with corn, carrots, peas, and green beans)

½–1 cup of your favorite teriyaki sauce (I like the Soy Vay brand, or see Jeff's Tips)

Sesame seeds (optional)

1 Add the sesame oil to the Instant Pot. Hit Sauté and Adjust so it's on the More or High setting. After 2 minutes of heating, add the chicken and onion and sauté for 3–5 minutes, until the chicken is pinkish-white in color.

2 Add the broth and stir, scraping the bottom of the pot to make sure any browned bits have come up.

3 Add the rice and top with the frozen veggies but *do not stir.* Just gently smooth the rice and veggies out so they're resting on top of everything else in the pot.

 To Serve 1–2 Simply halve the recipe. Cook times remain the same.

 4 Secure the lid, move the valve to the sealing position, and hit Manual or Pressure Cook on High Pressure for 2 minutes. When done, allow a 10-minute natural release followed by a quick release.

5 Add the teriyaki sauce (**see Jeff's Tips**) and mix until combined. Serve topped with sesame seeds, if desired.

JEFF'S TIPS Want to make your own teriyaki sauce? Fab! It's a few extra ingredients and one more step, but this one rocks the casbah. Whisk together the following in a bowl:

½ cup soy sauce, tamari, or coconut aminos (using tamari or coconut aminos will make the fried rice gluten-free)

¼ cup Shaoxing or sherry wine

¼ cup packed dark brown sugar

2 teaspoons squeeze ginger (it comes in a bottle) or minced ginger

3 cloves garlic, crushed or minced (1 tablespoon)

1 tablespoon honey

2 teaspoons sesame oil

¼ cup cold water plus ¼ cup cornstarch mixed together to form a slurry, then added to the bowl with the above ingredients.

When adding the teriyaki sauce to the rice, start with ½ cup and then feel free to add more to your liking. Remember, you can always add more of an ingredient but retracting isn't possible once added!

BROCCOLI CHEDDAR RISOTTO

 GF

 V + *(if using garlic or vegetable broth)*

For me, there are few things as comforting and delightful as a heaping bowl of cheesy risotto or finely creamed broccoli—so why not give them a wedding? This dish is essentially the risotto cousin to my yellow (*Simple Comforts*) book's broccoli-cheddar soup. And featuring just five key ingredients, it doesn't really get much simpler or more budget-friendly. Check out Jeff's Tip to see how to turn it into a creamy casserole.

Prep Time	Pressure Building Time	Pressure Cook Time	Optional Air Fry Time	Total Time	Serves
2 MIN	10–15 MIN	6 MIN	5–10 MIN	25 MIN	4–6

5 cups chicken, vegetable, or garlic broth (e.g., Garlic Better Than Bouillon)

2 cups arborio rice

1–2 pounds broccoli florets (fresh or frozen)

1 pound (4 cups) shredded Cheddar cheese (or any shredded cheese of your choice)

OPTIONAL CRUST

1 sleeve Ritz crackers, smashed and crumbled

4 tablespoons (½ stick) salted butter, melted

 JEFF'S TIP If you want to make this even creamier (and extra unconventional), add a creamy salad dressing in Step 2 along with the cheese. Ranch, creamy garlic, creamy Italian, blue cheese, or even Thousand Island dressing if the mood strikes! You can also keep it simple by just using some sour cream.

1 Add the broth and rice to the pot and stir. Top with the broccoli but *do not stir*. Secure the lid, move the valve to the sealing position, and hit Manual or Pressure Cook on High Pressure for 6 minutes. Quick release when done.

 To Serve 1–2 Simply halve the recipe. Cook times remain the same.

3 **For the optional crust:** Just before serving, use a fork to mix the crumbled crackers with the melted butter. Sprinkle the crumbs over the finished rice, add the Air Fryer Lid, and Broil (400°F) for 5–10 minutes, until the crust is golden brown. Alternatively, you can do this by placing the rice in a casserole dish and broiling in the oven for about 5 minutes, until the crust is golden brown (keep an eye on it as all ovens vary).

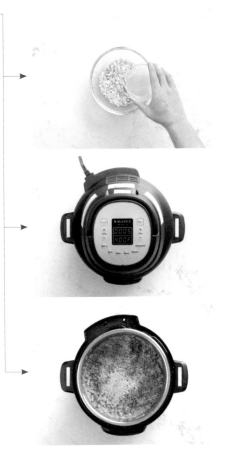

2 Add the Cheddar. Hit Cancel followed by Sauté and Adjust to the More or High setting. Stir until all is combined into cheesy amazingness, which will take about 2 minutes. The broccoli will have become creamed at this point, making for a lovely texture. Hit Cancel to turn the pot off and serve.

LASAGNA RISOTTO

(if using garlic broth and plant-based meat, see Jeff's Tip)

Risotto, although a member of the rice family, can sometimes pass for a member of the pasta family in terms of what it pairs with. For example: lasagna. While it's arguably one of the most delicious meals of all time, a lasagna can be a burden to assemble, not to mention quite messy. That all changes when you turn it into risotto, with little work and no layering required.

Prep Time	Sauté Time	Pressure Building Time	Pressure Cook Time	Total Time	Serves
5 MIN	10 MIN	10–15 MIN	6 MIN	30 MIN	4–6

THE RISOTTO

2 tablespoons extra-virgin olive oil

1 large yellow onion, diced

1½ pounds ground beef or meatloaf mixture

2 cups arborio rice

4½ cups chicken, beef, or garlic broth (e.g., Garlic Better Than Bouillon)

1½ cups marinara sauce (I like the Rao's and Victoria brands, but you can also use my Classic Red Sauce, page 28), preferably at room temperature

1 tablespoon seasoned salt (optional)

THE CHEESE

1 cup ricotta cheese

2 cups shredded mozzarella cheese, plus 1–2 cups for the optional baked topping

½ cup grated Parmesan cheese

1 large egg, lightly beaten

1 Pour the oil in the Instant Pot and hit Sauté and Adjust so it's on the More or High setting. After 3 minutes of heating, add the onion and sauté for 3 minutes, until lightly softened.

2 Add the meat and sauté until crumbled and lightly browned, about another 3 minutes, leaving the juices in the pot.

3 Add the rice and broth and stir everything together well, scraping the bottom of the pot to make sure it's cleared of any browned bits. Secure the lid, move the valve to the sealing position, hit Cancel, and then hit Pressure Cook or Manual on High Pressure for 6 minutes. Quick release when done.

4 Meanwhile, in a bowl, mix together all the cheese ingredients and set aside.

5 When the lid comes off the pot, stir in the marinara sauce and cheese mixture. The heat of the risotto will cook the egg in the mixture. Let rest for up to 5 minutes to thicken. Taste it. If you feel it needs the optional seasoned salt, stir it in now and serve.

JEFF'S TIP You can use any type of ground meat you wish, be it pork, turkey, chicken, or even a plant-based such as Impossible or Beyond (which will make it vegetarian).

To Serve 1–2 Simply halve the recipe. Cook times remain the same.

6 **For an optional baked ("al forno") lasagna finish:** Sprinkle an additional 1–2 cups shredded mozzarella on the risotto. Add the Air Fryer Lid and Broil (400°F) for 3–5 minutes, until the cheese is golden brown. Alternatively, you can do this by placing the risotto in a casserole dish, topping with the mozzarella, and broiling in the oven for 3–5 minutes, until a bubbly-brown cheesy layer has formed (keep an eye on it as all ovens vary).

STREET CART RICE

 DF

 GF

 VN + *(if using water or garlic broth)*

In New York City, it's super common to find street carts serving up Middle Eastern fare. The thing that always stands out to me at these tiny mobile kitchens is the rice. This dish is essentially a combination of the most vibrant flavors that stuck with me from the countless carts I've eaten from while strolling New York streets. I also love topping the rice with a creamy white or hot sauce (see Jeff's Tip) along with a side of falafel.

Prep Time	Sauté Time	Pressure Building Time	Pressure Cook Time	Natural Release Time	Total Time	Serves
5 MIN	7 MIN	5–10 MIN	3 MIN	10 MIN	30 MIN	4–6

¼ cup extra-virgin olive oil

2 large red onions, diced

2 cups basmati rice, rinsed

2 cups water, or chicken or garlic broth (e.g., Garlic Better Than Bouillon)

1 tablespoon curry powder

1 tablespoon seasoned salt

2 teaspoons cumin seed *or* ground cumin

2 teaspoons garlic powder

1 teaspoon turmeric

1 teaspoon ground cinnamon

1 Pour the oil in the Instant Pot and hit Sauté and Adjust so it's on the More or High setting. After 3 minutes of heating, add the onion and sauté for 3–5 minutes, until a bit softened and the color fades.

2 Add all the remaining ingredients to the pot and stir well. Secure the lid, move the valve to the sealing position, hit Cancel, and then hit Pressure Cook or Manual on High Pressure for 3 minutes. When done, allow a 10-minute natural release followed by a quick release.

JEFF'S TIP This goes great with a drizzle of tzatziki, creamy garlic dressing, or creamy Italian salad dressing along with some diced dill pickles. If you like it spicy, add hot sauce of your choice.

To Serve 1–2 Simply halve the recipe. Cook times remain the same.

3 Fluff the rice with a fork and serve.

HIBACHI-STYLE FRIED QUINOA

 (if using tamari or coconut aminos)
 (if using vegetable or onion broth)

My Hibachi Fried Rice from the orange (original *Step-by-Step*) book is a fan favorite: In fact, it's the recipe that put me on the Instant Pot map. Here, we make it lighter and even quicker by using some fluffy and springy quinoa instead of rice. And using a frozen vegetable blend makes it come together in a snap!

Prep Time	Pressure Building Time	Pressure Cook Time	Natural Release Time	Sauté Time	Total Time	Serves
5 MIN	5–10 MIN	1 MIN	10 MIN	9 MIN	30 MIN	4–6

2 cups quinoa, rinsed

2 cups chicken, vegetable, or onion broth (e.g., Sautéed Onion Better Than Bouillon)

2 tablespoons sesame oil

1 large white or yellow onion, diced

20 ounces frozen vegetable blend (one with corn, carrots, peas, and green beans)

3 large eggs, lightly beaten

⅓ cup low-sodium soy sauce, tamari, or coconut aminos

2 tablespoons sesame seeds, plus more for topping (optional)

1 Add the quinoa and broth to the Instant Pot and stir. Secure the lid, move the valve to the sealing position, and hit Manual or Pressure Cook on High Pressure for 1 minute. When done, allow a 10-minute natural release followed by a quick release.

2 When the quinoa is done, remove to a bowl and let rest. Don't worry if some grains are still in the pot as there's no need to rinse.

3 Add the sesame oil to the pot and hit Cancel followed by Sauté and Adjust so it's on the More or High setting. After 2 minutes of heating, add the onion and frozen veggies and sauté for 3–5 minutes, until slightly softened.

4 Move the veggies to one side of the pot. Pour the beaten eggs into the other side and stir constantly to scramble. After 1 minute of scrambling the eggs, mix them in with the veggies.

5 Hit Cancel to turn the pot off. Return the quinoa to the pot and top with the soy sauce and sesame seeds (if using). Stir until all is combined and top with additional sesame seeds, if desired.

To Serve 1–2 Simply halve the recipe. Cook times remain the same.

JEFF'S TIPS I shared these amazing and familiar Japanese steakhouse sauces for topping off your rice in my orange (*Step-by-Step*) book, but have to do so again for the sake of this recipe. Simply mix the ingredients for each sauce in separate bowls and use to top each serving:

JAPANESE MUSTARD SAUCE

- 1/4 cup low-sodium soy sauce, tamari, or coconut aminos
- 1/4 cup milk
- 2 tablespoons heavy cream
- 2 tablespoons ground mustard
- 1 1/2 teaspoons sugar
- 1 clove garlic, minced or pressed

JAPANESE GINGER SAUCE

- 1/2 cup low-sodium soy sauce, tamari, or coconut aminos
- 2 tablespoons minced ginger (I use squeeze ginger)
- Juice of 1/2 lemon
- 1 clove garlic, minced
- 1 1/2 teaspoons onion powder
- 1/2 teaspoon sugar
- 1/4 teaspoon white vinegar

JAPANESE MAYO (YUM-YUM) SAUCE

- 1 cup mayonnaise
- 2 tablespoons water
- 1 tablespoon melted butter
- 1 teaspoon tomato paste
- 1 teaspoon sugar
- 1/2 teaspoon paprika
- 1/2 teaspoon garlic powder
- 1/2 teaspoon salt

PESTO
· RISOTTO ·

Pesto is one of my favorite sauces ever. EVAH. Simply made from basil, olive oil, pine nuts, and Parmesan, it's green, it's a sight to be seen, and the taste is serene. Tossing it into a glorious risotto is one of the simplest and most magnificent dinner treats ever. Also, you guys, this recipe has only three (yes, *three*) core ingredients, two (yes, *two*) steps, and one happy Instant Pot.

Prep Time	Pressure Building Time	Pressure Cook Time	Total Time	Serves
2 MIN	10–15 MIN	6 MIN	20 MIN	4–6

2 cups arborio rice

5 cups chicken, vegetable, or onion broth (e.g., Sautéed Onion or Garlic Better Than Bouillon)

1½ cups pesto of your choice (Costco's Kirkland brand is my favorite pre-made, but see Jeff's Tips for how to make your own)

Mascarpone cheese, for topping (optional)

1 Add the rice and broth to the Instant Pot and stir. Secure the lid, move the valve to the sealing position, hit Cancel, and then hit Pressure Cook or Manual on High Pressure for 6 minutes. Quick release when done.

2 Stir in the pesto. Serve the risotto topped with dollops of mascarpone cheese, if desired.

 To Serve 1–2 Simply halve the recipe. Cook times remain the same.

JEFF'S TIPS

If you wish to make your own delicious pesto, place the following in a food processor and pulse until pureed:

2 cups loosely packed fresh basil leaves

6 cloves garlic, peeled and lightly smashed

¾ cup grated Parmesan cheese

½ cup extra-virgin olive oil

⅓ cup pine nuts (if you can't get your hands on pine nuts, use raw cashews, walnuts, almonds, or shelled pistachio nuts)

If you also wish to give this risotto a little tang, add the juice of 1 lemon, 2 teaspoons onion powder, and 1 teaspoon sugar in Step 1 while mixing the rice and broth.

PAD THAI

FRIED RICE

 DUMP & GO!   5 INGR. OR LESS! 3 STEPS OR LESS!

 DF

 GF

 V + *(if using garlic broth and if okay with fish sauce in pad thai sauce)*

I'm not gonna hedge my bets but will say that a classic pad thai is the most popular thing on the menu at practically every Thai restaurant here in the States. After all, with that sweet and peanut-laden sauce coating delicate rice noodles, it's the ultimate comfort in Thai cuisine. So how about we take it a step further by swapping in jasmine rice for the noodles, *and* make it easier by preparing it with only five ingredients? Of course, if you want it fancier and don't mind a few extra players, I've given you some optional classic toppings. And should you want it with a protein, check out Jeff's Tip.

Prep Time	Pressure Building Time	Pressure Cook Time	Natural Release Time	Sauté Time	Total Time	Serves
2 MIN	5–10 MIN	3 MIN	10 MIN	2 MIN	25 MIN	4–6

2 cups jasmine rice, rinsed

2 cups chicken or garlic broth (e.g., Garlic Better Than Bouillon)

⅓ cup fresh tarragon or Thai basil leaves, plus more for topping

3 large eggs, lightly beaten

1 cup pad thai sauce (I like the Pantai brand)

OPTIONAL TOPPINGS

1 (14-ounce) can bean sprouts, drained (you can use fresh as well)

8 ounces extra-firm tofu, diced

½ cup crushed peanuts

1 cup shredded carrots

1 bunch sliced scallions

Lime wedges

1 Add the rice and broth to the Instant Pot and stir. Top with the tarragon or basil. Secure the lid, move the valve to the sealing position, and hit Manual or Pressure Cook on High Pressure for 3 minutes. When done, allow a 10-minute natural release followed by a quick release.

2 Hit Sauté and Adjust to the More or High setting. Add the eggs and stir until combined and cooked into the rice, about 2 minutes.

JEFF'S TIP If you wish to add chicken or shrimp, do so in Step 2 along with the eggs. For chicken, use shredded pre-cooked rotisserie chicken; for shrimp, use raw or cooked of any size (tail on or off is fine). If using raw shrimp, stir until curled and opaque (2–3 minutes) which means they are ready to eat! Leftover Hoisin Pulled Pork (page 188) or the meat from the Beef Birria Tacos (page 198) also goes nicely with this rice when added in Step 2.

To Serve 1–2 Simply halve the recipe. Cook times remain the same.

3 Pour the pad thai sauce over the rice and mix until combined. Add any optional toppings of your choice and mix into the rice as well before serving and garnishing as desired.

· RISOTTO ·
FRANCESE

Oh *Fran-chezzzzzz*, my love! Forgive me for waiting until book *four* to include you in a recipe. It's high time you were paid your due in a lemony, buttery, eggy, creamy, dreamy risotto. My friends, if you're feeling like a lemony chicken francese–carbonara sleepover, add some optional bacon bits as a final touch; see Jeff's Tips.

(if using garlic broth and if you're okay with eggs)

Prep Time	Sauté Time	Pressure Building Time	Pressure Cook Time	Total Time	Serves
5 MIN	10 MIN	10–15 MIN	6 MIN	35 MIN	4–6

4 tablespoons (½ stick) salted butter

1 large Spanish or yellow onion, diced

1–1½ pounds boneless, skinless chicken breasts, tenderloins, or thighs, cut into bite-size pieces (optional)

5 cups chicken or garlic broth (e.g., Garlic Better Than Bouillon)

2 cups arborio rice

4 large eggs

Juice of 3 lemons

¼ cup heavy cream or half-and-half

1½ cups grated Parmesan cheese

1 Add the butter to the Instant Pot and hit Sauté and Adjust so it's on the More or High setting. Once melted and bubbling, add the onion and chicken (if using) and sauté for 3–5 minutes, until the onions are lightly softened and the chicken is pinkish-white in color.

2 Add the broth and stir everything together well, scraping the bottom of the pot to make sure it's cleared of any browned bits. Add the rice, but *do not stir*. Just smooth it out with a spatula. Secure the lid, move the valve to the sealing position, hit Cancel, and then hit Pressure Cook or Manual on High Pressure for 6 minutes. Quick release when done.

4 When the lid comes off the pot, give the risotto a stir. Hit Cancel followed by Sauté and Adjust so it's on the More or High setting. Once it begins to bubble, pour in the egg mixture and stir constantly for 2 minutes. This will ensure the eggs are cooked through. Add the cream and Parmesan and stir until combined. Hit Cancel and serve topped with additional Parmesan, if desired (and **see Jeff's Tips** for a fancy garnish).

3 Meanwhile, in a bowl, whisk together the eggs and lemon juice.

JEFF'S TIPS Want to add bacon bits? Go right ahead and add ¼–½ cup in Step 4 when adding the dairy. But try and use the real, pre-cooked Hormel or Oscar Meyer ones that come in a small canister or pouch. Or, you can use microwavable bacon and crush it up after. Just don't use the crunchy, fake bacon bits normally used as a salad topper. They will kill the consistency and flavor.

For an extra-fancy presentation, zest the lemons before juicing them. (Or after juicing the lemons, save the rind and slice into twists.) Then, top the plated risotto with the zest and/or twisted rinds. Lovely!

To Serve 1–2 Simply halve the recipe. Cook times remain the same.

SZECHUAN FRIED RICE

 DF
 GF
 VN + *(if using garlic broth)*

I just had to include a spicy fried rice in this chapter—and folks, this one brings the heat. Influenced by Chinese Szechuan fare, which is known for being generous with garlic, chiles, and other flavorful aromatics, this devilishly delicious rice dish is sure to please a spice-craving palate. In fact, you might ask yourself, "Is it fried rice or fired rice?!" Whatever you decide, it's just begging to have an icy Coke beside it.

Prep Time	Sauté Time	Pressure Building Time	Pressure Cook Time	Natural Release Time	Total Time	Serves
15 MIN	15 MIN	5–10 MIN	3 MIN	10 MIN	55 MIN	4–6

- 1 cup chili oil of your choice (see Jeff's Tips), divided
- 12 cloves garlic, roughly chopped
- 2 leeks, green tops, bottom stalks, and harder outer layers removed, sliced into 1-inch strips
- 3 red bell peppers, seeded and diced

- 4 jalapeño peppers or 4 red and/or green chile peppers, diced (keep the seeds intact for extra spice, or see Jeff's Tips for less heat)
- 1 large white or yellow onion, diced
- 2 cups chicken or garlic broth (e.g., Garlic Better Than Bouillon)

- 2 cups jasmine rice, rinsed
- ¼ cup sweet soy sauce or pad thai sauce (optional)
- ¼ cup low-sodium soy sauce, tamari, or coconut aminos (optional)

1 Add ¼ cup of the oil to the Instant Pot. (NOTE: For sautéing purposes, make sure it's mostly oil and light on the chili puree if it's in the oil you're using.) Hit Sauté and Adjust so it's on the More or High setting. After 3 minutes of heating, add the garlic and leek and sauté for 8–10 minutes, *just* until the leeks begin to get syrupy. Use a mixing spoon to remove the garlic and leek from the pot and place in a bowl (setting aside some for topping, if desired).

2 Add the peppers and onion to the pot and sauté for another 3 minutes, scraping the bottom to remove any browned bits.

3 Add the broth and rice to the pot. Smooth the rice out so it's mostly submerged, but *do not stir*. Secure the lid, move the valve to the sealing position, and hit Manual or Pressure Cook on High Pressure for 3 minutes. When done, allow a 10-minute natural release followed by a quick release.

JEFF'S TIPS

I like chili oil that has a combo of oil, pepper flakes, and a puree of spicy goodies in it. Chili oil can be found in the Asian section of most markets or, for greater variety, check out an Asian market or look online. My favorite brands are Lao Gan Ma and Lee Kum Kee—any of their chili oils are great (especially Spicy Chili Crisp).

If you want this crazy spicy, add 1–2 teaspoons cayenne pepper in Step 2. And if you want to go extreme, add a diced habanero pepper in Step 1. Now, whether you wish to add the seeds is up to you, depending on how masochistic you feel that day. Just be sure to wash your hands with some dish soap after handling because if you touch *any* part of your body after, you're gonna feel it.

Alternatively, to keep this on the milder side, forgo the chiles and only use the bell peppers (add a fourth pepper to make up for the lack of chiles) and only use 1–2 teaspoons (at most) red pepper flakes (or omit them).

Should you wish this rice to be even more abundant, add 10–20 ounces of frozen carrots, peas, or a vegetable mix in Step 4. You can also add water chestnuts and/or bamboo shoots. Just hit Sauté so the veggies get heated after a few moments of stirring with the rice.

The optional soy sauce and sweet soy sauce/pad thai sauce are to simply bring an element of savory and sweet to the spice of the rice.

4 Add the remaining ¾ cup chili oil (this includes the puree and pepper flakes if it's in your oil) and the sautéed veggies, along with the sweet soy sauce or pad thai sauce (if using) and soy sauce (if using), stirring until combined with the rice. Top with additional veggies for garnish, if desired.

To Serve 1–2

Simply halve the recipe. Cook times remain the same.

ARROZ AMARILLO

 (if using olive oil instead of butter)

 (if using a vegetarian broth and olive oil instead of butter)

(YELLOW RICE)

Many Spanish and Mexican restaurants offer up an *arroz amarillo* as a delicious side to their mains. Although pricey saffron is often used for flavor and to give it that yellow color, my budget-friendly version uses turmeric. (Speaking of turmeric, not only does it add flavor depth, but it also improves heart health and serves as an anti-inflammatory and antioxidant, making it one of the healthiest things you can put in your body.) However, if you'd rather the traditional saffron in place of the turmeric, you've got that option in the ingredients list. Try topping the rice with some jarred salsa, salsa verde, guacamole, sour cream, or Ginger-Scallion Oil (page 102). You can also toss in some rotisserie chicken before serving to make it a more complete meal.

Prep Time	Pressure Building Time	Pressure Cook Time	Natural Release Time	Total Time	Serves
2 MIN	5–10 MIN	3 MIN	10 MIN	25 MIN	4–6

2 cups jasmine or long-grain white rice (or <u>see Jeff's Tips</u>), rinsed

2 cups broth of your choice—chicken or garlic preferred

4 tablespoons (¼ stick) salted butter or ¼ cup extra-virgin olive oil (NOTE: You can also use half of each.)

½–1 tablespoon garlic salt (<u>see Jeff's Tips</u>)

1½ teaspoons turmeric or saffron

1 Add all the ingredients to the Instant Pot and stir. Secure the lid, move the valve to the sealing position, and hit *Manual* or *Pressure Cook* on High Pressure for 3 minutes. When done, allow a 10-minute natural release followed by a quick release.

2 Remove the lid, fluff with a fork, and serve.

JEFF'S TIPS If you'd rather use brown rice, pressure cook for 25 minutes with a 10-minute natural release for softer rice, or 15 minutes with a 5-minute natural release for firmer.

Whether you use butter or olive oil, I think the savory level of the dish is perfect as is. However, to be on the safe side, begin by adding ½ tablespoon garlic salt in Step 1 and then add up to ½ tablespoon more to taste in Step 2. You can also add any other seasonings you wish while fluffing.

To Serve 1–2 Simply halve the recipe. Cook times remain the same.

5

POULTRY

Each and every one of these winning recipes, whether creamy, light, deeply flavored, or bright, is truly a sight—and what's more, they're all absolutely clucking delicious. So get ready to expand your recipe rotation, because these poultry recipes are as simple as doing the chicken dance (which you'll likely do after tasting each dish)!

= DUMP & GO RECIPE

 = 5 INGREDIENTS OR LESS

 = 3 STEPS OR LESS

 = AIR FRYER LID

 K = KETO

P = PALEO

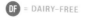 DF = DAIRY-FREE

GF = GLUTEN-FREE

V = VEGETARIAN

 VN = VEGAN

 + = COMPLIANT WITH MODIFICATIONS

CHICKEN PARMINARA

K + *(if using coconut flour, or see Jeff's Tips)*

GF + *(if using coconut or quinoa flour, or see Jeff's Tips)*

If you're a lover of Italian sauces but can't decide on white or red, you've just found a chicken dish that won't make you choose. This spectacular meal combines a creamy, cheesy, eggy Parmesan white sauce with a classic red sauce, which is then draped over tender chicken cutlets—giving it a fanfare of flavor. It naturally goes great over angel hair pasta or mashed potatoes, with some cheesy garlic bread. See Jeff's Tips for how to shave 10 minutes off the total time, and also how to repurpose the dish into an incredible pizza!

Prep Time	Sauté Time	Pressure Building Time	Pressure Cook Time	Total Time	Serves
10 MIN	10 MIN	10–15 MIN	5 MIN	35 MIN	4–6

2 pounds boneless, skinless chicken breasts, sliced into cutlets about ¼ inch thick

⅓ cup all-purpose, coconut, or quinoa flour (if desired, mix in about ¼ teaspoon each of seasoned salt, black pepper, and garlic powder for extra flavor)

¼ cup extra-virgin olive oil

1 cup chicken or garlic broth (e.g., Garlic Better Than Bouillon)

⅔ cup heavy cream or half-and-half

2 large eggs

1 cup grated Parmesan cheese, plus more for topping

1½ cups marinara sauce (I like the Rao's and Victoria brands, but you can also use my Classic Red Sauce, page 28), preferably at room temperature

1 (5.2-ounce) package Boursin cheese (any flavor) or ¾ cup Garlic Herb Cheese (page 21), cut into chunks (optional)

2 cups shredded mozzarella cheese (optional, for topping—see Jeff's Tips)

1 Set three dinner-sized plates next to each other. The first one will have the raw chicken cutlets, the second one the flour mixture, and the third should be empty. Dredge (coat) one chicken cutlet in the flour mixture so it's lightly dusted and set aside on the third plate. Repeat until the first plate is empty and the third plate is filled with coated cutlets.

2 Add the olive oil to the Instant Pot, hit Sauté and Adjust so it's on the More or High setting. After about 3 minutes of heating up, in batches, sear each side of the cutlets for about 1 minute, until lightly browned. Remove to a plate when done and repeat the process until all the chicken is browned.

3 Add the broth to the pot and stir well, scraping the bottom to get up any browned bits. Layer the chicken back into the pot, resting the cutlets on top of each other. Secure the lid, move the valve to the sealing position, hit Cancel, and then hit Manual or Pressure Cook on High Pressure for 5 minutes. Quick release when done.

CONTINUES

4 While the chicken's cooking, whisk together the cream, eggs, and Parmesan in a bowl; set aside.

5 Use tongs to carefully transfer the chicken to a serving dish. Hit the Cancel button, then hit Sauté and Adjust so it's on the More or High setting.

6 As the sauce is coming to a bubble, add the eggy cheese mixture and whisk for 1 minute—the heat of the pot will cook the egg. Then, add the marinara sauce and Boursin (if using) and stir until combined. Hit Cancel to turn the pot off.

7 Ladle the sauce over the chicken, top with some additional Parmesan, if desired, and serve over anything that makes you happy.

JEFF'S TIPS

For an optional cheesy top, make sure your serving dish is ovensafe. Sprinkle the shredded mozzarella evenly on top of the sauced chicken and broil in a preheated oven. Let the cheese melt for 3–5 minutes, until bubbly brown, but be sure to monitor it as all ovens vary.

Want to make this even quicker and save 10 minutes? If you don't mind not having flour-coated and slightly seared chicken cutlets, omit the flour mixture and olive oil and skip Steps 1 and 2. This will also make it keto and gluten-free!

Let's talk broth-to-pot ratios for a moment (and this goes for all chicken recipes that call for 1 cup of broth or less). If using a 6- or 3-quart Instant Pot, follow the recipe as is. If using an 8-quart pot, increase the broth by 1/2 cup more. Everything else remains the same.

If you're into making your own pizza and have your favorite baking method at the ready, the sauce and chicken are muses for the perfect pie. Slice the chicken into bite-size pieces. Then, ladle and smooth out 1/2–1 cup sauce on some stretched-out dough (either store-bought or homemade) and then top with a few cups shredded mozzarella and the chicken before baking into the ultimate pizza.

To Serve 1–2

Halve all of the ingredients, except for the broth—keep it at 1 cup so the pot properly comes to pressure. Cook times remain the same.

MISSISSIPPI CHICKEN

If you're a fan of the Mississippi Pot Roast in my yellow (*Simple Comforts*) book, just you wait until you try its struttin' counterpart. The tangy, peppery, sassy-yet-mild gravy cascading over juicy chicken is something I never get tired of. The flavors are deep, the gravy is rich, and when served over rice, it's twice as nice.

 DF + *(see Jeff's Tip)*

 GF + *(see Jeff's Tip)*

Prep Time	Sauté Time	Pressure Building Time	Pressure Cook Time	Total Time	Serves
10 MIN	**12** MIN	**10–15** MIN	**8** MIN	**40** MIN	**4–6**

THE CHICKEN

- **2 tablespoons (¼ stick) salted butter**
- **2 medium yellow onions, sliced longways into 1-inch-thick strips**
- **2 cups chicken or onion broth (e.g., Sautéed Onion Better Than Bouillon)**
- **1 tablespoon Worcestershire sauce**
- **1 (14- to 16-ounce) jar banana pepper rings (or 1 jar whole**

pepperoncini, stems removed), **divided with ½ cup of juice reserved**
- **1 (1-ounce) packet ranch dip mix**
- **1 (1-ounce) packet au jus or beef gravy mix**
- **3 pounds boneless, skinless chicken thighs (bone-in are fine too, just make sure they're skinless)**
- **2 tablespoons light or brown dark sugar**

THE GRAVY POTION

- **4 tablespoons (½ stick) salted butter, softened (NOTE: Zap in the microwave for 10 seconds if you don't feel like waiting for it to come to room temperature.)**
- **¼ cup all-purpose flour**
- ¼ teaspoon Zatarain's Concentrated Shrimp & Crab Boil (optional for extra spice, and a little goes a long way)

1 Add the butter to the Instant Pot and hit Sauté and Adjust so it's on the More or High setting. Once the butter's melted, add the onions and sauté for 3–5 minutes, until slightly softened.

2 Pour in the broth, Worcestershire sauce, and the pepper juice. Add the ranch and gravy mixes and stir until well-combined, followed by half of the peppers.

3 Add the chicken to the pot so it's nestled in the broth and top with the brown sugar. Secure the lid, move the valve to the sealing position, hit Cancel, and then hit Manual or Pressure Cook at High Pressure for 8 minutes. Quick release when done.

CONTINUES

4 Meanwhile, in a bowl, mix together the gravy potion ingredients until the consistency is smooth, not unlike a frosting.

5 Using tongs, remove the chicken to a serving platter.

6 Hit Keep Warm/Cancel and then hit Sauté again. Once bubbling, stir the gravy potion into the contents of the pot until everything is combined and thickened. Stir in the remaining peppers (reserving a few for garnish).

7 Drape the gravy over the chicken, top with reserved peppers, and enjoy! Goes great over Arroz Amarillo (page 142) or egg noodles.

JEFF'S TIP If you don't want a thicker gravy, or want an easy way to make this gluten free, skip the gravy potion altogether. It will still be rich in flavor—just a thinner sauce. If you make this adjustment and sub 2–3 tablespoons vegetable, canola, or extra-virgin olive oil for the butter in Step 1, you'll also make it dairy-free. But to keep it gluten-free with a slightly thicker gravy, use a GF gravy mix.

To Serve 1-2 Simply halve the recipe. Cook times remain the same.

BUTTER CHICKEN

This well-known Indian dish is one of the most fragrant, simple, and out-of-this-world-delicious things you'll make in your Instant Pot. Of course, the name doesn't lie: There's quite a bit of butter in there. In fact, there's so much, it may make Barbra Streisand think life's candy and the sun's a bowl of butter chicken. Enjoy it over Street Cart Rice (page 130).

 K + *(if you're okay with a cornstarch slurry)*

GF

Prep Time	Sauté Time	Pressure Building Time	Pressure Cook Time	Total Time	Serves
10 MIN	8 MIN	10–15 MIN	7 MIN	35 MIN	4–6

- 8 tablespoons (1 stick) salted butter
- 1 large Spanish onion, grated (or if you feel lazy, diced)
- 6 cloves garlic, minced or pressed
- 1 (14-ounce) can unsweetened coconut milk (shake can vigorously to mix before opening; it should be thin and watery, not thick and lumpy)

- 1½ cups canned crushed tomatoes, tomato puree, or tomato sauce (not marinara sauce), divided
- 2 tablespoons garam masala (I like Rani or Swad brands), divided
- 2½ pounds boneless, skinless chicken thighs (see Jeff's Tip), cut into bite-size chunks

- 2 tablespoons cornstarch plus 2 tablespoons cold water
- ½ cup heavy cream or half-and-half
- 2 teaspoons seasoned salt

1 Add the butter to the Instant Pot and hit Sauté and Adjust so it's on the More or High setting. Once melted, add the onion and sauté for 3 minutes. Add the garlic and sauté for 1 minute more.

2 Add the coconut milk, 1 cup of the canned tomatoes, and 1 tablespoon of the garam masala. Stir well, scraping the bottom to get up any browned bits. Add the chicken to the pot, smoothing it out so it's submerged in the liquid. Secure the lid, move the valve to the sealing position, hit Cancel, and then hit Manual or Pressure Cook on High Pressure for 7 minutes. Quick release when done.

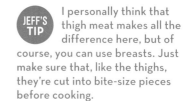

JEFF'S TIP I personally think that thigh meat makes all the difference here, but of course, you can use breasts. Just make sure that, like the thighs, they're cut into bite-size pieces before cooking.

3 Meanwhile, make a slurry by mixing the cornstarch and cold water.

4 Hit the Cancel button, then hit Sauté and Adjust so it's on the More or High setting. As the sauce is coming to a bubble, stir in the cornstarch slurry. Add the remaining ½ cup tomatoes, remaining 1 tablespoon garam masala, the cream, and seasoned salt. Stir and serve with some naan.

To Serve 1–2 Simply halve the recipe. Cook times remain the same.

CHEESY CHICKEN ROLL-UPS

This recipe is dedicated to everyone who loves cheesy chicken rolled up in a tortilla, but has no time to get fancy. I'll keep it as simple as this headnote: *four* (or five) ingredients; 10 minutes pressure cooking. Cheesy Chicken Roll-Ups are as addictive as they are a cinch to make.

Prep Time	Pressure Building Time	Pressure Cook Time	Sauté Time	Total Time	Serves
2 MIN	10–15 MIN	10 MIN	3–5 MIN	25 MIN	4–6

2½–3 pounds boneless, skinless chicken thighs, kept whole

1 cup chicken broth

1 pound (4 cups) finely shredded Mexican cheese blend (or any shredded cheese of your choice)

½ cup salsa verde (optional)

Flour or corn tortillas (I use burrito-size, but fajita-size will work for smaller portions)

1 Add the chicken and broth to the Instant Pot. Smooth out the chicken so it's as submerged in the broth as possible. Secure the lid, move the valve to the sealing position, and hit Pressure Cook or Manual at High Pressure for 10 minutes. Quick release when done.

2 Using tongs, remove the chicken to a large mixing bowl. Reserve ½ cup of the broth and discard the rest, returning the empty liner pot to the Instant Pot.

3 Using either two forks or a hand mixer, shred the chicken. Fold in the cheese and, if using the salsa verde, add it now and mix in.

4 Back to the Instant Pot, hit Cancel followed by Sauté and Adjust so it's on the More or High setting. Return the chicken mixture to the pot and stir often for 3–5 minutes so the cheese really melts and the chicken gets nice and hot. (NOTE: If you want the mixture a bit thinner, pour in some of that reserved broth and stir until you've hit the desired consistency.) Hit Cancel to turn the pot off.

5 Scoop some of that cheesy chicken into a tortilla, roll it up, and revel in the delicious simplicity! Even better with some salsa, sour cream, guacamole, and/or jalapeños rolled in.

 JEFF'S TIPS To make it keto in addition to gluten-free and low carb, use keto-friendly tortillas or egg wraps (the Crepini brand is great).

You can absolutely use chicken breasts in place of thighs. Just make sure they're no thicker than ½ inch (slice them if you need to) and pressure cook for 12 minutes instead of 10.

 To Serve 1–2 Halve all of the ingredients, except for the broth: Keep it at 1 cup so the pot properly comes to pressure. Cook times remain the same.

CHICKEN STROGANOFF

Beef Stroganoff is without a doubt one of my signature recipes. To set it apart from the rest, I use a garlic herb cheese that delivers far more than just a simple sour cream ending. Here's the chicken version—and with even fewer ingredients it's just as spectacular, yet quicker to make.

 (see Jeff's Tip)
 (see Jeff's Tip)

Prep Time	Sauté Time	Pressure Building Time	Pressure Cook Time	Total Time	Serves
10 MIN	8 MIN	10–15 MIN	7 MIN	35 MIN	4–6

- **4 tablespoons (½ stick) salted butter**
- **1 pound baby bella mushrooms, sliced**
- **6 cloves garlic, minced or pressed**
- **1½ cups chicken or mushroom broth (e.g., Mushroom Better Than Bouillon)**
- **2½ pounds boneless, skinless chicken thighs or breasts, cut into bite-size chunks**

- **1 (12-ounce) package wide egg noodles (see Jeff's Tip)**
- **¼ cup cornstarch plus ¼ cup cold water**
- **1 cup onion dip (NOTE: Not the dry mix. I'm talking the actual sour cream–based dip. It's usually found in a tub in the dip or refrigerated section of most markets, but it's sometimes near the chips.)**

- **1 (5.2-ounce) package Boursin cheese (any flavor) or ¾ cup Garlic Herb Cheese (page 21), cut into chunks**
- **2 teaspoons seasoned salt**
- 1 tablespoon Dijon mustard (optional)

1 Add the butter to the Instant Pot and hit Sauté and Adjust so it's on the More or High setting. Once melted, add the mushrooms and sauté for 5 minutes, until softened and browned. Add the garlic and sauté for 1 minute more.

2 Add the broth and stir the pot, scraping the bottom to get up any browned bits. Add the chicken, smoothing it out so it's submerged in the liquid. Secure the lid, move the valve to the sealing position, hit Cancel, and then hit Manual or Pressure Cook on High Pressure for 7 minutes. Quick release when done.

3 Meanwhile, separately cook the egg noodles on the stove according to package instructions and drain; and make a cornstarch slurry by mixing the cornstarch with the cold water.

JEFF'S TIP

You can also absolutely serve this creamy and unforgettable comfort dish over rice or veggies if you're trying to forgo noodles. Using cauliflower rice will also make it keto-friendly. And if going that route and using a gluten-free onion dip, this will also make the recipe gluten-free.

To Serve 1–2

Halve all of the ingredients, except for the broth—reduce it to 1 cup so the pot properly comes to pressure. Cook times remain the same.

4 Hit the Cancel button, then hit Sauté and Adjust so it's on the More or High setting. As the sauce is coming to a bubble, stir in the cornstarch slurry. Add the onion dip, Boursin, seasoned salt, and Dijon (if using). Stir and serve over the egg noodles.

THE CHICKEN RANCH

Folks, it doesn't get any easier (or tastier) than this quick recipe, which may as well be considered a hot version of a cold chicken salad. We're talking "dump and go" realness, and results loaded with cheesy, ranchy flavor. However you wish to serve it is totally your call, but I usually like to scoop some onto a potato slider bun or King's Hawaiian roll for a hearty sandwich, or enjoy as a topping to a green salad. Any way you slice it, the end result will be an addictive experience (especially with that optional bacon-bit touch).

Prep Time	Pressure Building Time	Pressure Cook Time	Sauté Time	Total Time	Serves
10 MIN	5–10 MIN	12 MIN	3–5 MIN	30 MIN	4–6

2 pounds ½-inch-thick boneless, skinless chicken breasts

1 cup chicken broth

2–4 cups shredded cheese of your choice (I use a Cheddar blend, see Jeff's Tips)

1 cup ranch dressing (I like Hidden Valley)

1 (5.2-ounce) package Boursin cheese (any flavor) or ¾ cup Garlic Herb Cheese (page 21)

½–1 cup bacon bits (optional, I use pre-bagged Hormel or Oscar Meyer)

1 Add the chicken to the Instant Pot and pour the broth over it. Secure the lid, move the valve to the sealing position, and hit Pressure Cook or Manual at High Pressure for 12 minutes. Quick release when done.

2 Using tongs, remove the chicken to a large mixing bowl. Reserve ½ cup of the broth and discard the rest, returning the empty liner pot to the Instant Pot.

3 Using either two forks or a hand mixer, shred the chicken. Fold in the cheese (which basically means to mix it in using a gentle, scooping-like motion—this tip may have helped David & Moira in Schitt's Creek).

4 Back to the Instant Pot, hit Cancel followed by Sauté and Adjust so it's on the More or High setting. Add the cheesy chicken mixture along with the ranch dressing and Boursin and cook for 3–5 minutes, stirring frequently so everything combines and the chicken gets nice and hot. If using the bacon bits, stir them in them now as well. (NOTE: If you want the mixture a bit thinner, pour in some of that reserved broth and stir until you've hit the desired consistency.) Hit Cancel to turn the pot off.

5 Serve on a bun, on a salad, over pasta, or on its own.

JEFF'S TIPS

Use any kind of shredded cheese: Pepper Jack is nice for a spicy touch and mozzarella is also good. How much cheese you wish is also up to you: Start with 2 cups and add more to your liking.

If you want a bit of a cool crunch factor, feel free to also add some sliced scallions, chopped celery, or whatever crunchy veggie you crave along with the bacon bits in Step 4.

To Serve 1–2

Halve all of the ingredients, except for the broth— keep it at 1 cup so the pot properly comes to pressure. Cook times remain the same.

GARLIC PARMESAN

CORNISH HENS
(OR WINGS)

DUMP & GO! *(if using wings)*

Some people go to Renaissance fairs to watch knights joust; I go to drink out of a metal chalice and to rip into juicy Cornish hens with my hands! Here, this smaller member of the poultry family that's essentially a personal-sized whole chicken is coated in a wondrous garlic-Parmesan sauce. It's all super easy and I also give you options for a crispy finish. In keeping with medieval tradition, forks are optional. Using Cornish hens will serve 2, but I provide directions in Jeff's Tips for making the recipe to accommodate 4–6 with wings or a whole chicken.

Prep Time	Sauté Time	Pressure Building Time	Pressure Cook Time	Natural Release Time	Crisping Time	Total Time	Serves
5 MIN	5–7 MIN	10–15 MIN	20 MIN (see Jeff's Tips for wing and whole chicken timing)	5 MIN	5–10 MIN	50 MIN	2

THE HENS

Seasoned salt (I use Lawry's)

2 Cornish hens, skin on

2 tablespoons (¼ stick) salted butter

1 cup chicken broth

THE GARLIC PARMESAN SAUCE

6 tablespoons (¾ stick) salted butter, melted

½ cup grated Parmesan cheese

3 cloves garlic, minced or pressed

1 teaspoon garlic powder

½ teaspoon black pepper

½ teaspoon dried parsley flakes

½ teaspoon Garlic Better Than Bouillon base (optional)

1 Lightly sprinkle seasoned salt on the hens and then rub it in.

2 Add the 2 tablespoons butter to the Instant Pot and hit Sauté and Adjust so it's on the More or High setting. Once melted, add the hens (either together or separately, depending on their size) and sear on all sides for about 3 minutes total, until the skin is lightly browned. Use tongs to remove to a plate to rest for a moment.

3 Set the trivet in the pot and add the broth. Set the Cornish hens on the trivet. Secure the lid, move the valve to the sealing position, hit Cancel, and then hit Manual or Pressure Cook on High Pressure for 20 minutes. Allow a 5-minute natural release followed by a quick release when done.

4 While the hens are natural releasing, make the garlic Parmesan sauce by combining all those ingredients, mixing well.

5 Use tongs to carefully transfer the hens to a plate. Remove the liner pot and drain the liquid (you can either discard or reserve as chicken broth for a later use).

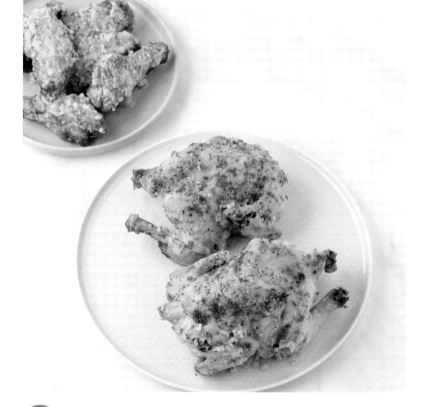

6 Crisp the hens in one of two ways:

To crisp in the pot: Rest the hens on the trivet in the pot and generously brush on the sauce. Place the Air Fryer Lid on top. Broil (400°F) for 6–10 minutes, until fully crisped.

To crisp in your oven: Place the hens on a foil-lined tray and generously brush on the sauce. Broil in the oven until the skin is crispy, 5–10 minutes (but keep an eye on them as all ovens vary).

JEFF'S TIPS

To make with 3–5 pounds chicken wings/ drumettes (feeds 4–6): In Step 1, rub the wings with seasoned salt. Skip Step 2. In Step 3, place the wings on the trivet in the pot. Pressure cook on High Pressure for 8 minutes. Quick release when done. When making the sauce in Step 4, add that 2 tablespoons butter from Step 2 (so you're using a whole stick, or 8 tablespoons). Continue with the rest of the recipe as written (same cook times for the crisping).

To make with a whole (5-pound-ish) chicken (feeds 2–4): Everything in the recipe remains the same as written, except the pressure cook time will be 30 minutes with a 10-minute natural release, followed by a quick release.

To Serve 1–2 This already serves 2, but check out Jeff's Tips to serve more.

CHICKEN ALFREDO

K + *(if using coconut flour instead of all purpose)*

GF + *(if using coconut or quinoa flour instead of all purpose)*

Alfredo sauce is one of those things that encapsulates what this book is all about: simple yet spectacular. Created with the basic ingredients of butter, Parmesan, and cream, the iconic Italian white sauce is indeed decadent and rich. But what puts this one over the top is the addition of garlic powder and the extra sinful, cheesy, garlic-y touch of Boursin (or my Garlic Herb Cheese). Naturally, this dish is perfect when served over pasta, rice, or veggies.

Prep Time	Sauté Time	Pressure Building Time	Pressure Cook Time	Total Time	Serves
5 MIN	**5** MIN	**10–15** MIN	**5** MIN	**30** MIN	**4–6**

2 tablespoons (¼ stick) salted butter, divided

2 pounds boneless, skinless chicken breasts, sliced into cutlets about ¼ inch thick and then into ¼-inch strips

1 cup chicken or garlic broth (e.g., Garlic Better Than Bouillon)

4 teaspoons garlic powder, divided

1 cup heavy cream or half-and-half

2 tablespoons all-purpose, coconut, or quinoa flour

1 cup grated Parmesan cheese

1 (5.2-ounce) package Boursin cheese (any flavor) or ¾ cup Garlic Herb Cheese (page 21), cut into chunks (optional, see Jeff's Tip)

Freshly cracked black pepper (optional)

1 Add the butter to the Instant Pot and hit Sauté and Adjust so it's on the More or High setting. Once melted, add the chicken and sauté until pinkish-white in color, about 3 minutes.

2 Add the broth and 2 teaspoons of the garlic powder to the pot. Stir well. Secure the lid, move the valve to the sealing position, hit Cancel, and then hit Manual or Pressure Cook on High Pressure for 5 minutes. Quick release when done.

3 Meanwhile, in a large bowl whisk together the cream, flour, Parmesan, and remaining 2 teaspoons garlic powder.

5 Serve topped with some cracked black pepper, if desired.

JEFF'S TIP Adding the optional Boursin will ensure a thicker sauce. But it can also be thickened with additional Parmesan or by mixing 2 tablespoons each of cornstarch and cold water to form a slurry and then adding it in Step 4 after the cream mixture.

4 Hit the Cancel button, then hit Sauté and Adjust so it's on the More or High setting. As the sauce begins to bubble, add the cream mixture. Stir until the sauce is combined, nicely coating the chicken. If using the Boursin, add it now and stir until melted into the sauce. Hit Cancel to turn the pot off.

To Serve 1–2 Halve all of the ingredients, except for the broth—keep it at 1 cup so the pot properly comes to pressure. Cook times remain the same.

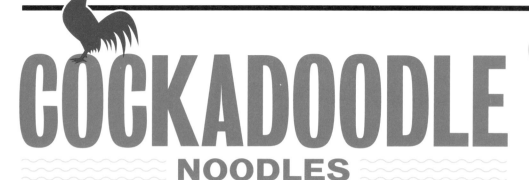

COCKADOODLE
NOODLES

3 STEPS OR LESS!

When I released this recipe to the world (okay, the internet) on a Sunday night, the tables were turned and it was actually the *roosters* who were awoken by the buzz. I can't say enough good things about this creamy, noodly chicken dish, but I'll start by noting that it's basically a warm hug in a bowl—like a chicken pot pie casserole. For the sake of this book, I've simplified it even further, and then provided you with additional flavorful options.

Prep Time	Sauté Time	Pressure Building Time	Pressure Cook Time	Natural Release Time (see Jeff's Tips)	Total Time	Serves
10 MIN	8 MIN	10–15 MIN	2 MIN	10 MIN	40 MIN	4–6

- **2 tablespoons (¼ stick) salted butter**
- **1½ pounds boneless, skinless chicken breasts, cut into bite-size pieces**
- **3½ cups chicken broth**
- **1 (12-ounce) bag egg noodles (I use wide ribbons)**

- **20 ounces frozen veggie mix (I use corn, carrots, peas, and green beans)**
- **1 cup heavy cream or half-and-half**
- **¼ cup ranch dressing (not the dry mix, but the actual dressing)**
- **2 cups shredded cheese blend of your choice (I like Colby or Cheddar Jack)**

- **½ cup grated Parmesan cheese**
- **1 (5.2-ounce) package Boursin cheese (any flavor) or ¾ cup Garlic Herb Cheese (page 21); or 4 ounces brick cream cheese cut into small chunks**

1 Add the butter to the Instant Pot. Hit Sauté and Adjust so it's on More or High setting. Once melted and bubbling, add the chicken and sauté for 5 minutes, until white in color.

2 Add the broth and stir well. Layer in the noodles, smoothing them with a spatula, followed by the frozen veggies, but *do not stir*. Secure the lid, move the valve to the sealing position, hit Cancel, and then hit Manual or Pressure Cook on High Pressure for 2 minutes. Allow a 10-minute natural release (or **see Jeff's Tips**), followed by a quick release.

3 Add the cream, ranch, shredded cheese, Parmesan, and Boursin. Stir until fully incorporated and serve. **See Jeff's Tips** for adding more flavor bombs to this already flavorful dish. They may just make you go "cock-a-doodle-doo!"

I personally like my egg noodles on the softer (but not mushy) side. If you want the noodles a bit firmer, go for a 5-minute natural release instead of 10.

With the finishing dairy touches, there's a lot of flavor already going on in this dish. However, should you wish to add even more flavor with additional seasonings that I'm willing to bet are already in your cupboard (especially if you're making many of the recipes in this book or my others), feel free to add any or all of the optional seasonings below. You can either add them in Step 2 with the broth or in Step 3 with the dairy for a more intense impact.

1–2 teaspoons seasoned salt or garlic salt (start with 1 and add more to taste)

1½ teaspoons Italian seasoning

1 teaspoon garlic powder

1 teaspoon onion powder

¼ cup hot sauce or buffalo wing sauce

Feel free to toss in any veggies you wish. If you want some sliced mushrooms, add 8–16 ounces and sauté them with the chicken in Step 1, adding another 2 tablespoons (¼ stick) of butter when doing so. If the bottom of the pot is a bit browned after, you can always clear that up with about 1 tablespoon Worcestershire sauce.

To Serve 1–2

Simply halve the recipe. Cook times remain the same.

SPINACH & ARTICHOKE  CHICKEN

 K + *(if using coconut flour)*

 GF + *(if using coconut or quinoa flour)*

The other day I found myself dipping chip after chip into the glorious Spinach & Artichoke Dip (page 242) that I was enjoying as an appetizer to a chicken entrée. The problem was, after filling up on the dip, I didn't have much room left over for the main dish. But then I thought to myself, wouldn't it be smart to just combine the two into a glorious spinach and artichoke chicken? Why yes, yes it would. As easy and quick to make as it is irresistible, this is sure to become your newest favorite.

Prep Time	Sauté Time	Pressure Building Time	Pressure Cook Time	Total Time	Serves
10 MIN	10 MIN	10–15 MIN	5 MIN	35 MIN	4–6

2 pounds boneless, skinless chicken breasts, sliced into cutlets about ¼ inch thick

⅓ cup all-purpose, coconut, or quinoa flour (if desired, mix in about ¼ teaspoon each of seasoned salt, black pepper, and garlic powder for extra flavor)

4 tablespoons (½ stick) salted butter

1½ cups chicken or garlic broth (e.g., Garlic Better Than Bouillon)

2 teaspoons garlic salt (I use Lawry's), optional

8–10 ounces baby spinach

½ cup heavy cream or half-and-half

1 (5.2-ounce) package Boursin cheese (any flavor) or ¾ cup Garlic Herb Cheese (page 21)

½ cup grated Parmesan cheese

2 cups shredded mozzarella cheese

1 (14-ounce) can artichoke hearts (see Jeff's Tips), drained and ripped apart by hand

1 Set three dinner-sized plates next to each other. The first one will have the raw chicken cutlets, the second one the flour mixture, and the third should be empty. Dredge (coat) one chicken cutlet in the flour mixture so it's lightly dusted and set aside on the third plate. Repeat until the first plate is empty and the third plate is filled with coated cutlets.

2 Add the butter to the Instant Pot. Hit Sauté and Adjust so it's on the More or High setting. Once the butter's melted, add the cutlets in batches and lightly brown on each side for 1 minute. Repeat until done and set aside.

3 Add the broth and really make sure you deglaze (scrape the bottom of the pot) so it's as smooth as you can get it. If you want a more savory touch, add the optional garlic salt and stir well. (NOTE: You can also add the optional garlic salt in Step 7 just before serving.)

CONTINUES

4 Return the chicken to the pot, allowing the cutlets to rest on top of each other. Top with the spinach. (NOTE: It will feel like you have a ton of spinach in there and it might come above the brim, but it will cook down to nothing.)

5 Secure the lid and move the valve to the sealing position. Hit Cancel and then hit Manual or Pressure Cook on High Pressure for 5 minutes. Quick release when done.

6 Brush the spinach off the chicken as best you can and transfer the chicken to a serving dish to rest.

7 Hit Cancel followed by Sauté and Adjust to the More or High setting. Add the cream, Boursin, Parmesan, mozzarella, and artichokes. Stir until well combined. Once bubbling, hit Cancel to turn the pot off.

8 Drape the sauce over the chicken and serve over rice or noodles— or even tortilla chips (**see Jeff's Tips**)!

JEFF'S TIPS If you want *more* artichokes, add up to another can and reserve some for topping when serving.

Want a thicker sauce? Mix 2 tablespoons cornstarch plus 2 tablespoons water to form a slurry and stir into the pot in Step 7 just before adding the dairy.

To make Spinach & Artichoke Chicken Nachos, slice the chicken into bite-size pieces in Step 6 and then return them to the pot when adding the artichokes in Step 7. Ladle the sauce over chips of your choice. Feel free to top with more shredded mozzarella and broil in the oven for a few minutes until the cheese is bubbly brown (don't go too far, though—we don't want burnt nachos!).

Or, for a nice (simpler) touch, top the chicken and artichokes with some crushed tortilla chips.

To Serve 1–2 Halve all of the ingredients, except for the broth —reduce it to 1 cup so the pot properly comes to pressure. Cook times remain the same.

COQ AU VIN

K+ *(if you're okay with wine and a cornstarch slurry)*

P+ *(if you're okay with wine and a cornstarch slurry)*

DF

GF

This classic French chicken dish is loaded with mushrooms, carrots, and pearl onions in a rich bacon-laden sauce with a touch of red wine. If that description didn't clue you in already, I'll spell it out for you: It's irresistible. This is a wonderful dish for entertaining: One taste and your guests will be inviting themselves back for dinner on the regular. My pressure-cooked version has you removing the skin, saving a few calories and searing time, but in Jeff's Tips I give you ways to sear your chicken with or without the skins as well as turning skin into schmaltz! If you're feeling decadent, pick up two bottles of red wine at the store; one for making the dish and another to enjoy alongside.

Prep Time	Sauté Time	Pressure Building Time	Pressure Cook Time	Total Time	Serves
10 MIN	**15** MIN	**10–15** MIN	**10** MIN	**45** MIN	**4–6**

8 ounces pancetta or thick-cut bacon, diced

1 pound button mushrooms, halved

10–14 ounces frozen pearl onions

6 cloves garlic, minced or pressed

¾ cup dry red wine (like a pinot noir)

1 cup beef, chicken, or garlic broth (e.g., Garlic Better Than Bouillon)

2 teaspoons dried thyme, plus more for topping (optional)

4 pounds bone-in chicken thighs and legs, mixed (NOTE: I prefer skinless chicken here. You can peel the skins off yourself if it doesn't come that way, but you can also keep the skins on—just make sure the cuts are bone-in. To turn that skin into schmaltz, see Jeff's Tips, page 172.)

1 (8-ounce) bag baby carrots (optional)

3 tablespoons cornstarch plus 3 tablespoons cold water

3 tablespoons tomato paste

2 teaspoons seasoned salt

1 (1-ounce) packet chicken or beef gravy mix (optional, and whichever flavor you prefer—I use beef)

1 On the Instant Pot, hit Sauté and Adjust so it's on the More or High setting. After 3 minutes of heating, add the pancetta or bacon and sauté for 8 minutes. Remove with a slotted spoon and place in a paper towel–lined bowl to rest, leaving the rendered fat in the pot.

2 Add the mushrooms and onions to the pot and sauté for 5 minutes, until the mushrooms are softened and lightly browned. Add the garlic and sauté for 1 minute more.

3 Add the wine and deglaze (scrape the bottom of the pot), getting up any and all browned bits. You should be able to see the bottom of the pot clearly once done.

CONTINUES

4 Add the broth and thyme (if using) and stir well. Nestle the chicken into the pot and top with the carrots (if using). Secure the lid, move the valve to the sealing position, hit Cancel, and then hit Manual or Pressure Cook on High Pressure for 10 minutes. Quick release when done.

5 Meanwhile, make a cornstarch slurry by mixing the cornstarch with the water.

6 Use tongs to carefully transfer the chicken to a serving dish. Hit the Cancel button, then hit Sauté and Adjust so it's on the More or High setting.

7 As the sauce is coming to a bubble, stir in the slurry until it thickens and combines. Follow with the tomato paste, seasoned salt, and the gravy packet (if using) and stir until melded into the sauce. Hit Cancel to turn the pot off and let the sauce rest for 2 minutes when it will thicken and come together.

8 Ladle the sauce over the chicken and top with the pancetta and additional thyme (if desired). Or, simply stir the pancetta into the sauce prior to ladling. Goes beautifully with Aligot (page 228).

CONTINUES

For a more traditional Coq au Vin with seared chicken (and if you have the extra time), just after Step 1, add 2 tablespoons salted butter to the pot and heat until it melts. Sear each side of the chicken in the butter and rendered fat for 30–60 seconds, until lightly browned (it's okay if some of the meat is still pink). Remove to a plate when done and repeat the process until all the chicken is flash-seared. (NOTE: If leaving the skin on the chicken, you'll need to sear it longer: 5–8 minutes or so, until all of the skin appears a bit browned.)

Turning chicken skin into schmaltz:
If you can only find bone-in thighs and legs with the skin still on, you can either leave it on, or you can simply peel and slice the skin and fat off prior to cooking. But rather than discarding those skins and fat, you can use them to make schmaltz—the Jewish-style rendered chicken fat that is a super flavorful (and super rich) substitute for any cooking oil (especially when used in matzo balls)!

Here's all you need:

2–4 cups chicken fat and skin (you can collect fat and skin and freeze for later, or use it freshly peeled and sliced off chicken—it's just best to have at least 2 cups)

1 large Vidalia (sweet) onion, peeled and quartered

Add the chicken fat and skin to an enamel-coated Dutch oven or nonstick pot (with no oil or butter added) and cook on low. Once the skins begin to render the fat into liquid and the skins start to lightly brown (10–20 minutes), add the onion. Raise the heat to medium-high and sauté, allowing the onion to break up and soften as the fat from the chicken skin continues to render. You want to cook until the onions begin to really soften and the chicken skin is crispy and begins to get quite browned, but not burned, another 10–15 minutes. From there, use tongs to remove the crisped skin and syrupy onions and discard (or place in a bowl and lightly salt for a crunchy, comforting snack). Let the fat cool for 20 minutes. Place a sieve or cheesecloth over a mason jar and pour the fat through it, discarding the cheesecloth when done. Cover the jar and place in the fridge where it will congeal and become schmaltz! It'll keep for up to 1 week in the fridge and 6 months in the freezer.

To Serve 1–2 Halve all of the ingredients, except for the broth and wine—reduce the broth to ¾ cup and the wine to ½ cup (a little more than half of what the original recipe calls for to keep a rich gravy). Cook times remain the same.

CHICKEN MURPHY

I was recently introduced to the Irish-pub staple known as Chicken Murphy while eating in rural northern New Jersey. Loaded with chicken, sausage, peppers, and onion, it's rich and hearty but surprisingly zesty, thanks to the addition of vinegar-laced cherry peppers. Make sure you save some of the pepper juice from the jar as instructed, as it adds a remarkable layer of flavor to the sauce. But if you want your Murphy mild, just leave the peppers and their juices out.

 (if you're okay with a cornstarch slurry)

Prep Time	Sauté Time	Pressure Building Time	Pressure Cook Time	Total Time	Serves
10 MIN	10 MIN	10–15 MIN	7 MIN	40 MIN	4–6

4 tablespoons (½ stick) salted butter

1 large Vidalia (sweet) onion, sliced longways into ¼-inch-thick strips

2 large bell peppers (I used 1 green and 1 orange but you can use any color), sliced into ¼-inch-thick strips

2 pounds Italian sausage (sweet, hot, or mixed), cut into ½-inch pieces

2 pounds boneless, skinless chicken thighs or breasts, cut into bite-size chunks

6 cloves garlic, minced or pressed

¾ cup dry white wine (like a sauvignon blanc; if not using, sub ¾ cup more broth)

¾ cup chicken or garlic broth (e.g., Garlic Better Than Bouillon)

1 (12- to 14-ounce) jar cherry peppers or pepperoncini, each sliced, with ½ cup of the juice reserved (see Jeff's Tips)

½–1 pound baby red or white potatoes (try to get the kind that are the size of ping-pong balls), skin on, quartered (optional)

6 tablespoons cornstarch plus 6 tablespoons cold water

OPTIONAL CREAMY FINISH

¼ cup heavy cream or half-and-half

1 (5.2-ounce) package Boursin cheese (any flavor) or ¾ cup Garlic Herb Cheese (page 21), cut into chunks

1 Add the butter to the Instant Pot and hit Sauté and Adjust so it's on the More or High setting. Once melted, add the onion and peppers and sauté for 3 minutes, until softened a bit.

2 Add the sausage, chicken, and garlic and sauté for 3–5 minutes more, until the chicken is pinkish-white in color.

3 Add the wine (or additional broth) and deglaze (scrape the bottom of the pot) to get any browned bits up. Add the broth and the ½ cup pepper juice (if using) and stir.

CONTINUES

4 Top with the cherry peppers or pepperoncini and baby potatoes (if using) but *do not stir.* Just smooth them out so they're evenly distributed and resting on top of everything else. Secure the lid, move the valve to the sealing position, hit Cancel, and then hit Manual or Pressure Cook on High Pressure for 7 minutes. Quick release when done.

5 Meanwhile, make a cornstarch slurry by mixing the cornstarch with the water.

JEFF'S TIPS

To keep it from caving in and getting a bit messy, a great tip for slicing raw sausage is popping it into the freezer for 5–10 minutes before slicing. This will help it keep its form.

Jarred cherry peppers are typically on the spicier side, but not overly so (think a 6 out of 10). Pepperoncini, even less so (3 or 4 out of 10). You can also sub in jarred sliced jalapeños, which are milder; or just leave the peppers out completely.

6 Hit the Cancel button, then hit Sauté and Adjust so it's on the More or High setting. As the sauce is coming to a bubble, stir in the cornstarch slurry and the sauce will thicken.

7 **If going for the optional creamy finish:** Add the cream and/or Boursin and stir until combined.

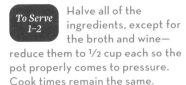

To Serve 1–2 Halve all of the ingredients, except for the broth and wine—reduce them to ½ cup each so the pot properly comes to pressure. Cook times remain the same.

8 Serve over mashed potatoes, rice, or pasta.

6

MEAT

Sure, I could tell you how the Instant Pot essentially "pressure braises" the most succulent, fork-tender, and fall-off-the-bone meat ever. But don't take my word for it: Seeing, trying, and tasting is truly believing. This chapter will bring you the best a carnivore could ask for, all coming together with little effort and loads of flavor.

= DUMP & GO RECIPE

 = 5 INGREDIENTS OR LESS

 = 3 STEPS OR LESS

 = AIR FRYER LID

 = DAIRY-FREE

= VEGAN

 = KETO

 = GLUTEN-FREE

+ = COMPLIANT WITH MODIFICATIONS

 = PALEO

 = VEGETARIAN

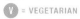

CHINESE-STYLE (CHAR SIU) SPARERIBS

 + *(if using tamari or coconut aminos and gluten-free hoisin and oyster sauces)*

When I was growing up, it wouldn't be a complete Chinese take-out meal in the Eisner household if there wasn't a red, foil-lined bag filled with huge, juicy spare ribs in a sweet, savory, and caramelized sauce—the Cantonese version of barbecue pork known as *char siu*. I've provided instructions for how to make your own char siu sauce, but feel free to use a pre-made one to save some time and shrink this tasty recipe down to just three ingredients!

Prep Time	Pressure Building Time	Pressure Cook Time	Natural Release Time	Optional Oven Time	Total Time varies, but typically	Serves
10 MIN	10–30 MIN	25 OR 30 MIN	5 MIN	3–5 MIN	1 HR 15 MIN	2–6

THE RIBS

2–6 pounds (up to 3 full racks) St. Louis ribs (recommended), spareribs, *or* baby back ribs (pork loin back ribs), unseasoned

2 cups apple juice (this stays the same no matter how many ribs you use)

Sesame seeds, for topping (optional)

THE CHAR SIU SAUCE (FOR 2 RACKS OF RIBS—HALVE OR DOUBLE AS NEEDED)

1/2 cup hoisin sauce

1/4 cup oyster sauce

1/4 cup honey

3 tablespoons soy sauce, tamari, or coconut aminos

3 tablespoons dark brown sugar

3 tablespoons Shaoxing or sherry wine

1 tablespoon sesame oil (any kind)

1 tablespoon Chinese five-spice powder

1/2 teaspoon red food coloring (optional, strictly for color)

1 Bend each rack of ribs into a coil and fit in the liner pot, resting against the perimeter of the pot. A 6-quart should be able to handle up to two racks of ribs, while the 8-quart can handle three full racks. The 3-quart may be able to fit one rack. If you wish to first cut each rack in half for easier removal when cooked (they'll be super tender), feel free to do so. Add the apple juice to the pot.

2 Secure the lid, move the valve to the sealing position, hit Cancel, and then hit Manual or Pressure Cook on High Pressure for 25 minutes for one rack (2–4 pounds) or 30 minutes for one-and-a-half to two racks (5–6 pounds). When done, allow a 5-minute natural release followed by a quick release.

3 Meanwhile, in a large bowl, whisk together the sauce ingredients until combined. Set aside. (**See Jeff's Tip.**)

4 The ribs will be *super* tender. Use either two sets of tongs, two serving forks, or one of each to carefully transfer the racks from the pot to a nonstick baking sheet lined with foil or parchment paper (see Step 5 NOTE), bone side down. (Don't stress if a rack splits in half—it's totally fine.)

5 Generously brush the char siu sauce all over the tops of the ribs until fully coated. They should be super saucy! (NOTE: If proceeding with Step 6, unlike in the photos, it's advisable to use foil instead of parchment paper as it's fully heat-proof and oven temperatures vary.)

6 **For a (strongly suggested) caramelized finish:** Pop the sheet with the ribs on the top rack of a preheated oven on broil and broil for 3–5 minutes. Keep an eye on them as all ovens vary. The sauce will caramelize onto the ribs. When done, remove the ribs from the oven and generously brush on more sauce.

7 Using a sharp knife, slice the ribs in between each bone (saucing the sides if desired). Top with sesame seeds, if desired. Grab lots of napkins and enjoy!

 JEFF'S TIP For the ultimate shortcut, you can buy char siu sauce. It's sold in some larger markets, at any Asian market, and online (I strongly recommend the Lee Kum Kee brand). A 14-ounce jar should do the trick for one saucy rack or two modestly sauced ones.

To Serve 1–2 See Step 2.

CHUCK & DIANE

A little ditty, about Chuck & Diane; one was a roast, and the other a sauce that's grand. This recipe is essentially taking a classic steak Diane and replacing the expensive filet mignon with a more affordable, more tender chuck roast that is kissed by that rich, creamy, brandy-based Diane sauce. One bite, and no matter your mood, life goes on.

 GF

Prep Time	Sauté Time	Pressure Building Time	Pressure Cook Time	Natural Release Time	Total Time	Serves
10 MIN	8 MIN	10–15 MIN	60 MIN	15 MIN	1 HR 45 MIN	4–6

- **1 (5- to 6-pound) chuck roast (get one that's nice and marbled), cut into five even pieces**
- **Kosher salt, for rubbing on the chuck roast**
- **6 tablespoons (¾ stick) salted butter, divided**
- **2 large shallots, diced**

- 1 pound baby bella mushrooms, sliced (optional)
- **6 cloves garlic, minced or pressed**
- **½ cup cognac, brandy, or sherry wine (see Jeff's Tips)**
- **¼ cup Worcestershire sauce**
- **¼ cup cornstarch plus ¼ cup cold water**

- **½ cup heavy cream**
- 2 tablespoons Dijon mustard (optional)
- 1 bunch fresh chives, sliced, for topping (optional)

1 Lightly rub the chuck roast with the kosher salt. (NOTE: I wouldn't use more than 1½ tablespoons total so as to not oversalt the dish.)

2 Add 4 tablespoons (½ stick) of the butter to the Instant Pot. Hit Sauté and Adjust so it's on the More or High setting. Once melted, sear the roast in the pot for about 1 minute on each side. Remove and set aside on a plate to rest.

3 Add the remaining 2 tablespoons (¼ stick) butter to the pot followed by the shallots and mushrooms (if using). Sauté for 2–5 minutes, until the shallots are softened and the mushrooms are lightly browned. Add the garlic and sauté for 1 minute longer.

CONTINUES

4 Pour in the cognac and Worcestershire sauce and deglaze (scrape the bottom of the pot) to get up any browned bits. Let simmer for 3 minutes. Then return the roast to the pot, secure the lid, and move the valve to the sealing position. Hit Cancel and then hit Manual or Pressure Cook on High Pressure for 60 minutes. When done, allow a 15-minute natural release followed by a quick release.

5 Meanwhile, make a slurry by mixing the cornstarch with the water.

6 Use tongs to carefully transfer the chuck roast to a carving board and slice it up. Hit the Cancel button, then hit Sauté and Adjust so it's on the More or High setting.

7 As the sauce is coming to a bubble, stir in the slurry until thickened. Add the cream and Dijon (if using) and stir. Hit Cancel to turn the pot off.

8 Return the roast to the pot so it's coated and resting in the sauce. If desired, top with the optional fresh chives and serve with Cacio e Pepe Pearls (page 90) or over Aligot (page 228) or any rice.

 JEFF'S TIPS If you don't want the wine, sub in 1/2 cup of a broth of your choice instead (beef makes sense).

Mushrooms and Dijon are common in a Diane sauce, but I'm making them optional here for those who don't fancy them.

 To Serve 1–2 With the exception of the cognac and Worcestershire sauce (keep those as is), halve the recipe (use 2½ pounds of chuck roast) and reduce the pressure cook time to 50 minutes. Same natural release time.

CHEESY STEAK FAJITA BAKE

This comforting dish, inspired by steak fajitas, is loaded with juicy flank steak and sautéed peppers and onions. We coat the meat and veggies in cheese (and salsa if desired), wrap in tortillas, and top with a creamy, queso-style sauce and more cheese. For an amazing and impressive (but easy) casserole-style fajita, bake to golden, ooey-gooey perfection.

Prep Time	Sauté Time	Pressure Building Time	Pressure Cook Time	Natural Release Time	Optional Oven Time	Total Time	Serves
10 MIN	10 MIN	10–15 MIN	12 MIN	5 MIN	10–20 MIN	1 HR–1 HR 10 MIN	4–6

- 4 tablespoons (½ stick) salted butter
- 3 pounds flank or flap steak, sliced against the grain into ¼-inch-thick strips
- 2 large yellow onions, sliced lengthwise into ¼-inch-thick strips
- 3 large poblano or bell peppers (any color), sliced lengthwise into ¼-inch-thick strips

- 2 (approximately 1-ounce) packets fajita seasoning, divided
- ¼ cup all-purpose flour
- 1 cup beef or garlic broth (e.g., Garlic Better Than Bouillon)
- 4 cups shredded Mexican cheese blend, divided
- ¼–½ cup red salsa (optional, see Jeff's Tip)

- 10–12 small flour or corn tortillas (fajita-size is best for this)
- 1 cup sour cream
- ½ cup crumbled cotija cheese (optional, you can use grated Parmesan if you can't find cotija)
- 1½ tablespoons cornstarch plus 1½ tablespoons cold water (optional)

1 Add the butter to the Instant Pot and hit Sauté and Adjust to the More or High setting. Once melted and bubbling, add the steak, onions, and peppers and sauté for 5 minutes.

2 Add one of the fajita seasoning packets and stir to coat for 1 minute. Then, sprinkle in the flour and stir continuously for 30 seconds more until all is coated.

JEFF'S TIP If using the salsa in Step 4 (which I recommend) start with ¼ cup and then, if you feel the filling is too thick, add more.

To Serve 1–2 Halve all of the ingredients, except for the broth—keep it at 1 cup so the pot properly comes to pressure. Cook times remain the same.

CONTINUES

3 Add the broth and stir well, scraping up any browned bits on the bottom of the pot. Secure the lid, move the valve to the sealing position, hit Cancel, and then hit Manual or Pressure Cook on High Pressure for 12 minutes. When done, allow a 5-minute natural release followed by a quick release.

4 Using a slotted spoon, transfer the steak and veggies to a large bowl. Add 2 cups of the shredded cheese and the salsa (if using) to the same bowl. Mix until the cheese melts into the meat and veggies.

5 Spray a 9x13-inch casserole dish with nonstick spray. Using a ⅓-cup measuring cup, scoop the steak and cheese mixture onto the tortillas. Roll each up, leaving the ends open, and arrange in the casserole dish, seam side down.

6 Hit Cancel and then Sauté and Adjust so it's on the More or High setting. Once bubbling, add the sour cream, cotija (if using), and remaining fajita seasoning packet. Whisk until combined.

7 **For a thicker sauce:** If, after whisking, you decide you want the sauce to be thicker, make a slurry by mixing the cornstarch with the water. Stir the slurry into the sauce; it will thicken immediately.

8 Hit Cancel to turn the pot off. Generously ladle the sauce over the wrapped tortillas in the casserole dish. Top with the remaining 2 cups shredded cheese.

9 **For a baked finish (recommended):** Bake uncovered in a preheated 350°F oven for 10–20 minutes, or until the cheese is lightly browned (keep an eye on it as all ovens vary). Goes great with Arroz Amarillo (page 142).

JEWISH Short Ribs

One of my biggest sources of pride when it comes to my first (orange) book is that my pressure-cooked version of a Jewish brisket was introduced into hundreds of thousands of homes that may have never tried one before. This time, short ribs are the star of the show, draped in a glorious sweet and sour sauce—and it's going to be one of the easiest and most unforgettable things you'll ever make. In fact, the super fun *Rachael Ray Show* asked me to make this dish in a "dinner doesn't have to be hard" segment, and it earned "oohs" and "aahs" from both Rachael and the audience.

Prep Time	Sauté Time	Pressure Building Time	Pressure Cook Time	Natural Release Time	Total Time	Serves
10 MIN	10 MIN	10–15 MIN	45 MIN	15 MIN	1 HR 30 MIN	4–6

THE SAUCE
1½ cups water
1½ cups ketchup
¾ cup white vinegar
¾ cup packed light or dark brown sugar

3 cloves garlic, minced or pressed
THE SHORT RIBS
5 pounds bone-in short ribs
Kosher salt, for rubbing on the short ribs

3 medium yellow onions, sliced into strips
3 tablespoons cornstarch plus 3 tablespoons cold water
1 (1-ounce) packet onion dip mix (optional)

1 In a large bowl, whisk together the sauce ingredients until combined. Set aside.

2 Lightly rub the short ribs with salt. Hit Sauté on the Instant Pot and Adjust so it's on the More or High setting. After 5 minutes of the pot heating, working in batches, flash-sear the short ribs for 30 seconds on each side. Set aside on a plate to rest.

3 Pour about ¼ cup of the sauce into the pot and deglaze (scrape the bottom of the pot) to get up any browned bits. Then, nestle in the short ribs, top with the onions, and pour the remaining sauce on top. Secure the lid, move the valve to the sealing position, hit Cancel, and then hit Manual or Pressure Cook on High Pressure for 45 minutes. When done, allow a 15-minute natural release followed by a quick release.

4 Meanwhile, make a slurry by mixing together the cornstarch and water.

5 Use tongs to carefully transfer the short ribs to a serving dish (they'll be so tender the meat will likely slide right off the bone). Hit the Cancel button, then hit Sauté and Adjust so it's on the More or High setting.

6 As the sauce is coming to a bubble, stir in the slurry and onion dip mix (if using). The sauce will thicken almost immediately. Hit Cancel to turn the pot off.

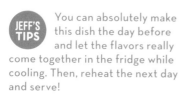

7 Ladle the sauce over the short ribs and enjoy with Truffle Hash (page 240) or Aligot (page 228).

JEFF'S TIPS You can absolutely make this dish the day before and let the flavors really come together in the fridge while cooling. Then, reheat the next day and serve!

If you want a more budget-conscious, yet incredibly tender and flavorful cut of meat, use 3–5 pounds chuck roast in place of the short ribs. Slice the roast into 4 or 5 equal pieces and pressure cook for 60 minutes at High Pressure; allow a 15-minute natural release followed by a quick release. Then, in Step 5, slice the meat into large chunks; return it to the pot in Step 7 once the sauce is complete and serve. Everything else in the recipe remains the same.

To Serve 1–2 Halve the recipe and reduce the pressure cook time to 35 minutes. Same natural release time.

HOISIN PULLED PORK

DUMP & GO!

DF

GF + *(if using tamari or coconut aminos, gluten-free hoisin sauce, and corn tortillas)*

Pulled pork is one of those things that couldn't be more satisfying—both on the taste buds and in its simplicity. While it's commonly cooked barbecue-style and placed in a bun with some slaw, we're deviating from the norm a bit here and using hoisin sauce instead of the 'cue and taking inspiration from Peking duck, that luscious duck meat wrapped in bao with scallions, hoisin, and cucumbers. You can do the bao here, or opt to stuff the pulled pork in a taco, or use as a topping on a salad!

Prep Time	Pressure Building Time	Pressure Cook Time	Natural Release Time	Total Time	Serves
10 MIN	10–15 MIN	60 MIN	10 MIN	1 HR 30 MIN	4–6

- 1½ tablespoons light or dark brown sugar
- 1½ tablespoons Chinese five-spice powder
- 1½ tablespoons garlic powder
- 3–4 pounds country-style ribs (boneless preferred—Costco has them), cut into 1-pound segments (NOTE: You can also use a boneless pork shoulder or butt.)

- ¼ cup low-sodium soy sauce, tamari, or coconut aminos
- 2 cups Coca-Cola, Dr Pepper, or beef broth
- 1 cup hoisin sauce, plus more for topping (see Jeff's Tips)
- 1 bunch scallions; most sliced, some cut longways into 1-inch matchsticks for topping

OPTIONAL FINISHES

Flour or corn tortillas (I use fajita-size), hard taco shells, or bao buns (see Jeff's Tips)

1 cucumber, sliced longways into 1-inch matchsticks for topping

1 On a large plate, mix together the brown sugar, five-spice powder, and garlic powder.

2 Brush the pork with the soy sauce and then roll it in the spices to coat. Set aside.

3 Add the trivet to the Instant Pot and pour in the remaining soy sauce and the soda or broth. Lay the pork on the trivet. Secure the lid, move the valve to the sealing position, and hit Manual or Pressure Cook on High Pressure for 60 minutes. When done, allow a 10-minute natural release followed by a quick release.

 Use tongs to transfer the very tender pork to a large mixing bowl (and remove the bone[s] if necessary). Reserve ½ cup of the juices from the pot and discard the rest.

 Shred the pork with a pair of forks or a hand mixer. Add the reserved juices, hoisin sauce, and scallions. Stir until combined.

6 Serve in tortillas, taco shells, or steamed bao buns and top with scallions, cucumber, and more hoisin, if desired.

JEFF'S TIPS How much hoisin is up to you. Start with 1 cup and add more to taste.

Bao buns can usually be found in the frozen section of many Asian markets. Just steam according to package.

To Serve 1-2 Halve the recipe and reduce the pressure cook time to 50 minutes with same natural release time.

MAGNIFICENT MEAT & POTATOES

You know when someone says they're a "meat and potatoes" person? This is the kind of meal they're talking about. The ingredients are basic and the flavors complex with a creamy gravy finish. This mouthwatering dish goes so nicely over a bed of egg noodles but also works over just about anything. The potatoes and carrots will become delicate and melt like butter as written, but see Jeff's Tips on how to keep them more substantial during the pressure cooking process.

K + *(see Jeff's Tips)*

GF + *(if using gluten free gravy mix)*

Prep Time	Sauté Time	Pressure Building Time	Pressure Cook Time	Natural Release Time	Total Time	Serves
10 MIN	10 MIN	10–15 MIN	60 MIN	15 MIN	1 HR 45 MIN	4–6

- 8 tablespoons (1 stick) salted butter, divided
- 1 large yellow onion, sliced lengthwise into ¼-inch-thick strips
- 3–5 pounds chuck roast, cut into bite-size pieces (you can also use beef stew meat)
- 2 cups beef or garlic broth (e.g., Garlic Better Than Bouillon)
- 1 pound baby potatoes (white and/ or red), skins on, halved
- 1 (8-ounce) bag baby carrots
- ¼ cup cornstarch plus ¼ cup cold water
- ½ cup heavy cream
- 1 (1-ounce) packet beef gravy mix
- 1 teaspoon Dijon mustard (optional)
- ½–1 tablespoon seasoned salt (optional)

1 Add 3 tablespoons of the butter to the Instant Pot. Hit Sauté and Adjust so it's on the More or High setting. Once melted, add the onion and sauté for 5 minutes, until slightly softened. Add the meat and sauté for 1–2 minutes, until lightly browned on each side.

2 Pour in the broth and scrape the bottom of the pot so it's nice and smooth. Top with the potatoes and carrots. Secure the lid, move the valve to the sealing position, hit Cancel, and then hit Manual or Pressure Cook on High Pressure for 60 minutes. When done, allow a 15-minute natural release followed by a quick release.

3 Meanwhile, make a slurry by mixing the cornstarch with the cold water.

4 When the meat's done cooking, remove the potatoes and carrots with a slotted spoon to a serving dish. Then, hit the Cancel button, then hit Sauté and Adjust so it's on the More or High setting.

5 As the sauce is coming to a bubble, stir in the slurry until thickened. Add the remaining 5 tablespoons butter, the cream, gravy mix, and Dijon (if using) and stir. Taste it. If you wish to add the seasoned salt, start with ½ tablespoon and stir it in now. Hit Cancel to turn the pot off.

6 Use a ladle to transfer the meat and a generous amount of gravy to the potatoes and carrots in the serving dish. From there, spoon over a bed of egg noodles and serve with some crusty French bread for dunking in the gravy.

JEFF'S TIPS To keep your potatoes and carrots a bit more firm during the pressure cooking process, wrap each in their own aluminum foil packet prior to pressure cooking when adding to the pot in Step 2. Once done cooking in Step 4, you can simply open the foil packets (use mitts) and put them directly into the sauce instead of transferring them to a serving dish (as they won't be as fragile during the final stirring steps).

If you want mushrooms, add 8 ounces of sliced or halved baby bellas along with the onion in Step 1.

Make it keto by omitting the potatoes. You can add steamed cauliflower in Step 5 in its place, if desired (this way it won't overcook during the pressure cooking stage).

To Serve 1–2 Halve the recipe (use 2 pounds of chuck roast) and reduce the pressure cook time to 50 minutes. Same natural release time.

BRISKET BULGOGI

DUMP & GO!

DF

GF + *(if using tamari or coconut aminos)*

A brisket is one of those meats that the Instant Pot does best—and in about a quarter of the time it would take in an oven or if braised. I'm known for my Jewish brisket (and now Jewish Short Ribs, page 186), but pairing brisket with a Korean-style sweet and savory sauce brings the succulent meat to a whole new level with the enzymes from pears further tenderizing the meat. Keep in mind that if you choose to marinate the brisket, it needs to go for at least 8 to 24 hours, so plan accordingly!

Prep Time	Optional Marinating Time	Pressure Building Time	Pressure Cook Time	Natural Release Time	Resting Time	Total Time (without marinating)	Serves
5 MIN	8–24 HRS	10–15 MIN	65 OR 75 MIN	25 MIN	10 MIN	2 HRS	4–6

THE MARINADE

2 (14- or 15-ounce) cans pears, fully drained

6 cloves garlic, roughly chopped

2-inch knob fresh ginger, peeled and roughly chopped (NOTE: You can also use 2 or 3 tablespoons minced ginger or squeeze ginger.)

3/4 cup low-sodium soy sauce, tamari, or coconut aminos

1 cup packed light or dark brown sugar

1/2 cup honey

1/2 cup hoisin sauce

2 tablespoons sesame oil (any kind)

2 teaspoons fish sauce (optional, and don't mind the pungent smell; the flavor is amazing when combined with everything else)

Sesame seeds, optional

THE BRISKET

1 (4- to 7-pound) beef brisket (don't trim the fat prior to cooking; see Jeff's Tips regarding cuts)

3 tablespoons cornstarch plus 3 tablespoons cold water (optional)

1 Add all the marinade ingredients to a food processor or blender and blend until puréed.

2 Cut the brisket in half against the grain (meaning perpendicular to the direction of the "strings" of the meat) so it will fit in your Instant Pot.

3 Place the brisket in a gallon freezer bag (use 2 bags if needed) and pour the marinade over it. Squeeze the air out of the bag and seal. Refrigerate for 8–24 hours (or **see Jeff's Tips**).

CONTINUES

4 When ready to cook, add the trivet to the Instant Pot. Use tongs to transfer the brisket from the bag to the trivet, stacking the two pieces fat side up. Pour the marinade from the bag all over it. Secure the lid, move the valve to the sealing position, and then hit Manual or Pressure Cook on High Pressure for 75 minutes if you want it super tender (shredding apart), or 65 minutes if you want it a little firmer and more sliceable. When done, allow a 25-minute natural release followed by a quick release.

5 Use tongs to carefully transfer the very tender brisket to a carving board, fat side up, and let rest for 10 minutes. (NOTE: Allow to rest for the full 10 minutes, otherwise it will shred apart when you try to carve it. While you wait, you can carefully slice off any undesired fat.)

6 Meanwhile, **for an optional thicker sauce:** Make a slurry by mixing the cornstarch with the cold water. Hit the Cancel button, then hit Sauté and Adjust so it's on the More or High setting. As the sauce is coming to a bubble, stir in the slurry. The sauce will thicken almost immediately. Hit Cancel to turn the pot off and then hit Keep Warm.

7 Once the brisket has cooled, use a carving knife to slice it against the grain into strips or chunks. Return the meat to the sauce and let it soak up the sauce for 10 minutes before serving. Top with sesame seeds, if desired. This goes nicely with kimchi (Korean-style fermented cabbage) and rice.

 JEFF'S TIPS If you wish to speed this along, you can skip the marinating (aka Step 3) and just pour the marinade over the brisket in the Instant Pot before cooking in Step 4. That said, I'd suggest marinating it just before you go to bed. It helps make the brisket even more tender and really optimizes the flavor (not to mention, it cuts down on prep time when you're ready to cook).

In the market, you may find some briskets are labeled as point cut or flat cut. The point cut will be fattier and more ideal for pastrami or for putting through a meat grinder, whereas a flat cut is less fatty or more ideal for slicing. Either will work.

If you choose to shred your brisket instead of slicing it, you can make outrageous brisket tacos, burritos, or even add to Ginger-Scallion Noodles (page 102).

 To Serve 1–2 Use 2–3 pounds of brisket, halve the recipe, and reduce the pressure cook time to 55 or 60 minutes with a 15-minute natural release time.

· THE ·
PERFECT TEN BURGER

DUMP
& GO!

K + (see Jeff's Tips)

GF + (if using gluten-
free onion dip
mix and buns)

In keeping with this book's directive of creating recipes with ten ingredients or less, I present to you the ultimate pressure-cooked burger. The end result is worthy of sinking your teeth into: So flavorful and oh-so juicy, you'll forget you even have a grill. The secret to the flavor is the bacon grease, although I do provide an alternative of butter. In addition to pressure cooking these, you can grill or air fry them (see Jeff's Tips on the next page).

Prep Time	Optional Bacon Cooking Time	Pressure Building Time	Pressure Cook Time	Total Time	Serves
10 MIN	15–25 MIN	10–15 MIN	10 MIN	30–45 MIN	4

2 slices white bread, crusts discarded, ripped into tiny pieces

¼ cup whole milk

3 tablespoons bacon grease, slightly warmed, or 3 tablespoons melted salted butter (see Jeff's Tips)

1½ pounds ground beef (80–85% lean preferred, or see Jeff's Tips)

2 tablespoons grated Parmesan cheese

½ (1-ounce) packet onion dip mix (so only use ½ ounce)

2 teaspoons hoisin sauce

1 teaspoon seasoned salt

1 teaspoon black pepper

4 hamburger buns

OPTIONAL TOPPINGS

Sliced cheese of your choice

Bacon

Lettuce

Tomatoes

Red onion (raw or sautéed)

Condiments of your choice

1 In a large mixing bowl, combine the white bread and milk. Mash with a fork for a minute until it becomes a paste-like consistency (when it looks like oatmeal, it's done).

2 Add the warm bacon grease or melted butter, beef, Parmesan, onion dip mix, hoisin, salt, and pepper. Mix/knead the meat mixture by hand until the ingredients are fully combined and evenly dispersed. The meat should be a bit sticky and easily form into a large meatball.

3 Shape the meat mixture into four burger patties by hand. Or use a hamburger patty press (easily found online), lining each press with parchment rounds so the patties don't stick to the press or to each other when stacked. The patties are now ready for immediate cooking, or they can stay in an airtight container in the fridge for up to 2 days.

CONTINUES

The Perfect Ten Burger is called that for a reason. It cooks in 10 minutes to medium juicy heaven whether pressure-steamed, grilled, or broiled in the air fryer. Here are two other ways to cook them:

- **To barbecue or grill:** Heat the grill with the lid closed to max temp for 5–10 minutes, until fully heated. Lower the heat to medium-high. Add the burger patties, cover, and grill for 10 minutes total. This means grill for 5 minutes on one side with the lid lowered and then flip with a spatula and grill for another 5 minutes also with the lid lowered. If adding cheese and/or wanting to toast the buns, place the cheese on top of the burgers and the buns face-down on the grill for the final 90 seconds of cooking.

- **To broil with the Air Fryer Lid on the Instant Pot:** Place the trivet in the liner pot with the tall side facing up and spray with nonstick cooking spray. Place the patties in one layer on the trivet (in batches, if necessary), add the lid, and Broil (400°F) for 10 minutes total, flipping the patties after 5 minutes. If adding cheese, lay it on the patties 90 seconds before the cook time is complete.

4 Remove the parchment paper and individually wrap each burger patty in foil sprayed with nonstick cooking spray. (NOTE: *Do not* add cheese to the raw patty before wrapping with the foil because it will stick to the foil—we'll deal with the cheese in Step 6.)

5 Place the trivet in the liner pot, add 1 cup water, and rest the foil-wrapped patties on the trivet, stacking as many as you wish. Secure the lid, move the valve to the sealing position, and hit Manual or Pressure Cook on High Pressure for 10 minutes (**see Jeff's Tips**). Quick release when done.

6 Place the patties on buns and top with any toppings your heart desires. (If you want a cheeseburger, now you can add the cheese to the cooked patty—the heat of it will melt the cheese a bit.) Enjoy one of the juiciest, most flavorful homemade burgers ever!

 JEFF'S TIPS If you don't already have some bacon grease stored in your fridge, start saving it up now! After you cook up some bacon, let the grease cool for 15 minutes. Then transfer it to a jar, cover, and place in the fridge. It will last up to a year and you can keep adding to it every time you have excess bacon grease. Bacon grease is wonderful to use in place of oil or butter in many dishes—especially when making scrambled eggs!

Don't eat red meat? Use ground turkey or ground chicken instead, and use butter instead of the bacon grease.

If you want your burgers more well-done, increase the pressure cook time to 15 minutes. Or, if you're doubling the recipe and cooking more burgers, up the cook time by 5 minutes per each two additional burgers.

To make keto, use keto-friendly bread or buns.

 To Serve 1–2 Halve all of the ingredients. (NOTE: The amount of water added in Step 5 will always be 1 cup no matter what, as that creates the steam for cooking.) Cook time remains the same.

BEEF BIRRIA TACOS

 K + *(if using keto-friendly tortillas)*

 P + *(if using paleo-friendly tortillas)*

 DF + *(if using olive oil)*

GF

The trendiest taco around, now from your Instant Pot! Birria is a deeply savory Mexican stew commonly made with goat meat, chiles, garlic, and spices. Quesabirria tacos are made with the stewed meat and melted cheese and dipped into the consommé braising liquid. But since goat meat can be difficult to source, I use one of *three* cuts of beef: short ribs, brisket, or chuck roast. Whichever you choose, the moment you bite into one of these special tacos will be unforgettable.

Prep Time	Sauté Time	Pressure Building Time	Pressure Cook Time	Natural Release Time	Taco Making Time	Total Time	Serves
10 MIN	10 MIN	10–15 MIN	45–65 MIN	15–20 MIN	2–4 MIN PER BATCH OF TACOS	1 HR 30 MIN–2 HRS	4–6

1 tablespoon chili powder

1 tablespoon ground cumin

1 tablespoon seasoned salt or adobo (any flavor), plus more to taste

Choice of one meat:

- *6–8 pounds bone-in short ribs*
- *5–6 pounds beef brisket (point cut preferably), cut into 4 large chunks*
- *1 (3- to 5-pound) chuck roast, cut into 4 large chunks*

3 tablespoons salted butter or extra-virgin olive oil

1 large Spanish onion, sliced lengthwise into ¼-inch-thick strips

12 cloves garlic, halved

2 cups beef broth

2 teaspoons dried oregano, optional

4 ounces dried guajillo or ancho chiles, stems and seeds removed

Corn tortillas (taco-size)

OPTIONAL TOUCHES (SEE JEFF'S TIPS)

Shredded Mexican cheese blend

Fresh cilantro

Sour cream

Guacamole

Finely diced red, yellow, or white onion

1 On a large plate, mix together the chili powder, cumin, and seasoned salt/adobo. Coat the meat in the seasoning.

2 Add the butter or olive oil to the Instant Pot, hit Sauté and Adjust so it's on the More or High setting. After 3 minutes of heating, flash-sear the meat for about 45 seconds on each side. Remove to a plate when done.

3 Add the onion and garlic to the pot and sauté for 5 minutes, until slightly softened and the garlic is lightly browned.

CONTINUES

JEFF'S TIPS

This recipe is designed specifically for corn tortillas. Flour tortillas won't cook or crisp the same way as the corn will when soaked in the birria broth and pan-fried. That said, you can totally use flour tortillas—but go for the smallest size you can find (generally fajita-sized).

Although the crispy, greasy taco shells are what make these tacos so special, you can save time and skip Steps 6 and 8 if you want to just use soft corn/flour tortillas or crunchy taco shells instead. From there, top your tacos as you wish!

4 Add the broth and oregano (if using) and deglaze (scrape the bottom of the pot), getting up any browned bits. Return the meat to the pot and top with the chiles. Secure the lid, move the valve to the sealing position, hit Cancel, and then hit Manual or Pressure Cook on High Pressure for the following times, depending on the meat:

Short ribs: 45 minutes with a 15-minute natural release followed by a quick release

Brisket: 65 minutes with a 20-minute natural release followed by a quick release

Chuck roast: 60 minutes with a 15-minute natural release followed by a quick release

5 When done, use tongs to transfer the chiles to a food processor or blender; then transfer the meat and onions to a large bowl (a slotted spoon will help with this). (NOTE: If you used short ribs, remove the meat from the bones—they'll slide right out.) Shred the meat with two forks or a hand mixer.

6 Ladle 1 cup of the consommé from the pot into a large bowl; set aside.

7 Ladle 1 more cup of the consommé from the pot to the food processor; blend with the chiles until pureed. Rest a fine-mesh strainer over the bowl of meat and pour the chile puree into it, pressing down with a mixing spoon so all the chile skin is caught as the puree strains into the bowl. Discard the skins. Taste the puree and add some more seasoned salt or adobo to taste, if desired. Mix the chile puree into the shredded meat to coat well.

8 Place a nonstick skillet on the stove over medium-high heat. Dip the corn tortillas into the bowl with the cup of reserved consommé. (NOTE: You can dip 2–4 at a time depending on how large your pan is.) The more saturated the tortillas are in those juices, the better they'll taste. Place in the pan and top with some of the shredded meat and cheese, if using. Fold the tacos into a classic crescent shape and cook for 1–2 minutes on each side, until the tortilla is crisped and golden brown (watch it so it doesn't burn). Repeat with more tortillas, shredded meat, and cheese (if using).

9 Serve with any toppings of your choice and dip in additional broth while enjoying.

To Serve 1–2 Simply halve the recipe. Shave 5 minutes off the cook time for each cut of meat.

BEER CHEESE BRATS

This dish dresses smoky bratwurst (or any smoked sausage, really) with a sweet, cheesy, brewy sauce. Whether you wish to serve it in a hero, over rice or pasta, or simply on its own with a few hot pretzels to dip into it, you're going to enjoy every bite (plus it's an excuse to crack open a beer or two).

V+ *(see Jeff's Tips)*

Prep Time	Sauté Time	Pressure Building Time	Pressure Cook Time	Total Time	Serves
15 MIN	**10** MIN	**10–15** MIN	**5** MIN	**40** MIN	**4–6**

4 tablespoons (½ stick) salted butter

2 large red and/or green bell peppers, diced

2 large carrots, peeled and diced

2–2½ pounds bratwurst, kielbasa, or any smoked sausage of your choice, sliced into ½-inch-thick pieces (see Jeff's Tips)

¾ cup beer (a lager or pale ale works best, or see Jeff's Tips)

2 teaspoons dried thyme

2–4 cups shredded Cheddar cheese (see Jeff's Tips)

¼ cup heavy cream or half-and-half

1 tablespoon Worcestershire sauce

1 teaspoon Old Bay seasoning or seasoned salt (optional)

1 teaspoon liquid smoke (optional)

OPTIONAL ACCOMPANIMENTS

Hero rolls (6 inchers work well)

Sauerkraut, drained

Sliced jalapeños

Rice or pasta (see General Cooking charts, page 22)

Hot pretzels (found in the frozen food section and prepared according to package)

1 Add the butter to the Instant Pot and hit Sauté and Adjust to the More or High setting. Once melted and bubbling, add the peppers and carrots and sauté for 5 minutes, until lightly softened. Add the sausage and sauté another 3 minutes.

2 Add the beer and thyme and stir, deglazing (scraping the bottom of the pot) to get up any browned bits.

3 Secure the lid, move the valve to the sealing position, hit Cancel, and then hit Manual or Pressure Cook on High Pressure for 5 minutes. Quick release when done.

CONTINUES

4 Stir in the cheese, cream, Worcestershire sauce, Old Bay or seasoned salt (if using), and liquid smoke (if using). Stir until it has become a glorious, beery, cheesy, bratty dish of beauty.

5 Serve as desired with any optional suggestions. NOTE: If making a hero, grab a 6-inch hero roll, slice the top lengthwise down the center (keeping the bottom intact to catch everything), and spread it open on a foil-lined sheet pan. Ladle in the beer cheese brats, top with things such as sauerkraut, jalapeños, roasted red peppers, and/or more shredded (or sliced) cheese. Then broil on the top rack in the oven for 1–2 minutes. You can also do this in the Instant Pot resting on the trivet with the Air Fryer Lid on Broil (400°F) for 1–3 minutes, until the cheese is browned and bubbling. Just be careful to keep an eye on it so as not to burn the cheese or bread!

JEFF'S TIPS

Bratwurst, kielbasa, and most smoked sausages are sold either pre-cooked or uncooked. I suggest pre-cooked since they will give off less liquid when pressure cooking, making for a thicker sauce. However, whichever you choose, all cook times will remain the same. You can also absolutely use chicken sausage, or any plant-based sausage of your choice to make it vegetarian.

Even though beer is a great way to flavor the sauce, if you want to try the recipe and prefer not to use beer, sub ½ cup of any broth of your choice (preferably ham; e.g, Ham Better Than Bouillon). If skipping alcohol, a non-alcoholic beer will work great here as well.

Personally, I like using all 4 cups of cheese for this recipe to give that sauce a "wow!" factor. But how cheesy you want the sauce is up to you (the more cheese, the thicker and richer the sauce). Start with 2 cups. Then, after Step 4 is complete, feel free to add up to 2 more cups. You can always thin the sauce out by adding more cream.

To Serve 1–2

Halve all of the ingredients, except for the beer— keep it at ¾ cup so the pot properly comes to pressure. Cook times remain the same.

LEMON ORZO PORK TENDERLOIN

K ⁺ *(see Jeff's Tips)*

P ⁺ *(see Jeff's Tips)*

DF ⁺ *(see Jeff's Tips)*

GF ⁺ *(see Jeff's Tips)*

I'm a bit infatuated with silky, eggy, lemony sauces. This sauce, here given the royal pork tenderloin treatment, was inspired by a Greek soup, avgolemono. It's perfect for dressing "the other white meat" in something light and bright, giving the pork wonderful flavor. If that wasn't enough, this recipe is made with no sautéing, only five ingredients, and just three simple steps.

Prep Time	Pressure Building Time	Pressure Cook Time	Natural Release Time	Sauté Time	Total Time	Serves
5 MIN	10–15 MIN	10 MIN	10 MIN	2 MIN	40 MIN	4–6

1¾ cups chicken broth

⅓ cup orzo

2 pounds pork tenderloin, sliced into ½- to 1-inch-thick medallions

5 ounces baby spinach (optional)

1 large egg

Juice of 2 lemons

¼–½ cup grated Parmesan cheese (optional)

1 Pour the broth and orzo into the Instant Pot and stir. Nestle in the pork and top with the spinach (if using). Secure the lid, move the valve to the sealing position, and hit Pressure Cook on High Pressure for 10 minutes. When done, allow a 10-minute natural release followed by a quick release. Using tongs, transfer the pork to a serving dish.

JEFF'S TIPS

2 In a small bowl, whisk together the egg and lemon juice. Hit Cancel followed by Sauté and Adjust to the More or High setting. Once bubbling, pour the mixture into the pot while stirring. After 1 minute, stir in the Parmesan (if using). Hit Cancel to turn the pot off.

3 Drape the sauce over the pork and serve.

Not adding the Parmesan will make it dairy-free.

Not adding the orzo will make it keto and gluten-free (reduce the broth to 1 cup).

Not adding both will make it paleo.

If you want the sauce eggier and a bit thicker, add a second egg.

If you want more Parmesan, go for it. Start with ¼ cup and work your way up.

To Serve 1–2 Halve all of the ingredients, except for the broth—reduce it to 1 cup so the pot properly comes to pressure. Cook times remain the same.

SHORT RIBS

CREAM OF MUSHROOM

I had to have a few short rib recipes in this book because they cook so perfectly in the Instant Pot (not to mention it's my favorite cut of meat). These short ribs are adorned with a creamy garlic and Parmesan sauce loaded with mushrooms and spinach, flavors common in regions of Tuscany. And in my kitchen.

Prep Time	Sauté Time	Pressure Building Time	Pressure Cook Time	Natural Release Time	Total Time	Serves
10 MIN	10 MIN	10–15 MIN	45 MIN	15 MIN	1 HR 30 MIN	4–6

6 tablespoons (¾ stick) salted butter, divided

5 pounds bone-in short ribs (see Jeff's Tips)

½ cup Marsala or sherry wine (see Jeff's Tips), divided

2 pounds baby bella mushrooms, 1 pound sliced and 1 pound halved

9 cloves garlic, minced or pressed

1 cup chicken or garlic broth (e.g., Garlic Better Than Bouillon)

2 teaspoons Italian seasoning

5 ounces baby spinach, optional

3 tablespoons cornstarch plus 3 tablespoons cold water

½ cup heavy cream

1 cup grated Parmesan cheese

1 (5.2-ounce) package Boursin cheese (any flavor), or ¾ cup Garlic Herb Cheese (page 21), optional

1 Add 3 tablespoons of the butter to the Instant Pot, hit Sauté and Adjust to the More or High setting. Once melted and bubbling, in batches, sear the short ribs for 30 seconds on each side. Set aside when done.

2 Add ¼ cup of the wine to the pot and deglaze (scrape the bottom of the pot), getting up any browned bits. Add the remaining 3 tablespoons butter along with just the sliced mushrooms and garlic and sauté for 5 minutes, until the mushrooms are lightly browned.

3 Add the remaining ¼ cup wine, plus the broth and Italian seasoning and stir, making sure the bottom of the pot is smooth and cleared of any additional browned bits. Nestle in the short ribs, stacking them on top of each other. Top with the halved mushrooms and the spinach (if using) but *do not stir*. (NOTE: You may need to press the spinach down in between the mushrooms so it fits.)

4 Secure the lid and make sure the valve is in the sealing position. Hit Cancel followed by Manual or Pressure Cook on High Pressure for 45 minutes. When done, allow a 15-minute natural release followed by a quick release. Meanwhile, make a slurry by mixing the cornstarch with the water.

5 Using tongs, carefully remove the ribs from the pot (they will be super tender) and place in a serving dish (try to keep most of the spinach and mushrooms in the pot). Hit Cancel followed by Sauté and Adjust so it's on the More or High setting. Once the sauce is bubbling, add the slurry, stirring immediately. Add the cream, Parmesan, and Boursin (if using). Stir until all is combined before hitting Cancel to turn the pot off. Let the sauce rest for 5 minutes.

To Serve 1–2 Halve all of the ingredients except for the wine and broth—reduce the wine to ¼ cup and broth to ¾ cup so the pot properly comes to pressure. Reduce the pressure cook time to 35 minutes, keeping the same natural release time.

6 Pour the sauce over the short ribs and serve over some rice or pasta along with crusty Italian bread to sop up the extra sauce.

JEFF'S TIPS If not using wine, sub ¼ cup more broth in Step 3.

If you want a more budget-conscious, yet incredibly tender and flavorful cut of meat, use 3–5 pounds chuck roast in place of the short ribs. Slice the roast into 4 or 5 equal pieces and pressure cook for 60 minutes at High Pressure; allow a 15-minute natural release followed by a quick release. Then in Step 5, slice the meat into large chunks and return to the pot in Step 6 once the sauce is complete and serve. Everything else in the recipe remains the same.

7

SEAFOOD

Making seafood in the Instant Pot not only cuts down on the work involved while making dinner super flavorful, it also makes sure your kitchen doesn't smell too pungent since the seafood is cooked under pressure!

This chapter will bring the sea to your plate in a variety of ways, from classic fare to pastas, soups, and stews to steams.

= DUMP & GO RECIPE

 = 5 INGREDIENTS OR LESS

 = 3 STEPS OR LESS

 = AIR FRYER LID

 K = KETO

P = PALEO

 DF = DAIRY-FREE

GF = GLUTEN-FREE

V = VEGETARIAN

 VN = VEGAN

+ = COMPLIANT WITH MODIFICATIONS

CRAB & CLAM DIP

This hot dip with a thick, creamy seafood base is usually one of the first things to go when I put it out at a party. It's incredibly simple to make and it'll be done in your Instant Pot without pressure cooking! Yup! We're just going to use the Sauté function for this one to show you how you can treat your Instant Pot like a pot on the stove, but do it anywhere (boats included).

Prep Time	Sauté Time	Total Time	Serves
10 MIN	15 MIN	25 MIN	4-6

- 4 tablespoons (½ stick) salted butter
- 1 medium yellow onion, diced
- 1 large carrot, peeled and diced
- 1 red bell pepper, seeded and finely diced
- 2 (6-ounce) cans lump crabmeat, drained
- 2 (6.5-ounce) cans chopped clams, drained

- 2 teaspoons Garlic (or any flavor) Better Than Bouillon base, divided (optional)
- 2 (8-ounce) bricks cream cheese
- 1 cup shredded mozzarella cheese
- 1 teaspoon garlic powder

OPTIONAL ACCOMPANIMENTS

A large, round bread, hollowed out to form a bread bowl to hold the dip (which doubles as a dipper since you can break off chunks as the dip disappears)

Pretzel chips, crackers, sliced baguette, etc.

Veggies of your choice (e.g., carrot sticks, celery sticks, sliced bell peppers, broccoli florets, cauliflower florets)

1 Add the butter to the Instant Pot and hit Sauté and Adjust so it's on the More or High setting. Once the butter's melted and bubbling, add the onion, carrot, and pepper and sauté for 5-10 minutes, until they become softened. (I don't like my veggies to be too hard and crunchy, but if you do, just sauté for less time.)

2 Add the drained crabmeat and clams. If using, add 1 teaspoon of the Better Than Bouillon. Stir until the seafood is heated through and combined with the Better Than Bouillon, about 1 minute.

3 Hit Cancel followed by Sauté and Adjust so it's on the **Less or Low setting.** Add the cream cheese and stir constantly until the cheese has melted into the dip and it has a creamy dip-like consistency. (NOTE: To speed the blending along, you can definitely up the temperature to Normal or Medium—just keep an eye on it while stirring so it doesn't burn or stick to the bottom of the pot.)

4 For the finishing touches, add the mozzarella, garlic powder, and remaining 1 teaspoon Better Than Bouillon (if using). Stir until fully combined.

5 Either serve the dip in the pot on the lowest setting to keep it warm, stirring every so often so it doesn't stick (**see Jeff's Tips**), or transfer to a bread bowl. Serve with your favorite chips, crackers, bread, or veggies and enjoy!

JEFF'S TIPS Since this recipe features a dip loaded with dairy, you may want to use the nonstick liner pot accessory for the Instant Pot to make for easier and smoother stirring/cleanup. But you can just as well get away with making this in the stainless steel liner that comes with the pot. Just stir the dip every so often when done and make sure it's only on the Keep Warm setting while resting.

You can also make this in an electric fondue pot, or on the stove in an enameled Dutch oven or nonstick skillet on medium heat.

To Serve 1-2 Simply halve the recipe. Cook times remain the same.

CIOPPINO

With its wonderfully rich tomato base, a cioppino is the ultimate fish stew in Italian cooking. The best part about making it yourself is that you are in control of which goodies from the sea make it into the pot. Simply allow my recipe to be your guide to a wonderful and comforting treat—and be sure to have plenty of crusty Italian bread nearby.

Prep Time	Sauté Time	Pressure Building Time	Pressure Cook Time	Total Time	Serves
10 MIN	10–15 MIN	10–20 MIN	1–3 MIN	35 MIN	4–6

THE BROTH

3 tablespoons extra-virgin olive oil

2 large shallots, diced

6 cloves garlic, minced or pressed

1 cup sherry or dry white wine (like a sauvignon blanc, see Jeff's Tips)

Juice of 1 lemon

4 cups vegetable or garlic broth (e.g., Garlic Better Than Bouillon)

1 (28-ounce) can crushed tomatoes

2 teaspoons seasoned salt, plus more to taste

2 teaspoons Italian seasoning

1 teaspoon Old Bay seasoning (optional)

¼–1 teaspoon crushed red pepper flakes, to taste (optional)

THE SEAFOOD OPTIONS (USE ANY AND/OR ALL—SEE JEFF'S TIPS FOR AMOUNTS)

Fresh mussels, rinsed and debearded (make sure to toss out any that have opened before cooking)

Cod, salmon, or halibut (or any fish you prefer), deboned and cut into bite-size pieces

Large or jumbo raw shrimp, peeled and deveined

Fresh scallops (any size)

Fresh calamari rings

Fresh or thawed frozen lump crabmeat, drained

1 Add the oil to the Instant Pot and hit Sauté and Adjust so it's on the More or High setting. After 3 minutes of heating, add the shallots and sauté for 3 minutes, until their color begins to fade. Add the garlic and sauté for 2 minutes longer.

2 Add the wine and lemon juice and deglaze (scrape the bottom of the pot), getting up any browned bits. Allow to simmer for 2 minutes.

3 Add the broth, crushed tomatoes, seasoned salt, and Italian seasoning and stir well. If using mussels, add them now, *but don't stir*! Just nestle them into the broth. Secure the lid, move the valve to the sealing position, then hit Cancel followed by Manual or Pressure Cook at High Pressure for 3 minutes without the mussels, or 1 minute with. (NOTE: This is so they don't overcook.) Quick release when done.

4 When done pressure cooking, if you added mussels, use a slotted spoon to remove them to a large bowl, then ladle about ½ cup broth over to keep them moist. Discard any mussels that failed to open. Hit Cancel followed by Sauté and Adjust so it's on the More or High setting. Taste the broth. Now you can decide if you want to add the Old Bay seasoning, crushed red pepper flakes, and/or additional seasoned salt to taste.

5 Now to add the seafood! Regardless of which you go with, once the pot's bubbling, add it in this order for these amounts of time:

Fish: 2 minutes (or 5 minutes if only cooking fish)

Shrimp, scallops, and/or calamari: 2 minutes (3 minutes if only cooking shellfish)

Crabmeat: no longer than 1 minute

6 Hit Cancel and then Keep Warm. If you cooked them, return the mussels to the pot. Ladle the stew into bowls and enjoy with some crusty Italian bread.

 JEFF'S TIPS Using sherry instead of a dry white wine will give the cioppino a slightly richer taste. Or you can use ½ cup of each. But if you don't want any wine, that's just fine. Sub an additional 1 cup broth in Step 2.

If using mussels in Step 3, you can use up to 3 pounds. If using one or two seafood options in Step 5, feel free to add 1–1½ pounds of each. But if using three or more, go with about ¾ pound of each, tops, so as not to overcrowd the pot!

If using any seafood that's frozen, just rinse it in a colander under cold water until thawed while the broth is being pressure cooked.

To Serve 1–2 Simply halve the recipe. Cook times remain the same.

SEAFOOD ALFREDO

Since my take on a richer-than-a-millionaire Alfredo is something I can make with minimal focus and one hand tied behind my back, it felt entirely fitting to include a seafood version in this chapter. To make it even better, virtually any shellfish can be tossed in at the end.

DUMP & GO! · 3 STEPS OR LESS!

Prep Time	Pressure Building Time	Pressure Cook Time	Sauté Time	Total Time	Serves
5 MIN	10–15 MIN	6 MIN	5 MIN	30 MIN	4–6

- 3–4 cups (<u>see Jeff's Tips</u>) garlic or chicken broth (e.g., Garlic Better Than Bouillon)
- 1 pound ziti, ziti rigati, gemelli, or medium shells
- 8 tablespoons (1 stick) salted butter, cut into 8 pats, divided

- ¾ cup heavy cream (preferred) or half-and-half, plus more if needed (<u>see Jeff's Tips</u>)
- 1 cup grated Parmesan cheese
- 1 teaspoon garlic powder
- 1 teaspoon black pepper
- 1 (5.2-ounce) package Boursin cheese (any flavor) or ¾ cup Garlic Herb Cheese (page 21)

THE SEAFOOD OPTIONS (UP TO 2 POUNDS TOTAL, MIXED AND MATCHED OR SINGULAR—<u>SEE JEFF'S TIPS</u>)

- Large or jumbo raw shrimp, peeled and deveined
- Fresh scallops (any size)
- Fresh calamari rings
- Fresh or thawed frozen lump crabmeat, drained

1 Add the broth to the Instant Pot as well as the pasta, smoothing it out so it's mostly submerged in the broth (it's okay if some sticks above it). Top with 3 pats of the butter.

2 Secure the lid, move the valve to the sealing position, and hit Manual or Pressure Cook at High Pressure for 6 minutes (regardless of which pasta you choose). Quick release when done.

3 When the lid comes off, give everything a stir. Hit Cancel followed by Sauté and Adjust so it's on the More or High setting. Add the remaining 5 pats butter and the cream. Stir everything in the pot with a wooden spatula until the butter's melted. Add the seafood you chose and stir into the pasta and remaining broth. Cook for 3–5 minutes. **(NOTE: If using shrimp, once it becomes opaque and curls, it's done.)** Hit Cancel to turn the pot off. Add the Parmesan, garlic powder, pepper, and Boursin and stir until totally melded, about 1 minute. Let the pasta rest for 5 minutes to fully come together. Serve immediately, topping with freshly cracked black pepper, if desired.

 JEFF'S TIPS Remember, a rich dairy sauce such as this will continue to be absorbed by the pasta as the dish rests. But for a thicker sauce after pressure cooking, use 3 cups of broth and for a thinner sauce, use 4 cups. That said, you can always add more cream (up to ½ cup) to thin out the sauce before serving or when reheating leftovers.

If using any seafood that's frozen, just rinse it in a colander under cold water until thawed while the broth is being pressure cooked.

Whichever seafood you choose, keeping it to 2 pounds max makes the most sense considering you don't want the seafood to overwhelm the pasta.

 To Serve 1–2 Simply halve the recipe. Cook times remain the same.

CRAB BISQUE

Be it summer, fall, winter, or spring, crab bisque always makes me sing. With loads of lump crabmeat mixed into a lush, velvety, and creamy veggie-laden broth, it's no wonder that folks can't get enough of this delicious soup. The sherry is optional but gives the bisque a deep flavor.

 GF

Prep Time	Sauté Time	Pressure Building Time	Pressure Cook Time	Total Time	Serves
5 MIN	10 MIN	10–15 MIN	2 MIN	35 MIN	4–6

- 4 tablespoons (½ stick) salted butter
- 2 large shallots, diced
- 1 bunch scallions, sliced, some reserved for topping
- 3 cloves garlic, minced or pressed
- ½ cup sherry wine (optional; if not using, sub ½ cup more broth)
- 1½ cups chicken, fish, or garlic broth (e.g., Fish or Garlic Better Than Bouillon)

- 1 teaspoon dried thyme, plus more to taste
- 2 cups heavy cream or half-and-half
- 1 tablespoon Worcestershire sauce
- 2–4 tablespoons tomato paste (start with 2 and add more to taste)

- 1–2 teaspoons Old Bay seasoning or seasoned salt (optional and to taste)
- 1 pound refrigerated or thawed frozen lump crabmeat (see Jeff's Tips), drained

OPTIONAL ACCOMPANIMENTS

Oyster crackers

Croutons

1 Add the butter to the Instant Pot and hit Sauté and Adjust so it's on the More or High setting. Once the butter's melted and bubbling, add the shallots and scallions and sauté for 3 minutes, until the color of the shallots begins to fade. Add the garlic and sauté for 1 minute more.

2 Add the wine (or ½ cup broth) and deglaze (scrape the bottom of the pot), getting up any browned bits. Allow to simmer for 2 minutes.

3 Add the broth and thyme and stir well. Secure the lid and move the valve to the sealing position, then hit Cancel followed by Manual or Pressure Cook on High Pressure for 2 minutes. Quick release when done and give the pot a good stir.

4 Hit Cancel followed by Sauté and Adjust to the More or High setting. Add the cream, Worcestershire sauce, and 2 tablespoons tomato paste and stir. (NOTE: I like my bisque a little frothy, but if you don't want it that way, leave the cream out until the end of Step 5.)

5 Take an immersion blender and blend until pureed (or blend in batches using a blender). Taste the soup to see if you want to add more tomato paste or thyme, or add Old Bay seasoning or seasoned salt. If so, add and blend once more. (NOTE: If you waited to add the cream post-blending, stir it in now.)

6 Add the crab and stir it into the bisque. Allow it to heat for 1 minute. Hit Cancel and then Keep Warm and let the soup rest for 5 minutes so that any bubbles from the blending subdue. Serve the bisque topped with the reserved sliced scallions, a few shakes of additional Old Bay, and oyster crackers or croutons, if desired.

JEFF'S TIPS For the lump crabmeat, I usually buy a 1-pound refrigerated or frozen tub at Costco, but you don't have to use a fancy lump crab. Three or four (6-ounce) cans crab (drained) is perfectly fine too!

To cut down on the dairy, you can use an unsweetened nondairy milk such as almond, soy, oat, or cashew. You can also use unsweetened coconut milk (just make sure you shake it well, so it's thin like water and not thick and lumpy).

 To Serve 1–2 Simply halve the recipe. Cook times remain the same.

STEAMED CLAMS
IN BUTTERY WINE SAUCE

One of the joys of Instant Potting is how convenient it is to get mollusks to play a game of "open sesame"—especially since they do it so politely, steamed to tender bliss without you even realizing it. This recipe will give you a broth that you'll want to slurp like a soup—or sop up with some bread. The clams also go gorgeously over a bed of angel hair pasta.

DUMP & GO!

Prep Time	Sauté Time	Pressure Building Time	Pressure Cook Time	Total Time	Serves
5 MIN	8 MIN	10–15 MIN	2 MIN	25 MIN	4-6

4 tablespoons (½ stick) salted butter

3 large shallots, diced

9 cloves garlic, minced or pressed

¾ cup dry white wine

2 tablespoons dried parsley flakes

1 teaspoon garlic powder

½ teaspoon Old Bay seasoning (optional)

3–5 pounds (or about 3 dozen) fresh clams (look for smaller clams, like Manila), rinsed (toss any that have opened before cooking)

1½ cups chicken or garlic broth (e.g., Garlic or Fish Better Than Bouillon)

Juice of 2 lemons

1 Place the butter in the Instant Pot and hit Sauté and Adjust to the More or High setting. Once melted and bubbling, add the shallots and cook for about 2 minutes, until softened. Add the garlic and sauté for 1 minute longer.

2 Add the wine and stir, scraping up any browned bits from the bottom of the pot. Let simmer for 1–2 minutes, until slightly thickened. Stir in the parsley, garlic powder, and Old Bay (if using).

3 Add the clams. (NOTE: It's fine to fill the pot to about 1 inch below the brim.) Pour the broth and lemon juice over them. Secure the lid, move the valve to the sealing position, and hit Manual or Pressure Cook at High Pressure for 2 minutes. Quick release when done.

4 Serve immediately, topping with freshly cracked black pepper if desired.

JEFF'S TIPS

Mollusks such as clams and mussels really do need to be cooked within an hour or two after purchase in the store (where they'll usually be on ice). Keeping them in your fridge all day will cause them to open prematurely, rendering them not fit to cook.

If you want the broth spicy, add ½–1 teaspoon crushed red pepper flakes and/or ⅛–½ teaspoon Zatarain's Concentrated Shrimp & Crab Boil in Step 2 along with the seasonings.

To Serve 1–2

Use 1–2 pounds of clams. Cook times remain the same.

SHRIMP SCAMPI

Are y'all ready to cook scampi like a champ(i)? The classic pasta in a lemon-wine-Parmesan sauce is as simple to make as it is tasty. In this case, we add the shrimp after the pasta cooks to ensure it reaches tender perfection. To get a little fancy, serve topped with some fresh parsley alongside some garlic-cheese toast or cheese sticks.

Prep Time	Pressure Building Time	Sauté Time	Pressure Cook Time	Total Time	Serves
10 MIN	10–15 MIN	12 MIN	6 MIN	40 MIN	4–6

8 tablespoons (1 stick) salted butter, divided

2 large shallots, diced

6 cloves garlic, minced or pressed

¼ cup dry white wine (like a chardonnay)

Juice of 1 lemon

3½ cups chicken or garlic broth (e.g., Garlic Better Than Bouillon)

2 teaspoons dried basil

1 pound linguine (see Jeff's Tip)

1–2 pounds large or jumbo raw shrimp, peeled, tails on or off, and deveined (if frozen, rinse with cold water through a colander until thawed)

½ cup grated Parmesan cheese, plus more for topping if desired

1 Add 6 tablespoons (¾ stick) of the butter to the Instant Pot and hit Sauté and Adjust so it's on the More or High setting. Once the butter's melted and bubbling, add the shallots and sauté for 3 minutes, until the color begins to fade. Add the garlic and sauté for 2 minutes longer.

2 Add the wine and lemon juice and deglaze (scrape the bottom of the pot), getting up any browned bits. Allow to simmer for 2 minutes.

JEFF'S TIP Normally, a scampi is served over angel hair or capellini pasta. But since that pasta cooks the fastest of them all, it's a wee-bit delicate when cooked under pressure and so I chose a sturdier linguine. If you want to try the angel hair, just lower the pressure cook time to 3 minutes (it may break apart easily, though). Or if you want to use a thicker, hollowed-out spaghetti called bucatini (or perciatelli), up the pressure cook time to 12 minutes. Whatever you choose, just make sure you break the noodles in half and lay in a crisscross fashion like the linguine, so they fit and cook evenly in the pot.

3 Add the broth and dried basil. Stir well, giving the bottom of the pot a final scrape. Break the linguine in half and layer in a crisscross fashion so it's mostly submerged in the sauce but *do not stir*. Top with the remaining 2 tablespoons butter. Secure the lid and move the valve to the sealing position, then hit Cancel followed by Manual or Pressure Cook on High Pressure for 6 minutes. Quick release when done and give the pot a good stir. (NOTE: The linguine may be a little clumped together and perhaps a bit al dente but that's how it should be. It will separate and continue to cook as it's stirred.)

4 Hit Cancel followed by Sauté and Adjust so it's on the More or High setting. Add the shrimp and stir with the pasta and remaining broth. Once the shrimp become opaque and curl, 3–5 minutes, add the Parmesan and stir until combined into the sauce. Hit Cancel to turn the pot off. Serve immediately.

To Serve 1–2 Simply halve the recipe. Cook times remain the same.

CATCH
OF THE DAY

The name of this recipe says it all. You can choose virtually any type of fish fillet and then dress it up with any marinade or sauce of your liking. The best part? This fork-tender protein of the sea has just *two* ingredients (because water doesn't count) and *five* minutes of cooking time. While all the recipes in this book are designed to be super simple, this one is arguably the simplest.

Prep Time	Pressure Building Time	Pressure Cook Time	Total Time	Serves
2 MIN	10–15 MIN	5 MIN	20 MIN	4–6

4–6 boneless fish fillets of your choice (see Jeff's Tips), ¼–½ inch thick, fully thawed if frozen

Any store-bought marinade or sauce of your choice (½–1 cup should do the trick), such as:

- *Teriyaki*
- *Lemon pepper*
- *Herb & garlic*
- *Italian*
- *Chimichurri*
- *Sesame ginger*
- *Any sauce from Chapter 1 (page 26)!*

1 Place the trivet in the Instant Pot, handle side up, and pour in 1½ cups water. Place a parchment round on the trivet. Lay the fillets on the parchment, generously brushing the marinade or sauce of your choice on top of each as you stack them in a crisscross fashion (or season lightly with your favorite seasonings for a more subtle flavor).

2 Secure the lid, move the valve to the sealing position, and hit Manual or Pressure Cook at High Pressure for 5 minutes. Quick release when done.

3 Carefully remove the trivet with the fillets and transfer them to a plate (they will be very delicate). Top with additional marinade or sauce, if desired. Goes great with Green Bean Casserole (page 232) or pick a rice from Chapter 4 (page 116).

 JEFF'S TIPS While any of the most common fillets will work here, those that are especially well-adapted are tilapia and salmon. But mahi mahi, cod, haddock, and halibut are also good options. Just make sure the fillets are no thicker than 1/2 inch for them to cook properly.

Speaking of which, if for whatever reason your fish appears a bit underdone after pressure cooking, simply add it back to the pot and give it 1–2 minutes more pressure cook time. It's always wiser to undercook fish at first than to overcook it!

 To Serve 1–2 Use as many fillets as you'll eat. Cook times remain the same. (NOTE: The amount of water added in Step 1 will always be 1½ cups no matter what, as that creates the steam for cooking.)

8

VEGGIES, SIDES & BITES

This chapter focuses on all things sides, snacks, and vegetarian. Some recipes are simple and classic, others a bit over the top and more inventive. Regardless of how fancy the dish, they're all simple crowd-pleasers and take minimal time to prepare (not to mention consume).

A fine-mesh steamer basket works best for some of these recipes; they're easily found (and affordable) online. Just Google "Instant Pot steamer basket."

= DUMP & GO RECIPE

 = 5 INGREDIENTS OR LESS

 = 3 STEPS OR LESS

 = AIR FRYER LID

K = KETO

P = PALEO

 DF = DAIRY-FREE

GF = GLUTEN-FREE

V = VEGETARIAN

 VN = VEGAN

+ = COMPLIANT WITH MODIFICATIONS

DEVILED 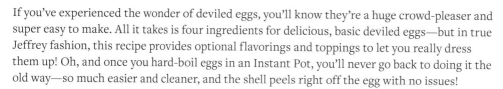 EGGS

If you've experienced the wonder of deviled eggs, you'll know they're a huge crowd-pleaser and super easy to make. All it takes is four ingredients for delicious, basic deviled eggs—but in true Jeffrey fashion, this recipe provides optional flavorings and toppings to let you really dress them up! Oh, and once you hard-boil eggs in an Instant Pot, you'll never go back to doing it the old way—so much easier and cleaner, and the shell peels right off the egg with no issues!

Prep Time	Pressure Building Time	Pressure Cook Time	Natural Release Time	Mixing & Filling Time	Optional Chilling Time	Total Time	Serves
5 MIN	5–10 MIN	5–6 MIN	5 MIN	10 MIN	1 HR	30 MIN	4–6

THE EGGS

6 extra-large or jumbo eggs

¼ cup mayonnaise

⅛–¼ teaspoon seasoned salt or celery salt

A dash of black pepper

OPTIONAL FILLING FLAVORINGS

1–2 tablespoons horseradish (I use Gold's)

1–2 tablespoons bacon bits or crumbles (make sure they're super tiny—chop them super small if need be)

1–2 tablespoons finely chopped dill pickles

1 teaspoon hot sauce

½ teaspoon dried dill

¼ teaspoon mustard powder

¼ teaspoon paprika (smoked or regular)

OPTIONAL TOPPINGS

Bacon crumbles or bits

Grated or finely shredded cheese of your choice

Paprika (smoked or regular), sprinkled

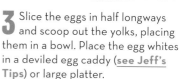

1 Add the trivet to the Instant Pot and pour in 1 cup water. Rest the eggs on top of the trivet. Secure the lid, move the valve to the sealing position, and hit Manual or Pressure Cook on High Pressure for 5 minutes (6 minutes for a slightly firmer yolk). When done, allow a 5-minute natural release followed by a quick release.

2 Carefully place the eggs in an ice-water bath to chill for 90 seconds, then peel them (**see Jeff's Tips**).

3 Slice the eggs in half longways and scoop out the yolks, placing them in a bowl. Place the egg whites in a deviled egg caddy (**see Jeff's Tips**) or large platter.

4 Add the mayo, seasoned salt, and pepper (and any of the optional flavorings) to the bowl with the yolks. Blend together very well with a fork. This will make for smoother piping.

5 Fasten a wide star tip with a frayed design on a piping/frosting bag (this will make it look pretty). Place the bag in a tall drinking glass with the top of the open bag spilling over the sides of the glass and add the yolk filling to the bag. (Alternatively, you can place the filling in a sandwich baggie with one small corner cut off.) Squeeze the mixture into the divot where each egg yolk was. Garnish with any optional toppings of your choice. (NOTE: You can skip the piping altogether and simply spoon the mixture into the egg whites' divots—they just won't look as profesh.)

6 For best results before serving, pop the deviled eggs into the fridge for 1 hour so the filling sets nicely!

JEFF'S TIPS My friend Rachael Ray taught me the best way to peel cold water–shocked hard-boiled eggs: Smash them on the counter and roll them under your palm with a little pressure applied. The shell will be fully cracked and will peel right off!

You can use any fillings and toppings you love. Just make sure the hole in the piping bag (and the tip you use) is wide enough to squeeze everything through so it doesn't clog and then shoot everywhere once pressure is applied.

A deviled egg caddy is so convenient, not only to make sure the deviled eggs don't directly stack on top of each other, but also for transporting!

To Serve 1–2 Halve all of the ingredients. (NOTE: The amount of water added in Step 1 will always be 1 cup no matter what, as that creates the steam for cooking.) Cook time remains the same.

ALIGOT
(CHEESY MASHED POTATOES)

Aligot (pronounced *ahLEE-go*) is a French-style side dish that essentially takes common mashed potatoes to the next level. Actually, it's not just next level, but the cheesiest level you've ever thought your potatoes could be. In fact, it's so cheesy and fondue-like, the potatoes stretch like taffy due to all the cheese combined with the already creamy, buttery starch. When I made this with Rachael Ray on her show, the "WOW!" look on her face said it all. All we could do was laugh because it's that showy and that unreal. I mean, is it potatoes with cheese or cheese with potatoes? Whatever you decide, this should be served with any meat dish that has a succulent gravy to mix in with it, such as my Jewish Short Ribs (page 186) or Mississippi Chicken (page 149).

Prep Time	Pressure Building Time	Pressure Cook Time	Sauté Time	Total Time	Serves
5 MIN	10–15 MIN	8 MIN	5 MIN	30 MIN	4–6

2¼ pounds Yukon Gold or Idaho (russet) potatoes, peeled and quartered

8 tablespoons (1 stick) salted butter, cut into pats

1 cup heavy cream

6 cups (24 ounces) shredded Gruyère/Swiss or mozzarella cheese, or a mix of the two (see Jeff's Tips)

Kosher salt and black pepper, to taste (optional, I used about 1 tablespoon salt and 1 teaspoon black pepper)

1 Pour 1 cup water into the Instant Pot. Place the potatoes in a steamer basket and lower into the pot. (You can also use the trivet, but the basket is easier.) Secure the lid, move the valve to the sealing position, and hit Manual or Pressure Cook on High Pressure for 8 minutes. Quick release when done.

2 Using oven mitts, remove the basket and drain the liner pot. Return the liner pot to the Instant Pot, and add the potatoes back in. Using a potato masher, mash the potatoes right in the pot until most of the big chunks are gone.

3 Hit Cancel followed by Sauté and Adjust so it's on the **Normal or Medium setting.** Add the butter and mix in with the potatoes. Then, pour in the heavy cream and stir until combined.

4 In a couple of batches, add all the shredded cheese and stir in using a silicone spoon. (NOTE: Silicone-coated utensils work best with melty cheese as they won't stick.) Keep stirring constantly and, like magic, you'll see the potatoes begin to take on a stretchy, taffy-like consistency and officially become aligot. As you mix, taste and season as needed with the optional salt and pepper. Keep stirring until it gets nice and hot and super stretchy (about 5 minutes).

5 When done, hit Cancel followed by Keep Warm. Leave the aligot in the pot while serving as the heat is essential to keep that cheesy stretch going; it will firm up if left at room temperature for too long. To that point, once plated, enjoy sooner rather than later for best results.

JEFF'S TIPS I used 4 cups shredded Gruyère/Swiss and 2 cups shredded mozzarella, but you can just as well use Gouda, Cheddar, Colby Jack, Mexican/taco blend, or Monterey Jack. Any melty cheese will do!

If you want your aligot to be a bit creamier, simply add up to another cup of cream in Step 4 when it begins to stretch.

If you *really* want to make these potatoes over the top, add a package of Boursin or ¾ cup Garlic Herb Cheese (page 21) when adding the cheese in Step 4.

To Serve 1–2 Halve all of the ingredients. (NOTE: The amount of water added in Step 1 will always be 1 cup no matter what, as that creates the steam for cooking.) Cook time remains the same.

CACIO E PEPE
BRUSSELS SPROUTS

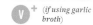

(if using garlic broth)

If you're going to try and feed me Brussels sprouts when raw, you may as well try to figure out how to stop paying taxes: It's never gonna happen. But once those sprouts are pressure cooked in a cheesy, buttery, peppery sauce? You don't have to ask me twice. This is a side dish that I never get bored of. The optional roasted finish, when they become crispy and slightly charred, is worth the extra step. And if you happen to have some creamy salad dressing around, I won't be mad if you drizzle some into the final product for even more joy.

Prep Time	Pressure Building Time	Pressure Cook Time	Sauté Time	Optional Crisping Time	Total Time	Serves
5 MIN	10–15 MIN	1 MIN	2 MIN	10–15 MIN	20 MIN	4–6

2–3 pounds Brussels sprouts, stems trimmed, halved

½ cup chicken or garlic broth (e.g., Garlic Better Than Bouillon)

8 tablespoons (1 stick) salted butter, cut into 8 pats (1 tablespoon each) and divided

½ cup grated Parmesan and/or Pecorino Romano cheeses (see Jeff's Tip)

1 tablespoon freshly cracked pepper (or more or less to taste)

OPTIONAL CREAMY FINISH

Any creamy salad dressing of your choice (such as Caesar, ranch, creamy garlic, creamy Italian, or blue cheese)

JEFF'S TIP I use equal parts Parmesan and Pecorino Romano as that's typical in a cacio e pepe, but you can use one or the other. You can also add more or less cheese to taste.

1 Add the Brussels sprouts, broth, and 4 pats of the butter to the Instant Pot. Secure the lid, move the valve to the sealing position, and hit Manual or Pressure Cook on High Pressure for 1 minute. Quick release when done.

2 Hit Cancel followed by Sauté and Adjust so it's on the More or High setting. Add the remaining 4 pats butter and mix in with the sprouts. Add the cheese and pepper and stir until combined. Hit Cancel to turn the pot off.

To Serve 1–2 Halve all of the ingredients except for the broth—keep it at ½ cup so the pot properly comes to pressure. Cook time remains the same.

4 **For an optional creamy finish:** When ready to serve after Step 2 or 3, stir in the optional dressing of your choice (start with ⅓ cup and add more to taste) or just drizzle some on top of each portion when serving.

3 **For an optional crispy finish:** If you have the Air Fryer Lid, place it on top of the pot and Broil (400°F) for 10–15 minutes, until slightly charred and crispy. Or, you can place the Brussels sprouts on a foil-lined baking sheet and roast in a preheated 400°F oven for 10–15 minutes, until they reach the desired crispness (keep an eye on them as all ovens vary).

GREEN BEAN CASSEROLE

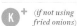 K+ *(if not using fried onions)*

 GF+ *(if not using fried onions)*

 V

A green bean casserole is a classic, beloved side on many holiday tables, and with good reason. It's quick, easy, and so delish. My version doesn't have you using canned soup, which is all too common in this dish; instead, I call for a combo of cream and herb cheese to give it a rich and creamy finish—setting it apart from the rest. Of course, the crispy fried onions are here to stay.

Prep Time 5 MIN	Pressure Building Time 10–15 MIN	Pressure Cook Time 1 MIN	Sauté Time 2 MIN	Optional Crisping Time 5–10 MIN	Total Time 20 MIN	Serves 4–6

4 (14.5-ounce) cans cut and/or French-style green beans, drained, 1 cup of their juices reserved

8 ounces baby bella mushrooms, sliced (optional)

½ cup heavy cream or half-and-half

1 (5.2-ounce) package Boursin cheese (any flavor) or ¾ cup Garlic Herb Cheese (page 21), cut into chunks

2–3 cups shredded mozzarella cheese (see Jeff's Tips)

1 (6-ounce) container French's fried onions

1 Add the green beans and 1 cup juices to the Instant Pot and smooth them out with a mixing spoon/ spatula. (If using the mushrooms, top with them now but *do not stir*.) Secure the lid, move the valve to the sealing position, and hit Manual or Pressure Cook on High Pressure for 1 minute. Quick release when done.

2 Hit Cancel followed by Sauté and Adjust so it's on the More or High setting. Add the cream, Boursin, and mozzarella and stir until fully combined with the green beans.

3 Stir 1–1½ cups of the fried onions into the green beans and dairy. Top with the remaining onions.

JEFF'S TIPS You can certainly use 3–4 pounds of fresh green beans instead of canned—it'll just take a bit longer. Make sure you trim the ends of the beans, add 1 cup of a broth of your choice to account for liquid, and up the pressure cook time to 10 minutes. Everything else remains the same.

Start with 2 cups of the shredded mozzarella in Step 2. If a very thick consistency is your thing, add that third cup.

4 **For an optional crispy finish:** If you have the Air Fryer Lid, before transferring the creamy green beans to a serving dish, place the fried onions on top. Add the Air Fryer Lid and Broil (400°F) for 5–10 minutes, until the onions brown a bit. Or, you can place the beans in a casserole dish, top with the onions, and pop into a preheated 400°F oven for 5–10 minutes, until the onions reach the desired crispness (keep an eye on it as all ovens vary).

To Serve 1–2 Halve all of the ingredients except for the shredded mozzarella and juices from the canned beans—keep it at 1 cup so the pot properly comes to pressure. All cook times remain the same.

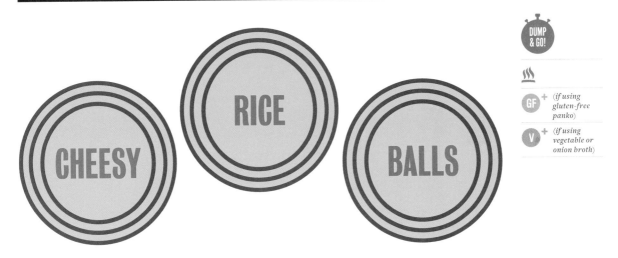

CHEESY RICE BALLS

DUMP & GO!

GF + (if using gluten-free panko)

V + (if using vegetable or onion broth)

Chances are if you're invited over for pizza at an old-school Italian-American Brooklynite home, you're getting rice balls, too. Also known as arancini, these balls of deliciousness are simply creamy cooked-and-cooled risotto rolled into balls, coated in breadcrumbs, and baked or fried. Be sure to dip them into your favorite sauce (see Chapter 1, page 26). These are loaded with cheesy goodness and are sure to please even your friend who hails from Bensonhurst.

Prep Time	Pressure Building Time	Pressure Cook Time	Cooling Time	Crisping Time	Total Time	Serves
10 MIN	10–15 MIN	6 MIN	2 HRS	3–25 MIN	2 HRS 30 MIN–3 HRS	4–6

2 cups arborio rice

5 cups chicken, vegetable, or onion broth (e.g., Sautéed Onion Better Than Bouillon)

1 (5.2-ounce) package Boursin cheese (any flavor) or ¾ cup Garlic Herb Cheese (page 21)

1 cup grated Parmesan cheese, divided, plus more for topping

1 cup panko breadcrumbs

2 teaspoons dried parsley flakes (optional, for color)

½ cup olive oil

1 Add the rice and broth to the Instant Pot and stir. Secure the lid, move the valve to the sealing position, hit Cancel, and then hit Pressure Cook or Manual on High Pressure for 6 minutes. Quick release when done.

2 Stir in the Boursin and ¾ cup of the Parmesan until blended into the rice. Hit Cancel to turn the pot off. Let cool and firm up for 2 hours. (NOTE: To speed this up, cover with foil and place in the fridge.)

3 Meanwhile, place the breadcrumbs, parsley (if using), and remaining ¼ cup Parmesan on a large plate and mix together with a fork until blended.

4 Using clean hands, grab some of the rice mixture and roll it into a ball the size of a plum. Dip the ball in a small bowl of olive oil and lightly rub the oil all over the ball. Then, roll the ball around the plate of seasoned panko until coated. Repeat with remaining rice mixture.

5 Now it's time to get crunchy:

To get crunchy with an Air Fryer Lid: Place a layer of rice balls (about six at a time) directly in the liner pot (no basket required). Place the Air Fryer Lid on top of the pot and Broil (400°F) for 10–20 minutes, until the balls are slightly charred and crispy. (NOTE: You'll need to do this in two batches.)

To get crunchy with an air fryer: Spray the bottom of your air fryer's basket with nonstick cooking spray. Place a layer of rice balls in the basket. Air fry at 400°F for 15–25 minutes, until the balls are slightly charred and crispy. (NOTE: Depending on the size of your air fryer, you may need to do this in more than one batch.)

To get crunchy in the oven: Coat a foil-lined baking sheet with nonstick cooking spray and place the rice balls in a single layer. Roast in a 400°F preheated oven for 10–15 minutes, until they reach the desired crispness (keep an eye on them as all ovens vary).

To get crunchy by deep frying: Add enough vegetable or canola oil to your deep fryer to meet its maximum fill line. Heat the oil to 375°F (usually takes about 20 minutes). One by one, drop in the balls (you should be able to fit about 6 balls in at a time). Fry for 3–5 minutes, until golden. Let drain on a paper towel–lined sheet. Repeat to fry all the balls.

 JEFF'S TIPS If you want these rice balls cheesier, feel free to add up to 2–3 cups shredded mozzarella in Step 2.

The beautiful thing about this recipe is that the rice balls can be made with any risotto and/or their leftovers! Once the risotto you make is fully prepared, let cool as in Step 2 and then pick up with Step 3 to complete the recipe. Try it with Sausage Risotto (page 120).

 To Serve 1–2 Simply halve the recipe. Cook times remain the same.

BUFFALO CAULIFLOWER

BOMB

DUMP & GO! 5 INGR. OR LESS! 3 STEPS OR LESS!

DF GF V

Are you ready for the simplest, most sensational health-ified junk food treat? We're gonna slather a buffalo hot sauce all over a head of cauliflower, pressure cook it to soften it, and then give it a roasted finish by air frying or baking. Of course, if buffalo-style isn't your bag, I've got you covered in Jeff's Tip with suggestions to make it with any flavor you prefer.

Prep Time	Pressure Building Time	Pressure Cook Time	Crisping Time	Total Time	Serves
2 MIN	10–15 MIN	2 MIN	10–20 MIN	35–45 MIN	4–6

1 large head cauliflower, stalk intact but large green leaves removed

1 (12- to 16-ounce bottle) buffalo wing sauce, divided (I use Sweet Baby Ray's)

OPTIONAL SERVING SUGGESTIONS
Blue cheese or ranch dressing
Blue cheese crumbles
Carrot sticks
Celery sticks

1 Add the trivet and 1 cup water to the Instant Pot. Rest the cauliflower on the trivet, stalk side down, giving it a light brushing with the buffalo sauce. (NOTE: You should still have plenty of sauce left after this.) Secure the lid, move the valve to the sealing position, hit Cancel, and then hit Pressure Cook or Manual on High Pressure for 2 minutes. Quick release when done.

2 Roast in one of two ways:
To roast with the Air Fryer Lid: Remove the trivet and, using tongs, carefully place the cauliflower on a plate. Drain the liner pot, pat dry, and return it to the Instant Pot along with the trivet. Carefully use tongs to rest the cauliflower on the trivet. Generously brush most of the remaining sauce on the cauliflower. Place the Air Fryer Lid on top of the pot and Broil (400°F) for 10–15 minutes, until slightly charred and crispy.
To roast in the oven: Coat a foil-lined baking sheet with nonstick cooking spray and place the cauliflower on it, then generously brush on much of the remaining sauce. Roast in a preheated 400°F oven for 15–20 minutes, or until roasted to your desire (keep an eye on it as all ovens vary).

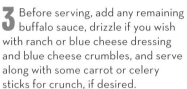

JEFF'S TIP

If you aren't into buffalo sauce, by all means, feel free to make this with any marinade or sauce you desire! Some flavor suggestions: sesame ginger, teriyaki, bourbon, herb and garlic, or BBQ.

To Serve 1–2

Halve all of the ingredients. (NOTE: The amount of water added in Step 1 will always be 1 cup no matter what, as that creates the steam for cooking.) Cook time remains the same.

3 Before serving, add any remaining buffalo sauce, drizzle if you wish with ranch or blue cheese dressing and blue cheese crumbles, and serve along with some carrot or celery sticks for crunch, if desired.

PIEROGI POUTINE

DUMP & GO!

5 INGR. OR LESS!

3 STEPS OR LESS!

V *(if using garlic or onion broth)*

Pierogi is the Polish name for the classic potato- or cheese-filled dumplings that originated in Eastern Europe and are beloved everywhere. On a recent visit to one of my favorite foodie cities, Montreal, I was eating poutine (French fries topped with gravy and cheese) and became inspired to try slathering a bunch of buttery pierogi with a gravy-cheese sauce—and it worked wonders. I give you my take on the ultimate snack, Pierogi Poutine.

Prep Time	Pressure Building Time	Pressure Cook Time	Sauté Time	Optional Baking Time	Total Time	Serves
2 MIN	10–15 MIN	1–3 MIN	2 MIN	3–10 MIN	20 MIN	4–6

2 cups chicken, garlic, or onion broth (e.g., Garlic or Sautéed Onion Better Than Bouillon), **divided (see Jeff's Tip)**

28 ounces frozen or refrigerated pierogi (any flavor)

1 (1-ounce) packet chicken, beef, or brown gravy mix

1 (5.2-ounce) package Boursin cheese (any flavor) or ¾ cup Garlic Herb Cheese (page 21), cut into chunks

2 cups shredded mozzarella cheese or cheese curds, plus more for optional topping

1 Pour 1½ cups of the broth into the Instant Pot. Place the pierogi in a steamer basket and lower into the pot. Secure the lid, move the valve to the sealing position, and hit Manual or Pressure Cook on High Pressure for 1 minute for refrigerated pierogi and 3 minutes for frozen. Quick release when done. Using an oven mitt, remove the steamer basket from the pot, then use tongs to place the pierogi on a serving platter.

2 Hit Cancel followed by Sauté and Adjust so it's on the More or High setting. Add the remaining ½ cup broth (or **see Jeff's Tip**) and the gravy mix, Boursin, and mozzarella. Stir until all the dairy is fully combined into a thick and cheesy gravy.

3 Once thickened, drape the gravy all over the pierogi, top with additional mozzarella if you like, and serve immediately.

4 **For an optional baked finish:** If you have the Air Fryer Lid, return the pierogi to the pot, stir them into the gravy, and place an additional 1–2 cups shredded cheese or cheese curds on top of the pierogi. Add the Air Fryer Lid and Broil (400°F) for 5–10 minutes, until the cheese is bubbly-brown. Or, you can place the pierogi with the gravy in a casserole dish and top with more cheese, then broil in the oven for 3–5 minutes, until the cheese is bubbly-brown (keep an eye on it as all ovens vary).

 For a richer experience, sub in ½ cup heavy cream or half-and-half for the ½ cup broth in Step 2.

 Simply halve the recipe. Cook times remain the same.

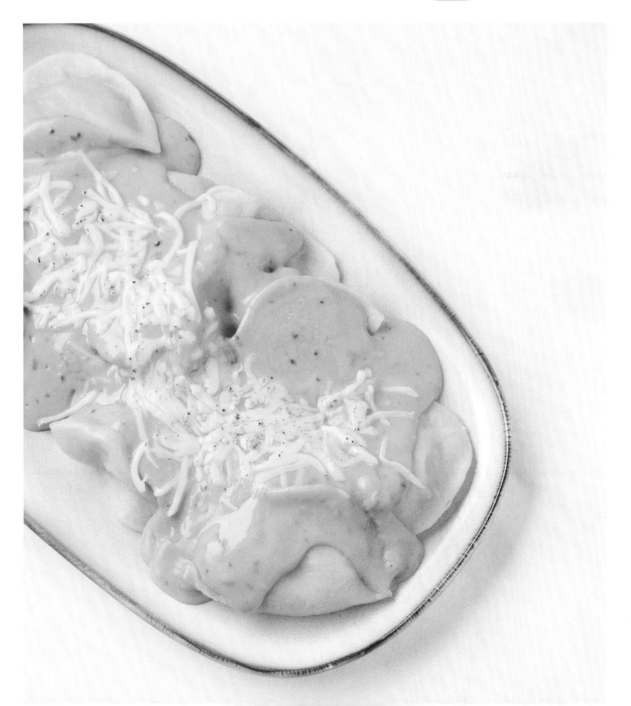

TRUFFLE ·HASH·

3 STEPS OR LESS!

GF

V

I love a potato dish loaded with goodies. This one features tender baby potatoes tossed with a bunch of juicy mushrooms, shallots, and sweet bell peppers. Then, it's finished off with a lovely drizzle of truffle oil. It goes so nicely on top of a thick slice of toasted bread with a runny egg for breakfast, or as a side to a dish such as Chuck & Diane (page 180) for dinner.

Prep Time	Sauté Time	Pressure Building Time	Pressure Cook Time	Total Time	Serves
15 MIN	**15 MIN**	**10–15 MIN**	**10 MIN**	**50 MIN**	**4–6**

- 6 tablespoons (¾ stick) salted butter, divided
- 1½ pounds baby bella mushrooms, sliced or halved
- 2 large shallots, diced

- 2 large green bell peppers, diced
- 3 cloves garlic, minced or pressed
- 1½ pounds baby potatoes (I use a mix of white and red), unpeeled, quartered

- 1 teaspoon garlic salt
- 1 teaspoon Italian seasoning
- 1 teaspoon black pepper
- 2 tablespoons truffle oil (white or black—see Jeff's Tips)

1 Add 4 tablespoons (½ stick) of the butter to the Instant Pot and hit Sauté and Adjust so it's on the More or High setting. Once the butter's melted and bubbling, add the mushrooms, shallots, and peppers. Sauté for 5 minutes, until the mushrooms begin to soften, cook down, and brown. Add the garlic and potatoes and sauté for 2 minutes longer.

2 Transfer the sautéed veggies to a fine-mesh steamer basket (see page 224). Add 1 cup water to the pot and rest the steamer basket in it. Secure the lid and move the valve to the sealing position, then hit Cancel followed by Manual or Pressure Cook on High Pressure for 10 minutes. Quick release when done.

 JEFF'S TIPS You can add more or less truffle oil to taste. Speaking of which, you don't need the fancy stuff. You can get a good one for about $10 a bottle, and it should last you a while.

You can also give this hash a slight crisp by adding the Air Fryer Lid when done with Step 3 and Broil at 400°F for 10–15 minutes, stirring halfway through.

3 Using oven mitts, carefully remove the steamer basket, drain the liner pot, and then return it to the Instant Pot. Add the remaining 2 tablespoons butter to the pot and hit Cancel followed by Sauté and Adjust so it's on the More or High setting. Once the butter's melted, dump the veggies from steamer basket into the pot. Add the garlic salt, Italian seasoning, black pepper, and truffle oil. Stir until combined and sauté for 2 minutes before serving.

 To Serve 1–2 Halve all of the ingredients. (NOTE: The amount of water added in Step 2 will always be 1 cup no matter what, as that creates the steam for cooking.) Cook time remains the same.

SPINACH & ARTICHOKE

 DUMP & GO! 3 STEPS OR LESS!

GF

V⁺ *(if using garlic broth)*

This famous dip needs no introduction. It makes appearances in pubs, restaurants, and living rooms basically everywhere. The one thing I could never get past when making it "the old-fashioned way" was using frozen spinach and having to thaw it and then squeeze out the water before cooking it with the dairy. Using wet, soppy spinach was just never appealing to me. Here, the spinach is fresh and, once pressure cooked to wilted perfection, it sets the stage for the cheesy, creamy finish! This one is truly spectacular.

Prep Time	Pressure Building Time	Pressure Cook Time	Sauté Time	Total Time	Serves
5 MIN	10–15 MIN	2 MIN	5 MIN	25 MIN	4–6

8–10 ounces baby spinach

1 cup chicken or garlic broth (e.g., Garlic Better Than Bouillon)

½ cup Alfredo sauce (I used a roasted garlic flavor—see Jeff's Tips) or Tuscan Sauce (page 38)

½ cup sour cream

½ cup mayonnaise

8-ounce brick cream cheese or 2 (5.2-ounce) packages Boursin cheese or 1½ cups Garlic Herb Cheese (page 21) (see Jeff's Tips), cut into chunks

½ cup grated Parmesan cheese

2 cups shredded mozzarella cheese

1 (14-ounce) can artichoke hearts, drained, then ripped up by hand

1–3 teaspoons garlic powder (optional)

OPTIONS TO SERVE

Hollowed-out sourdough bread bowl (get one from the market or Panera)

Chips/veggies of your choice for dipping

1 Add the spinach to the Instant Pot and pour the broth over it. Secure the lid and move the valve to the sealing position, then hit Manual or Pressure Cook on High Pressure for 2 minutes. Quick release when done.

2 The spinach will have wilted significantly so give it a good stir. Hit Cancel followed by Sauté and Adjust so it's on the More or High setting. Add the Alfredo, sour cream, mayonnaise, cream cheese or Boursin, Parmesan, and mozzarella and stir until blended. This will take a good 3–5 minutes of stirring.

3 Once all the dairy has blended into the spinach, add the artichokes and garlic powder (if using—start with 1 teaspoon and add more to taste). Transfer to a serving bowl or hollowed-out sourdough bread bowl and serve with chips and/or veggies.

JEFF'S TIPS

I personally feel that including Alfredo sauce sets this dip apart from the rest. But if you want to save on an ingredient, omit the Alfredo and increase the sour cream and mayo to ¾ cup each (instead of just ½ cup).

If you want some variety, instead of cream cheese or Boursin, use both! But then use just 4 ounces cream cheese and 1 package Boursin.

If you really love artichokes, add more—up to an entire second can. And if you aren't into them, leave them out (but re-name it Creamy Spinach Dip... or something).

To Serve 1–2 Halve all of the ingredients, except for the broth—keep it at 1 cup so the pot properly comes to pressure. Cook times remain the same.

SPAGHETTI SQUASH

MARINARA

K
P
DF
GF
VN

The thing I love about spaghetti squash is not only how lightning quick it is to prepare under pressure, but that it's also a fabulous, low-carb, and yet slightly sweeter alternative to actual spaghetti. This recipe only requires two ingredients to get a tasty, nutritious, and speedy meal on the table in no time.

Prep Time	Pressure Building Time	Pressure Cook Time	Sauté Time	Total Time	Serves
3 MIN	10–15 MIN	6 MIN	5 MIN	25 MIN	4–6

1 (3- to 4-pound) spaghetti squash, halved, seeds scooped out

1–2 cups marinara sauce (I like the Rao's and Victoria brands, but you can also use my Classic Red Sauce, page 28), preferably at room temperature

1 Place the trivet in the Instant Pot and pour in 1 cup water. Place the squash halves on the trivet, skin side down. Secure the lid and move the valve to the sealing position, then hit Manual or Pressure Cook on High Pressure for 6 minutes. Quick release when done.

2 Carefully remove the squash from the Instant Pot and use a fork to rake through the softened squash meat and shred it into spaghetti. Drain the water from the liner pot and return the liner to the Instant Pot.

3 Add the sauce to the Instant Pot and hit Sauté, adjusting to the More or High setting. Once the sauce is bubbling, add the shredded spaghetti and stir to coat with the sauce. Serve topped however you wish (grated Parmesan, fresh or dried oregano, etc.).

JEFF'S TIP Don't feel like using a red sauce? Use any prepared sauce from the sauce chapter (page 26). Now it's Spaghetti Squash du Jour!

To Serve 1–2 Halve all of the ingredients. (NOTE: The amount of water added in Step 1 will always be 1 cup no matter what, as that creates the steam for cooking.) Cook time remains the same.

MAGICAL MACARONI SALAD

DUMP & GO!

V + *(if using garlic broth and if you're okay with Worcestershire sauce)*

My favorite side dish at any summer event is macaroni salad, but the thing that just about kills it for me is when there's too much of a vinegary aftertaste. That's not going to happen here. This macaroni salad is already easy to make, but to keep things extra simple and customizable, I give you full control over what goodies you want to toss in to make it just the way you like it!

Prep Time 10 MIN	Pressure Building Time 10–15 MIN	Pressure Cook Time 6 MIN	Chilling Time 3–4 HRS	Total Time 30 MIN (3½–4½ HRS WITH CHILLING TIME)	Serves 4–6

1 pound elbow macaroni

2½ cups chicken or garlic broth (e.g., Garlic Better Than Bouillon)

1½ cups mayonnaise

½ cup sour cream

⅓ cup whole milk

2 tablespoons white vinegar

2 teaspoons Worcestershire sauce

1 (15-ounce) jar Miracle Whip (or see Jeff's Tips)

OPTIONAL MIX-INS

1 (16-ounce) jar bread and butter or dill pickles, drained (with ¼ cup of the juices reserved) and diced

1 (10-ounce) jar sweet relish

1 (6-ounce) can pitted black olives, drained and diced

1 bunch scallions, chopped

1 large bell pepper (any color), seeded and diced

1 (10-ounce) bag shredded carrots

2–3 ribs celery, diced

8 ounces Colby Jack (or any) cheese, diced

½ pound ham (any kind), sliced ½ inch thick by the deli, diced

Kosher salt and black pepper to taste (celery salt is a nice touch here)

1 Add the macaroni and broth to the Instant Pot (it's fine if some of the pasta isn't fully covered). Secure the lid and move the valve to the sealing position, then hit Manual or Pressure Cook on High Pressure for 6 minutes. Quick release when done.

2 Stir the pasta (it may appear a bit clumped but this will change when mixed in Step 4). Remove the liner pot and place on a trivet on the counter to rest until the pasta cools, about 10 minutes.

3 Meanwhile, prepare the dressing in a very large mixing bowl by combining the mayo, sour cream, milk, vinegar, Worcestershire sauce, and pickle juice (if using). Mix together well.

4 If any broth is left (there probably won't be), drain the macaroni in a colander. Then, add the macaroni to the dressing bowl. Mix together well, until the macaroni is coated with dressing and becomes unclumped. (NOTE: The dressing may seem thin now, but it will mostly get absorbed by the pasta in Step 5.) If you want to add any of the optional toppings (and you should), do that now and mix until coated and mixed with the macaroni and dressing.

5 Refrigerate the macaroni salad for 3–4 hours so it really sets. (NOTE: For best results, it's probably best to either make this first thing in the morning for an afternoon/evening meal or before bed and let it sit in the fridge overnight.)

6 When ready to serve, take the macaroni out of the fridge and mix in the Miracle Whip. Taste it and decide if you wish to add salt or pepper before serving.

JEFF'S TIPS Not a fan of Miracle Whip? Instead of the final toss with it, feel free to just add an additional 1 cup mayo and another ½ cup sour cream with 1 tablespoon granulated sugar.

The beautiful thing about macaroni salad is you can add whatever veggies/items you see fit! The choice is totally yours but I *do* highly recommend using the pickles with a splash of some pickle juice—it really sets it apart!

I also suggest you leave the liquids/mayo/sour cream/Miracle Whip exactly as I've listed as this will give you the perfect macaroni salad consistency without that bitter vinegar aftertaste!

To Serve 1–2 Simply halve the recipe. Cook times remain the same.

⑨

DESSERT

This book ain't over 'til dessert is served. These decadent yet simple sweet endings (or snacks for any time of day—breakfast counts) are sure to not only please those you serve them to, but boost your sense of accomplishment as well.

Sweet treats have never been tastier (or easier), but these treasures come with a warning: They may leave you wanting more. A silicone sling (page 20) is going to come in very handy in this chapter.

NOTE: I largely left instructions for halving these recipes out as it's harder to pull off. Plus, you'll almost always regret not having made the full amount!

= DUMP & GO RECIPE

 = 5 INGREDIENTS OR LESS

 = 3 STEPS OR LESS

 = AIR FRYER LID

K = KETO

P = PALEO

 DF = DAIRY-FREE

 GF = GLUTEN-FREE

V = VEGETARIAN

 **VN** = VEGAN

+ = COMPLIANT WITH MODIFICATIONS

THE DEEP-DISH CHOCOLATE CHIP COOKIE

A visit to Chicago inspired me to make this outrageous dessert. Seeing how deep-dish pizza can be found every which way you turn there, can you blame me? We're talking a chocolate chip cookie that's more a brownie/blondie/cake than a cookie. And if you take it to the next level by scooping your favorite ice cream on top of a slice and adding a luscious topping to make the ultimate sundae? See you in the morning.

DUMP & GO!

V

Prep Time	Pressure Building Time	Pressure Cook Time	Natural Release Time	Cooling Time	Total Time	Serves
10 MIN	10–15 MIN	40 MIN	10 MIN	15 MIN	1 HR 25 MIN	4–8

8 tablespoons (1 stick) salted butter, softened (see Jeff's Tips)

¼ cup plus 2 tablespoons white sugar

¼ cup plus 2 tablespoons tightly packed light brown sugar

½ teaspoon salt

½ teaspoon baking soda

1 teaspoon vanilla extract

1½ teaspoons pure maple syrup (optional)

1 large egg

1 cup plus 2 tablespoons all-purpose flour (no need to sift)

6 ounces (approximately 1 cup) chocolate chips of your choice (see Jeff's Tips)

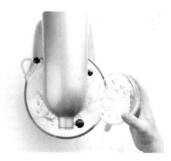

1 Add the softened butter to a stand mixer with the paddle attached (or a large bowl if using a good hand mixer). Lower the paddle into the bowl, lock it, and place on the lowest speed setting (stir setting) for about 5 seconds; then work your way to speeds 2 and then 4 until the butter is totally creamed. This whole mixing process should only take between 10 and 15 seconds. Unlock the stand mixer, lift the head, and use a rubber spatula to push any of the butter from the paddle into the bowl.

2 Next, add both sugars, the salt, baking soda, vanilla, and maple syrup (if using) to the bowl. Lower the paddle back into the bowl, lock it, and mix everything for another 20 seconds on speed 2. As it's mixing, add the egg and mix together for another 20 seconds. Unlock the stand mixer, lift the head, and use a rubber spatula to push any of the batter from the paddle to the bowl.

3 Lower the paddle back into the bowl and lock it. Go to the lowest speed and add half the flour. (NOTE: You must keep it on the lowest speed when adding flour or it will go all over the place.) Once the flour is fully incorporated, add the rest of the flour and mix until fully combined. Once it is, up the speed to 2 for 10 seconds. Unlock the stand mixer, lift the head, remove the paddle, and use a rubber spatula to push any of the dough from the paddle to the bowl.

CONTINUES

4 With a spatula, mix the chocolate chips into the thick cookie dough until fully combined and evenly dispersed.

5 Use nonstick spray or butter to grease the bottom and sides of a 7x3-inch springform pan (it must be this exact size and it must be springform). Lay in a 7-inch round of parchment and grease that too. Place the cookie dough in the prepared pan and press it down so it's as even as possible (it doesn't have to be perfect). Loosely cover the pan with foil.

6 Add 1½ cups water to the Instant Pot. Place the springform pan in a silicone sling and lower into the pot (you can also use a trivet). Secure the lid, move the valve to the sealing position, and hit Manual or Pressure Cook at High Pressure for 40 minutes. When done, allow a 10-minute natural release followed by a quick release. Using oven mitts, carefully remove the pan from the Instant Pot and let cool on the counter for 15 minutes.

7 When ready to serve, carefully open the springform latch and remove the sides of the pan. Slice the cookie as you would a cake and serve as is, or check out Jeff's Tips to make the ultimate sundae!

JEFF'S TIPS

I prefer salted butter over unsalted for better flavor. And the butter *must* be softened, which you can achieve by setting out at room temperature for a few hours or by placing the cold, firm butter in the microwave for 10–15 seconds tops—don't let it melt!

I used semi-sweet morsels, but you can use milk chocolate chips or white chocolate chips, or go for toffee chips, peanut butter chips, walnuts, M&Ms, etc.—however you choose to mix and match, 6 ounces should be the max.

To make it the ultimate deep-dish cookie sundae, top with vanilla ice cream (or your favorite flavor) and any other toppings of your choice (whipped cream, hot fudge, cherries, nuts, sprinkles, cherries—the sky's the limit!).

Leftovers store well in an airtight container. If you want it a little warmed up, zap a slice in the microwave for **only** 5–10 seconds (it could burn otherwise due to the high flour and sugar content).

To Serve 1–2

Just invite Cookie Monster over. He'll finish it if you won't.

CROISSANT PUDDING
· WITH WHISKEY GLAZE ·

Once while on a blissful trip to Costco, I came across their amazing croissants, which are sold by the dozen. I didn't know why I'd need that many and then it hit me: "I'm gonna make a serious bread, no—*croissant* pudding with you," I said. After which I grabbed a bottle of whiskey and some confectioners' sugar, and gave that pudding a sweet icing glaze that worked wonders. Now, although this ingredient list may seem longer than most in this book, don't be fooled. The glaze repeats a few ingredients used in the bread pudding itself.

Prep Time	Sauté Time	Resting Time	Chilling Time	Pressure Building Time	Pressure Cook Time	Cooling Time	Total Time	Serves
10 MIN	3–5 MIN	15–20 MIN	1 HR	10–15 MIN	25 MIN	15 MIN	2 HRS 20 MIN	4–8

THE CROISSANT PUDDING
2 tablespoons (¼ stick) salted butter, plus more for greasing

2 cups whole milk

3 tablespoons white sugar

3 tablespoons light brown sugar

1½ teaspoons vanilla extract

3 large eggs, beaten

¼ teaspoon ground cinnamon

6 cups cubed croissants or challah or brioche (I used 6 croissants from Costco that come in packs of 12)

THE WHISKEY GLAZE
2 cups confectioners' (powdered) sugar

2 tablespoons (¼ stick) salted butter, melted

3 tablespoons whole milk, half-and-half, or heavy cream

1 tablespoon whiskey (see Jeff's Tips)

1 teaspoon vanilla extract

1 Add the butter to the Instant Pot and hit Sauté and Adjust so it's on the **Normal or Medium setting.** When the butter is melted, add the milk, white and brown sugars, and vanilla extract. Stir together for just a few moments until warmed, about 3 minutes. (NOTE: Do *not* let the milk bubble—we want it just warm enough so that everything comes together easily.)

2 Hit Cancel to turn off the pot and remove the liner pot to sit on a protected countertop surface until cool, 15–20 minutes. (Or pop in the fridge to speed up the cooling if you have the space.) The mixture *must* be cooled before we add the eggs or they will cook from the heat and we definitely don't want that! Once the mixture is cool to the touch, add the eggs and cinnamon and whisk together to form our custard.

3 Place the cubed croissant in a large mixing bowl and pour the custard over it. Mix together well so that all of the croissant is sopping up the custard. Pop in the fridge for 1 hour to fully cool and set. Clean out the liner pot and then return to the Instant Pot.

CONTINUES

4 Spray a 6-cup Bundt pan with nonstick cooking spray—don't forget the center. Once the custard-soaked bread cubes are cool, transfer them to the Bundt pan and distribute evenly, packing it all into the pan. Cover the pan with foil and poke a hole through the center of the Bundt for the steam to easily circulate.

5 Pour 1½ cups water in the Instant Pot. Place the Bundt pan in a silicone sling (or on the trivet) and lower into the pot. Secure the lid, move the valve to the sealing position, and hit Manual or Pressure Cook on High Pressure for 25 minutes. Quick release when done.

6 Meanwhile, in a separate bowl, whisk together all of the whiskey glaze ingredients. Set aside.

7 Use oven mitts to carefully remove the pan from the Instant Pot and let cool on the counter for 15 minutes. Place a plate larger than the Bundt's diameter over the top of the Bundt, hold together securely, and quickly flip upside down. Gently tap with a mixing spoon so the bread pudding easily slides out onto the plate. (NOTE: If the croissant pudding has issues coming out of the pan, gently wedge a silicone spatula in between the pudding and along the sides of the pan. Then, gently move the spatula all the way around the pan to help ensure it loosens.)

8 Take the whiskey glaze and pour it over the croissant pudding, icing it along the sides. Cut a slice and serve alongside a nice hot cup of coffee, tea, or cocoa!

 JEFF'S TIPS If you don't want whiskey in your glaze, simply leave it out! And if you want a more sugary, flavored glaze, such as with honey or peanut butter, use that instead of the confectioners' sugar.

I think the glaze's consistency is perfect as written, but you can make it thinner or thicker to your liking. The more milk/cream you add to the glaze, the thinner it will be. The more powdered sugar, the thicker!

This also makes a lot of glaze (because I love it so much and also love dunking the croissant pudding into it). But you can totally halve it if you wish by simply halving the whiskey glaze ingredients.

 To Serve 1–2 Save half for you and give the other half to your favorite delivery driver.

PINEAPPLE UPSIDE-DOWN CAKE

DUMP & GO!

V

Get ready to turn your world upside down (but, like, in a delicious way). Pineapple upside-down cake was a huge hit in the '70s and it's making a comeback today. This cake is moist, densely loaded with pineapple, and infused with the most amazing juicy, brown-sugar glaze on top...or is that the bottom?

Prep Time	Pressure Building Time	Pressure Cook Time	Natural Release Time	Total Time	Serves
5 MIN	10–15 MIN	50 MIN	30 MIN	1 HR 35 MIN	4–8

- 1 (15.25-ounce) box pineapple cake mix (I use Duncan Hines Pineapple Supreme)
- 1 (3.4-ounce) packet Jell-O Vanilla Instant Pudding Mix (make sure it's "Instant")
- 3 large eggs

- ½ cup canola oil (vegetable oil is fine too but I suggest canola for this)
- ¼ cup seltzer
- 1 (20-ounce) can pineapple rings, all the syrup or juice from the can reserved

- 6 tablespoons (¾ stick) salted butter
- ¾ cup packed dark brown sugar
- Maraschino cherries, stems removed

1 In a stand mixer or in a mixing bowl using a hand mixer, combine the cake mix, pudding mix, eggs, oil, seltzer, and the juice or syrup from the pineapple (but not the pineapple itself). Blend well until all of the lumps are out and it's nice and smooth. Set aside.

2 Place the butter in a bowl and melt in the microwave for 1 minute. Add the brown sugar and mix together well.

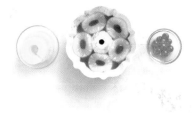

3 Lightly spray a 6-cup Bundt pan with nonstick cooking spray along the bottom and all sides (don't forget the center). Pour the buttery brown sugar mixture into the pan so that it coats the entire bottom. Lay in five pineapple rings and put a cherry in the hole of each, then fill in any other spaces with more cherries.

4 Pour in the batter until it's about ¼ inch under the rim of the pan (it's fine if you have batter left over), cover the pan with foil, and use your finger to poke a hole through the center of the Bundt pan for the steam to easily circulate.

5 Add 1½ cups water to the Instant Pot. Place the Bundt in a silicone sling and lower into the pot (you can also use the trivet). Secure the lid, move the valve to the sealing position, and hit Manual or Pressure Cook on High Pressure for 50 minutes. Allow a 30-minute natural release followed by a quick release.

6 Use oven mitts to carefully remove the pan from the Instant Pot and let cool for about 5 minutes. Remove the foil, place a plate larger than the pan's diameter over the top, hold together securely, and quickly flip upside down. The cake will simply slide right out of the pan and transfer beautifully to the plate. Check out **Jeff's Tip** and serve.

JEFF'S TIP You can have a slice as soon as it comes out of the pan (because, let's face it, you're not going to be able to wait). But if you keep it at room temperature for a while the cake will begin to soak in that incredible brown butter sauce and the experience will be taken to the next level! Cover leftovers in a cake caddy or an airtight container.

To Serve 1–2 Eat one slice today and two more tomorrow. And give any leftovers (yeah, right) to someone you love. There, it's halved.

LAVA CAKES

Lava cakes from the Instant Pot have become quite a popular dessert, with many iterations out there, so this ain't the first and certainly won't be the last! And it makes sense: With just a few basic ingredients, you can make four individual soufflé-like, volcano-shaped cakes that, once you pierce the cake part, produce a flowing river of sweet, decadent (not too hot) lava that will trigger a major "oooh" factor. This recipe lets you customize your lava cakes' flavor by giving a choice of any type of meltable morsel you desire (see Jeff's Tips). Having four 6-ounce oven-safe ramekins is key to making this edible volcano erupt. Serve with ice cream and any other toppings you wish!

Prep Time	Pressure Building Time	Pressure Cook Time	Total Time	Serves
10 MIN	10–15 MIN	8–10 MIN	30 MIN	4

4 large eggs

1 cup confectioners' (powdered) sugar

2 tablespoons heavy cream

8 tablespoons (1 stick) salted butter

1 cup morsels/chocolate chips of your choice (see Jeff's Tips)

1/3 cup all-purpose flour

1/8 teaspoon salt

OPTIONAL TOPPINGS
Confectioners' (powdered) sugar, for dusting

Scooped ice cream of your choice

Any ice cream toppings you love (such as hot fudge, caramel, Magic Shell, whipped cream, sprinkles, and, of course, cherries!)

1 In a large bowl, whisk together the eggs, sugar, and cream. Set aside.

2 Place the butter and morsels in a large microwave-safe bowl. Microwave in four 30-second intervals (2 minutes total), stirring at each break. Once fully melted into sweet, buttery amazingness, pour the egg and sugar mixture into the chocolate mixture. Whisk until combined.

3 Add the flour and salt. Whisk until everything is fully incorporated.

4 Spray four 6-ounce glass or ceramic ramekins (Pyrex is best) with nonstick cooking spray. Evenly distribute the batter between the ramekins.

5 Add the trivet to the Instant Pot and pour in 1 cup water. Set three of the ramekins on top of the trivet and rest the fourth on top of the center of the three below it. (There's no need to cover them with foil.) Secure the lid, move the valve to the sealing position, and hit Manual or Pressure Cook on High Pressure for 8 minutes for runnier cakes, or 10 minutes for firmer (9 minutes is a happy medium). Quick release when done.

6 Use oven mitts and tongs to carefully remove the ramekins from the trivet. Carefully place a plate on top of each ramekin and then quickly flip it so the lava cake slides right onto the plate! Top with any of the optional suggestions, if desired, and dig in immediately!

JEFF'S TIPS The go-to lava element for this is semi-sweet chocolate chips/morsels. But you can absolutely use any kind of meltable morsel/chip out there, be it peanut butter, dark chocolate, milk chocolate, white chocolate, or butterscotch. You can also mix them up! Whatever you go for, just make sure you use 1 cup total.

To make these lava cakes red velvet–style, for the chocolate, use 1/2 cup semi-sweet chips/morsels and 1/2 cup white chocolate chips/morsels in Step 2. Then, add 1 teaspoon red food coloring in Step 3. Everything else in the recipe remains the same.

To Serve 1–2 Okay, *this* dessert recipe you can halve. (NOTE: The amount of water added in Step 5 will always be 1 cup no matter what, as that creates the steam for cooking.) Same cook times.

 # JAM TODAY

 DUMP & GO!   5 INGR. OR LESS!

 DF

 GF

 V

I was recently watching that trippy *Alice in Wonderland* from the '80s featuring all those stars of yesteryear. The one scene that stood out is when Carol Channing, as the iconic White Queen, turns into a sheep. It may have been nightmare fuel as a child (and fever-dreamish as an adult), but before she goes baa-baa, she sings a song about jam and how you can have it tomorrow or yesterday but never (ever) jam today. Now I love me some Carol Channing, but we're going to prove her wrong by not only making jam today, but by making it with only five ingredients and any berry you choose—be it strawberry, blueberries, or raaaaaaaaspberries!

Prep Time 10 MIN	Resting Time 10–15 MIN	Pressure Building Time 10–15 MIN	Pressure Cook Time 1 MIN	Natural Release Time 10 MIN	Sauté Time 5 MIN	Chilling Time 4–8 HRS	Total Time 50 MIN (5 TO 9 HRS WITH COOLING TIME)	Serves 4–6

2 pounds any berry you want, stems removed (NOTE: If using strawberries, halve them as well.)

1 cup white sugar

Juice of 1 lemon

1 teaspoon vanilla extract

3 tablespoons cornstarch plus 3 tablespoons cold water

1 Add the berries, sugar, lemon juice, and vanilla to the Instant Pot and stir until the berries are coated. Let rest for 10–15 minutes so the sugar draws the juice out from the berries, creating the liquid needed for the pot to come to pressure. Secure the lid, move the valve to the sealing position, and hit Manual or Pressure Cook on High Pressure for 1 minute. When done, allow a 10-minute natural release followed by a quick release.

2 Meanwhile, in a bowl, combine the cornstarch and cold water until a slurry forms.

3 Once the lid comes off the pot, stir the mixture—the berries will be a perfect, softened consistency. Now, to thicken into jam! Hit Cancel followed by Sauté and Adjust so it's on the More or High setting. Once bubbling, stir in the cornstarch slurry and let bubble for 2 minutes, until thickened into a jam-like consistency. Hit Cancel to turn the pot off.

4 Transfer the jam to mason jars (I use 4- and 8-ounce sizes) and let rest *uncovered* for 15 minutes. Then, place a lid on top of each jar and pop in the fridge to cool completely (another 4–8 hours—overnight is best). When ready to serve, spread it on biscuits, scones, toast, muffins, you name it!

JEFF'S TIPS

We don't need pectin to make this jam because the cornstarch slurry does the trick!

If using frozen berries, rinse them under a colander so they thaw out before pressure cooking. However, you may need an immersion blender in the beginning of Step 3 to mix the jam.

This jam will last in the fridge for up to 2 weeks and can be frozen for up to 6 months.

To Serve 1–2

Just follow the recipe as is. One can never have too much jam on hand!

· COOKIES & CREAM ·
CHEESECAKE

I can never turn down an Oreo cheesecake—so I'm glad I finally get to put mine in a book. Since there are about a bajillion Oreo flavors nowadays, you can get really creative with this one. Use any flavor you choose to make this ultimate cheesecake match your mood and personality. You'll see a bunch of the ingredients call for being at room temperature. Don't overlook this (see Jeff's Tips for why).

Prep Time 10 MIN	Pressure Building Time 10–15 MIN	Pressure Cook Time 40 MIN	Natural Release Time 30 MIN	Resting Time 30 MIN	Chilling Time 5 HRS	Total Time 1 HR 30 MIN (7 HRS WITH RESTING/ CHILLING TIME)	Serves 4–8

1 (14.3-ounce) package Oreo cookies (see Jeff's Tips)

4 tablespoons (½ stick) salted butter, melted, plus more for greasing

2 (8-ounce) bricks cream cheese, at room temperature

⅔ cup white sugar

¼ cup sour cream, at room temperature

¼ cup heavy cream, at room temperature

2 tablespoons all-purpose flour

2 large eggs, at room temperature

1 Generously grease a 7x3-inch springform pan all over with butter. Line the bottom with a 7-inch round of parchment paper and grease the parchment as well.

2 To make the crust, blitz 16 Oreos (with the cream still in the middle, of course) in a food processor; or place in a freezer bag and crush with a mallet or rolling pin. Place the crushed Oreos in a bowl with the melted butter and mix with a fork until combined. Dump the mixture into the greased pan and, using the bottom of a drinking glass, flatten the crumbs to form a crust that is even on the bottom and slightly climbs up the sides of the pan. Pop in the freezer for at least 15 minutes to set.

3 Using a stand mixer with the paddle attached (a hand mixer won't do for this), lower the paddle into the bowl and lock it. Add the cream cheese and beat on low until smooth and creamy. While the mixer is still running, add in this order: the sugar, sour cream, heavy cream, flour, and eggs (one at a time). Keep mixing on low speed until super thick and creamy and no lumps remain. Lift the paddle and stir in 8 more Oreos that have been lightly broken up or smashed.

4 Take the pan out of the freezer and pour/spoon in the batter, leaving about ½ inch room from the brim of the pan. Smooth the top with a spatula and cover the pan with foil.

5 Add 2 cups water to the Instant Pot. Place the pan in a silicone sling (or on the trivet) and lower into the pot. Secure the lid, move the valve to the sealing position, and hit Manual or Pressure Cook at High Pressure for 40 minutes. When done, allow a 30-minute natural release followed by a quick release. Using oven mitts, carefully remove the pan from the Instant Pot and remove the foil (the cake should be slightly jiggly). Let rest in the sling or on the trivet on the counter for 30 minutes. Then, place in the fridge, still in the springform pan, and chill for *at least* 5 hours before serving. This will ensure it firms up.

6 When ready to serve, use a sharp knife to separate the cake edges from the pan sides and slowly unlatch and remove the sides of the pan.

To Serve 1–2 Come on. Watch a few episodes of *The Golden Girls* and the next thing you know, this cheesecake will have vanished.

7 Top with 6–10 additional Oreos that are a mix of halved, crumbled, and crushed (for variety) and serve with a glass of cold milk!

JEFF'S TIPS Notice this recipe doesn't require vanilla extract? It's definitely not necessary and allows the cookies & cream flavor to really shine! But if you're a purist, feel free to add 1 teaspoon in Step 3 after the eggs.

Like I said in the headnote, use any Oreo flavor you desire. Or mix it up so you use different ones for the crust, filling, and topping. Just make sure you use the regular size and not the double- or mega-stuffed for the crust as that can throw things off.

The cream cheese, sour cream, and eggs must be at room temperature so that they blend into a batter properly. If they're too firm, it's gonna make for a sad cheesecake. Two hours on the counter should do the trick.

Here's a little bonus for you in case you wanted to know how to use your pot with a bit more detail than shown in the graphic on page 11.

1. PLOT THE POT. Always make sure the removable

stainless steel liner pot is resting in the Instant Pot prior to cooking. If it isn't and you add food or liquid, it's going to go directly on the heating element and seep out the bottom, and that's not good. Also, *never* place your Instant Pot directly on a stovetop: if you accidentally turn it on or place the pot on a still-hot burner, the plastic bottom will melt.

2. PLUG AND PLAY. When the Instant Pot is first plugged

in (if the cord on your model is detachable, make sure it's firmly plugged into both the pot and the outlet), the display will read Off. So even though the screen is *on* and the device is now powered, the cooking element itself is *off*.

3. SAUTÉ AWAY. One of the most brilliant things about the Instant Pot is that you can sauté directly in the pot before pressure cooking, treating it as if it's a pot or pan on the stove. If a recipe calls for it (and many do), hit the Sauté button, then adjust the temperature to the More or High setting (which is what the recipes in this book call for most of the time). To adjust the temperature settings: If your model has an Adjust or

arrow button, hit that one; if it doesn't, hit the Sauté button again to adjust the temperature to either Less/Low, Normal/Medium, or More/High. If your model has only buttons, once you hit Sauté it will say On after a few moments and begin to heat up. If it has a knob or a Start button, hit that button to begin the process.

4. SWITCH GEARS. When done sautéing, hit the Cancel or the Keep Warm/Cancel button, depending on your model. Think of this as the Home button on a smartphone. This will make sure your pot is back in the Off position so you can then select a different function.

5. PUT A LID ON IT. The gasket (the silicone ring under the lid) is the key to the Instant Pot sealing properly. Before pressure cooking, make sure the gasket is firmly in the metal grooves or it will not come to pressure and steam may escape from the sides. Once all is good, secure the lid by locking it into place. Make sure the valve is moved from the venting position to the sealing position. Some models automatically seal the pot for you once the lid is secured, but other models require you to do this manually.

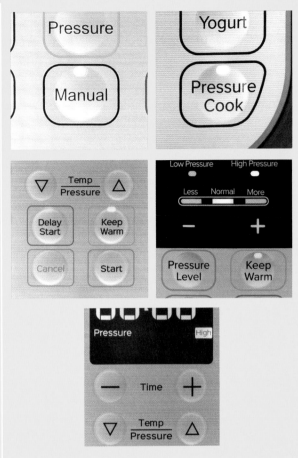

6. PRESSURE LUCK. Depending on your model, hit either the Manual or Pressure Cook button (different from the Pressure Level button if your model has one). Then, to adjust the time, use the +/- buttons or knob (if yours has one) to go up or down in time. If your Instant Pot model has only buttons, it will say On within a few moments of hitting the Manual or Pressure Cook button and begin to heat. If it has a knob or a Start button, you'll need to hit that button to begin the process. So when reading the instructions for each recipe, make sure you hit that Start button as well, should your model have one. Additionally, upon starting a pressure cooking cycle, check that the Keep Warm button is lit, as this means the pot will switch to keeping your food warm once the pressure cooking cycle is complete.

When the pot is On, that means it's building pressure. The higher the volume of ingredients in the pot, the longer it will take to come to pressure (I've specified the pressure building time for each recipe). Once there is enough steam built up inside the pot, the little metal pin in the lid will pop up, locking the lid. From there, a few moments (or minutes) later the display will shortly begin to count down from the pressure cook time you set it for. When finished, and if the Keep Warm button is lit when you set the pressure cook time, the pot will read 00:00 or L0:00 depending on your model, and then will begin to count up, showing how much time has elapsed since the pressure cooking cycle was completed. This comes in handy for measuring the time if a recipe calls for a natural release. Speaking of which...

7. RELEASE WITH PEACE. You've reached the final step in the pressure cooking process—releasing the steam! We use two ways to release the steam from the pot in this book:

Quick release. Once the pressure cooking is complete, move the valve or press the button/slide the switch to the venting position and the steam will release. Just be careful not to have your hand directly over the valve while this happens or you could be in for a quick singe. When all the steam is released, the pin will drop, unlocking the lid for safe removal.

Natural release. Once the pressure cooking cycle is complete, let the pot sit, undisturbed, for the specified amount of time so the steam dissipates on its own. For example, if the recipe calls for a 5-minute natural release, do nothing until the display reads L0:05 or 00:05, depending on your model. After that, finish with a quick release. If a recipe calls for a full natural release, it means you do nothing until the pin in the lid drops and the lid can be opened. This can take anywhere from 5 to 45 minutes depending on the volume of food in the pot.

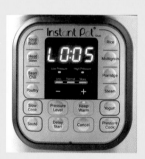 

NOTE While this is unlikely to happen with my recipes, if for whatever reason the valve begins to spit out some liquid while releasing due perhaps to altitude or another factor, either throw a dish towel over it or allow a full natural release. But make sure to never allow a full natural release for pasta or rice, as they will overcook.

8. TRY AN AIR FRY. One of the most genius things about the Instant Pot is that you can swap lids and transform it into an air fryer. A few recipes in this book call for that option and when they do, I provide clear instructions on just how to use it.

Whether you buy a stand-alone Air Fryer Lid (currently for 6-quart only) or the Duo Crisp or Duo Pro models (6- or 8-quart), they all come with a resting disk to place the hot lid on once you're done cooking. When not using, flip the disk over and, once the Air Fryer Lid is cooled, you can lock the open end of your lid with the bottom of the disk for easy storing and protection of the heating element.

Alternatively, if you don't have an Air Fryer Lid, you can use your oven for a crispy finish; simply place the food in an oven-safe casserole dish and broil until the desired level of crispiness is reached.

ACKNOWLEDGMENTS

This book, like my others, wouldn't be here without the champion efforts of the various teams in my life.

———

Team Home: Richard & Banjo—Because that's what you are: my home. I love you both more than you love Auburn football and cheese. You light up my days and make life better, funnier, and that much more special.

Team Family: Mom, Dad, Amanda, David, Levi, Stevie, and Mack—The best and craziest family a guy could ask for. I constantly look forward to our family outings and really look forward to the day when the kids start to actually eat more than just pizza and chicken nuggets again. (Have them start with the Alphabet Soup on page 58. From there, they'll graduate to the Coq au Vin on page 169 in no time.)

Team Voracious/Little, Brown/Gernert: Michael Szczerban, Nicole Tourtelot, Thea Diklich-Newell, Pat Jalbert-Levine, Laura Palese, Deri Reed, Nyamekye Waliyaya, Lauren Ortiz, and Katherine Akey—Thank you, once again, for (painstakingly) shepherding my complex vision to beautiful, simplistic life. I could not be more proud of book 4 and look forward to whatever else may be in store.

Team Photoshoot: Aleksey Zozulya and Carol J. Lee—Did we seriously shoot over 100 recipes in just 16 days (with each day averaging just 6 hours)? I'm going to just say you're both prodigies because I'm pretty sure we're the only team of three who's been able to achieve something of this crazy (and highly efficient)

magnitude in such a short time. Our lightning-fast work on this shoot is a true testament to time-saving meals. What you've designed and captured is so stunning and magical, it belongs in a book. So it's a good thing it's happened yet again.

Team Rachael Ray Show: Thank you to Rachael herself for the endless fun when she has me on her show as well as for her great generosity in championing my books. And to Erin Fitzpatrick Rose for being the most wonderful and buttoned-up producer to present and work with me on such golden opportunities. These experiences have truly changed my life.

Team Friends: Sometimes they come and go, but the true ones always stick around. Thank you to all of you for your love, trust, loyalty, and support (you know who you are). I love you.

Team Fans: That's all of you—Thank you. Thank you. THANK YOU. From the bottom of my heart. I've said it a zillion times but I'll say it forever—neither this book (nor the other three) would be here if it weren't for your encouragement, enthusiasm, caring, and sharing. You are the reason I do this and I hope that this book gives you exactly what you've asked for: dinner done quickly and hassle-free (with perhaps a little fun mixed in). Now go make something delicious and let us all know what you thought!

INDEX

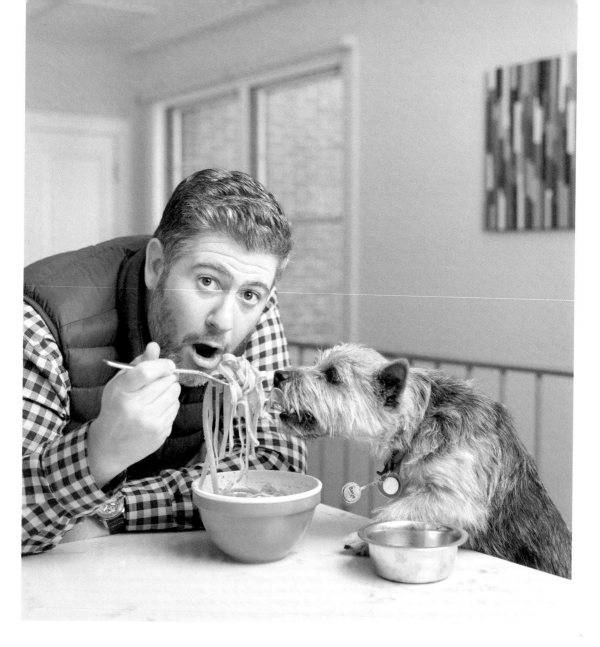

ABOUT THE AUTHOR

JEFFREY EISNER is a multiple #1 bestselling author of the *Step-by-Step Instant Pot* series of cookbooks; he was the top-selling debut cookbook author of 2020, when people were cooking at home more than ever. His trusted and signature recipes have earned him numerous recurring appearances on national and international television. He develops and tests his recipes in both the rural farmlands of northern New Jersey and the bustling borough of Queens, New York. When not cooking, he enjoys traveling with his partner, Richard, and spoiling their dog, Banjo the Norwich Terrier. He also loves pinball and theatre.